SOAR to College Success and Beyond

First Edition

KENNETH A. KIEWRA, PH.D.

University of Nebraska - Lincoln

cognella®

SAN DIEGO

Bassim Hamadeh, CEO and Publisher
Jennifer Codner, Senior Field Acquisitions Editor
Susana Christie, Senior Developmental Editor
Michelle Piehl, Senior Project Editor
Abbey Hastings, Production Editor
Jess Estrella, Senior Graphic Designer
Trey Soto, Licensing Coordinator
Natalie Piccotti, Director of Marketing
Kassie Graves, Vice President of Editorial
Jamie Giganti, Director of Academic Publishing

Cover image: Copyright © 2019 iStockphoto LP/nirat.

Printed in the United States of America.

Portions of this book were previously published by Pearson Education, Inc. in the title *Learn
How to Study and SOAR to Success*.

 cognella® | ACADEMIC PUBLISHING

3970 Sorrento Valley Blvd., Ste. 500, San Diego, CA 92121

Brief Contents

Detailed Contents

7   SOAR for Reading, Writing, Arithmetic, and Beyond   157

8   The Mighty Ms   181

9   Life and Time Management   212

Preface

Welcome, Students! So Glad You're Here!

Whether you've come from just down the road, another state, or another country, whether you're first-gen or fourth-gen, first-year or fourth-year, student athlete or theater major, undeclared or pre-med, Democrat or Republican, regular or decaf ... you're all here now, sharing three goals:

1. **College Success.** You want passing grades ... great grades ... A+ grades.

2. **Independent Learning.** You want to become a more effective learner who can learn on your own: any time, any place, in college and beyond.

3. **Learning Enjoyment.** You want to enjoy the learning process. Learning need not be drudgery. It can be fun to learn about the intricacies of the cell or the expansiveness of the cosmos when you know what you're doing.

Sounds good, but why now, you wonder. "Why a book on how to learn when I'm in college?" The reason is simple. Although you've been in school for 12 or more years, you've likely not been taught how to learn. Most teachers teach content such as mathematics and science but not how to learn such content. Most teach skills such as how to add mixed fractions or how to balance chemical equations but not the skill of learning. Most never teach students how to record notes, construct graphic organizers, create associations, assess learning, boost motivation, manage time, and rock a growth mindset. Most teachers focus on the products of learning, not the processes.

And why is that? Many teachers believe that students naturally know how to learn, that learning skills develop as naturally as height or weight and need not be taught. But that's wrong. Just as violin, golf, chess, and equestrian skills must be taught, practiced, and perfected, so must academic skills, such as note-taking and self-testing.

Now here's the good news. The teaching of academic skills can occur at any time; it's not too late. Moreover, the teaching of such skills is not remedial—how can it be, if the skills have not been taught before—but enriching. Now's the time to enrich your knowledge of how to learn, so that you become an independent learner who excels in college and beyond and who loves doing it.

I hope you entrust me to lead you on this learning-to-learn journey. I believe I'm a qualified guide. I was once a college student, like you, shortly after the inventions of paper and building-climbing ivy. I struggled at first, until I took an educational psychology class that stressed academic skills like note-taking. I learned a lot and was twice named Notetaker of the Year Runner Up. Inspired by educational psychology, and not ready to choose a cable plan, I went to graduate school and earned a Ph.D. in educational psychology. Full disclosure: That was only after a hand injury loosened my grip on my real dream—becoming a get-back coach. My focus, in graduate school and now, is on learning: how students learn in the classroom and beyond, perhaps as they try to master chess or swimming or strive to excel in the workplace.

The strategies you're about to acquire in this book have been taught successfully to thousands of college students at my own university, and to students worldwide through books and articles I've written. Much of what's taught, such as SOAR, note-taking, graphic organizers, life and time management, and talent development, is a product of my own research.

This is a book about how to learn. It is not a book about college adjustment, such as how to get financial aid or how to settle a roommate dispute. There are books that address college adjustment issues, but my sense is that they can only hope to transform a troubled first-year student with a 2.0 GPA into a less troubled fourth-year student with a 2.0 GPA. This book aims to teach learning.

So pull up a chair, shine a light on these pages, and open your mind to learning how to learn, so you might become a more effective and joyous learner in college and beyond.

A Special Note to Instructors

Welcome to You, Too!

Were you listening in? Good. Together, we can help your students learn how to learn.

I have two tips. First, you may or may not want to cover the chapters in the order they appear. Their given order makes sense because SOAR, and its components and applications covered in Chapters 2–7, is at the heart of academic success and this book. Or you might want to cover Chapters 8 and 9 first, as those chapters on the Mighty Ms—mindset and motivation—and on life and time management are the support topics your students might need right away. A sensible argument could be made either way. You choose.

Second, perhaps do both. As you teach content chapter by chapter, whatever the order, I suggest that you also embed strategy training on the fly as needed. When students retreat to the rear of the classroom, a quick, impromptu lesson on sitting front and center is in order. When laptops and phones command their attention during class, the time is ripe to warn them about digital distractions and to suggest longhand note-taking. When students are assigned a long-range project, why not tell them then about the "invest early" and "invest daily" time-management principles? You get the idea: In addition to chapter-to-chapter coverage, embed strategy training on the fly as needed.

Thanks for choosing this book and for helping students succeed in college and beyond. Let's get to it!

Acknowledgments

Thank you to the influencers who shaped this book.

Thank you, colleagues, for helping me investigate the science of learning. Thank you, students, for teaching me what works and what does not.

Thank you, University of Nebraska, for supporting my work the past 34 years. A special thanks to Emily Slattery and Cindy DeRyke for your valuable production help on this and other projects.

Thank you, reviewers, for your many insightful suggestions. You certainly made this a better book:

Thank you, Cognella, for adopting this book and bringing it to life. A special thanks to Jennifer Codner, Senior Field Acquisitions Editor; Michelle Piehl, Senior Project Editor; Abbey Hastings, Production Editor; David Rajec, Associate Editor; Trey Soto, Licensing Specialist; Jess Estrella, Senior Graphic Designer; and Tiffany Mok, Senior Content Marketing Specialist.

As always, a special thank you to my loving and supportive family: Christine, Keaton, Anna, and Samuel. You're my inspiration.

Dedication

To my mentors, Dr. Nelson DuBois and Dr. Harold Fletcher. Thank you for opening my eyes to the wonders of educational psychology and for showing me the path.

CHAPTER 1

Some Success Stories to Start You on Your Way

OVERVIEW

Objectives

1. Make the argument that talent is made, not born.

2. Describe the four SOAR components and the intended outcome for each.

3. Describe the relative benefits of having a growth mindset versus a fixed mindset.

Focus Questions

1. Retell the Mozart story showing that talent is made, not born.

2. Why did students practicing the cup-and-ball game not improve initially? What helped them finally improve?

3. According to what was found in the SOAR study, how do college students usually study?

4. What are SOAR's four components, and what is the outcome of each?

5. What do the cup-and-ball game story and the SOAR story have in common?

6. Why are students not taught how to learn?

7. What do the Hoyt and Sartore motivation stories have in common?

8. What is a growth mindset, and what are its benefits?

9. Name some things productive scholars do to maximize time.

10. What's the main point of all the chapter stories?

This book is about success—success in college and beyond. This book is for you. It's intended to make you successful in college and for a lifetime. That's a lofty intention, but it's completely doable. Thousands of college students have learned the ideas in this book and applied them successfully in the classroom and beyond. You will too. Here are some important success stories to start you on your way.

The Talent Story

Most people think talent is born. A gift from the gods.

For years, Amadeus Mozart has been held up as the poster child for innate ability. How else could he play piano at 3, learn violin at 4, and compose at 5?

I'll tell you how. Mozart was born into a musical home and tutored from the opening movement by his father Leopold, who was himself an accomplished musician and composer and who literally wrote the book on violin instruction the year Mozart was born. Mozart practiced relentlessly, trying to catch up to his older sister Anna and to earn his father's praise, and because he loved music.

Mozart's talent wasn't born; it was made. Made by an early start, excellent instruction, and massive practice.

Of course, we're not talking about a Mozart solo here. These are some of the everyday chords that turn the ordinary into the extraordinary in any domain. It's how Tiger came to roar in golf. Tiger's father, Earl, was a golf fanatic. Earl placed toy clubs in the young cub's crib and moved Tiger's high chair into the garage so he could watch his father hit golf shots into a net. He had Tiger playing golf out on the course as a toddler. And, throughout Tiger's career, no one practiced longer and better—he spent 9 hours a day putting, shaping shots on the range, and lifting weights to add precious yards to his drives. Tiger wasn't born with some golfing gene; he earned his stripes.

And, should you think from these two stories that talent futures are always shaped by doting parents with a hand already dipped in the eventual talent pool, think again. Here's Bobby Fischer's story. Fischer is America's only world chess champion. But if not for a couple of chance occurrences, Fischer might have never pushed a pawn. As a child, Fischer lived with his mother and sister in Arizona before the family, by chance, moved to New York, which happened to be the chess mecca in the United States. By chance, Fischer was soon introduced to chess when his older sister brought home a plastic chess set from a local store for herself and Bobby to try. Bobby enjoyed playing and was soon reading about the game and playing for hours on his own. But it was because Bobby lived in New York City that he had access to some of the best chess clubs and players in the world. It was in those clubs that Bobby honed his game nightly. Did Fischer's mother lend support? Not really—in fact, she actually spoke with a psychologist about how to curb Bobby's chess passion. It was a chance introduction to the game, the fact that New York was a center of chess excellence, and his unbridled passion that made Bobby king.

Benjamin Bloom was among the first to study talent development. He studied 120 top American performers across six domains: piano, sculpture, mathematics, neurology, tennis, and swimming. His overriding conclusion was this: What any person in the world can learn, almost all persons can learn if provided with the appropriate conditions of learning (Bloom, 1985).

Like Benjamin Bloom, I've studied talent development at its highest levels. I've chronicled the talent paths of Olympic gold medalists, professional athletes, award-winning artists, high-school phenoms, child prodigies, champion coaches, master teachers, and nurturing parents across a wide array of talent domains.

My conclusions are like Bloom's. Talent is made, and it's within your reach. The seeds of talent development reside not in your genes but in the palm of your hand. You control talent growth. As Ralph Waldo Emerson said, "Every artist was first an amateur" (Emerson, 1904).

But what are those "appropriate conditions" Bloom spoke of that allow talent to blossom? Let's examine some more stories and find out.

Activity 1.1

Think of someone in the public eye, living or deceased, whom you admire. It could be someone in music, sports, science, or any domain. Do some quick internet research to uncover the factors that made him/her so talented or successful.

The Cup-and-Ball Story

Have you ever played the cup-and-ball game before? If not, perhaps some of your ancestors have. It's been around since the 14th century. In its most basic form, it's a cup on a stick with a ball hanging down on a string, as seen in Figure 1-1. The goal of the game is simple: Using just the hand holding the stick, swing the ball up into the cup. Easier said than done.

In a recent class I taught on talent development, I gave a cup-and-ball game to each student. The purpose was to show the benefit of proper practice. Students were to take a 20-attempt

Figure 1-1 Cup-and-Ball Game

baseline test at the start, practice each day for 15 minutes, and take a weekly 20-attempt test to chart their progress. All the students were unfamiliar with the game and recorded scores between 0–2 on the baseline test. The average score on the week 1 test was 2; it was 3 in week 2, and no one scored better than 6. Practice was not paying off as planned. In week 3, all students reported scoring under 5 on the weekly test, except for one student who reported scoring 19. What was happening? Why was practice not effective, and was there a cup-and-ball cheater in our midst?

I had students bring their games to class the following week and gave them time to practice, in order to see things for myself. As they did, it was evident there were two distinct styles of playing. Most students swung the ball upward in a big arc with the string fully extended. Their swing was smooth and accurate, from all the practice, but the ball would invariably land in the cup and then bounce out. Meanwhile, the student who posted the high score the previous week had a completely different style. Rather than swinging the ball out and up with maximum circumference, she simply thrusted her stick-holding hand upward, sending the ball straight up, barely above the cup, and guiding it softly and securely inside the cup.

Activity 1.2

Take a baseline measurement of your ability for some simple task. It could be flipping playing cards into a pot, tossing a tennis ball into a garbage can, or balancing a stick on your finger. After that, practice the same activity for 7 days and chart your practice. Did you improve your practice techniques and performance?

I had our expert model her playing style for the class. They were in awe of her prowess but easily recognized that her unique and simple practice technique was the secret. She wasn't some sort of cup-and-ball savant; she simply knew a better way to practice and execute the skill. The other students tried her practice method, and after just a few minutes of effective practice, their scores skyrocketed. Most left that day getting 10 out of 20. Within 2 weeks, the class average was 16. The moral of this story: Not all practice is effective, but proper practice is effective.

The SOAR Story

In an experiment that Tareq Daher and I conducted on study methods, we gave college students five online texts to study, each about a different type of ape (Daher & Kiewra, 2016). An abbreviated version of three of those texts is shown in Table 1-1. Before students studied the ape texts, we asked them how they typically study text material. Most reported that they traditionally take notes as they read and then use rote memory techniques such as rehearsing certain facts over and over.

Table 1-1 ABBREVIATED APE TEXTS USED IN SOAR STUDY

Gibbons	Orangutans	Gorillas
Gibbons are dexterous while moving in the trees. Almost no predators can catch them. This ape moves from one tree to another, reaching speeds of 35 mph. Because of their small sizes, their only protection comes from brachiating away when confronted. They are about 2 feet tall and weigh about 20 pounds. They cannot swim, but because they are omnivores that eat both plants and meat, they can survive in several areas of a forest living in the trees.	Orangutans weigh an average of 200 pounds with an average height of 5 feet. They can move on the ground at a speed of 15 mph. Only when under attack have these omnivores been known to gather in their groups and make loud noises to scare away others. Although they are known to swing in trees, they spend most of their lives on the ground. Their name means "man of the forest." They are known for caring for their young as a group.	Gorillas are large apes that weigh 300 pounds and are, on average, 6 feet tall. Despite their size, they rarely attack other animals. In fact, gorillas are herbivores, eating mostly plant material. They are the least aggressive of the apes, despite their size. When an intruder disturbs them, they may gather in their group and make a lot of noise as a display of power. Males are called silverbacks. They reach about 10 mph swinging in trees but spend their lives largely on the ground.

Source: Tareq A. Daher and Kenneth A. Kiewra, "An Investigation of SOAR Study Strategies for Learning from Multiple Online Resources," *Contemporary Educational Psychology*, vol. 46, p. 11. Copyright © 2016 by Elsevier B.V. Reprinted with permission.

We next conducted training for 30 minutes. We gave all students three brief texts about various topics other than apes and had half of them practice using their typical learning strategies (which, indeed, turned out to be brief note-taking and repetitive memorization techniques like rewriting key ideas). The other half were trained to use an unfamiliar strategy called SOAR. SOAR is an acronym that stands for the method's four components: select, organize, associate, and regulate. Selection is carried out by recording complete notes, like those in Table 1-2 for the three ape texts in Table 1-1. Organization is carried out by creating graphic organizers—spatial displays that organize information in ways that allow for easy comparison among topics. Table 1-3 is a graphic organizer for the three ape texts. Association is carried out by identifying relationships among text ideas, and graphic organizers are especially helpful in identifying relationships. Examining the Table 1-3 organizer, this associative relationship is readily apparent: The heavier the ape, the slower its speed in trees. Notice that this simple association encompasses six discreet facts (gorillas weigh 300 pounds, orangutans weigh 200 pounds, gibbons weigh 20 pounds, gorillas travel through trees at 10 mph, orangutans travel through trees at 15 mph, gibbons travel through trees at 35 mph) that most students are likely to try to memorize separately and ineffectively. Finally, regulation is carried out by self-testing, asking and answering one's own practice questions before the teacher tests students for real, using questions like: How do orangutans defend themselves? Or: What's the relationship between apes' weight and tree speed? Table 1-4 shows the four SOAR components.

Table 1-2 COMPLETE NOTES FOR THE APE TEXTS

Complete Notes	
Gibbons	Speed in trees: 35 mph Weight: 20 lbs. Height: 2 ft. Diet: Omnivores Defense: Brachiate away Habitat: Live in trees Unique facts: • Cannot swim • Dexterous in trees
Orangutans	Speed in trees: 15 mph Weight: 200 lbs. Height: 5 ft. Diet: Omnivores Defense: Make loud noises in groups Habitat: Ground Unique facts: • Name means man of the forest • Group cares for their young
Gorillas	Speed in trees: 10 mph Weight: 300 lbs. Height: 6 ft. Diet: Herbivores Defense: Gather in groups Habitat: Ground Unique facts: • Least aggressive ape • Males called silverbacks

Source: Tareq A. Daher and Kenneth A.Kiewra, "An Investigation of SOAR Study Strategies for Learning from Multiple Online Resources," *Contemporary Educational Psychology*, vol. 46, p. 12. Copyright © 2016 by Elsevier B.V. Reprinted with permission.

Table 1-3 GRAPHIC ORGANIZER FOR THE APE TEXTS

	Gorillas	Orangutans	Gibbons
Weight (lbs.)	300	200	20
Height (ft.)	6	5	2
Tree speed (mph)	10	15	35
Diet	Herbivores	Omnivores	Omnivores
Defense	Gather in groups	Loud noises in groups	Brachiate away
Habitat	Ground	Ground	Trees
Unique facts	Least aggressive ape Males called silverbacks	Name means man of the forest Group cares for their young	Cannot swim Dexterous in trees

Source: Tareq A. Daher and Kenneth A.Kiewra, "An Investigation of SOAR Study Strategies for Learning from Multiple Online Resources," *Contemporary Educational Psychology*, vol. 46, p. 12. Copyright © 2016 by Elsevier B.V. Reprinted with permission.

Table 1-4 THE FOUR SOAR COMPONENTS

Select	Recording complete notes
Organize	Creating graphic organizers
Associate	Identifying relationships
Regulate	Self-testing

Following this training period, all students were presented the five ape texts via computer, each on a separate web page, and told to study them for 30 minutes in preparation for a test. They were given notepads and told that anything they wrote on their notepads could be studied for an additional 10 minutes before testing occurred. The brief SOAR training paid off in terms of study strategies, as evidenced by the notepads. The SOAR-trained group used more SOAR strategies than those using their typical study methods. Regarding selection, SOAR studiers recorded 12% more notes. Regarding organization, 92% of SOAR studiers created a graphic organizer, compared to just 21% of typical studiers. Moreover, the graphic organizers of SOAR studiers were more complete. Regarding association and regulation, SOAR studiers created a handful of associations and practice questions, whereas typical studiers created zero of each. The big benefit of SOAR training, though, was in the test results. SOAR-trained students scored 20% higher—that's two letter grades higher. Table 1-5 summarizes the SOAR study findings.

Table 1-5 SUMMARY OF SOAR STUDY FINDINGS

	SOAR-Trained Group	Typical Study Methods Group
Select	12% more notes	
Organize	92% created graphic organizer Organizer more complete	21% created graphic organizer
Associate	Created associations	Created no associations
Regulate	Created practice questions	Created no practice questions
Test Performance	Scored 20% higher	

Activity 1.3

Try using SOAR strategies. Below is some information about bees and wasps. Try creating an organizer to compare them. Then generate some associations and some potential test questions.

Bees have hairy bodies and legs, whereas wasps have smooth bodies and legs. The abdomen and thorax of a bee is round, whereas in the case of a wasp, it is cylindrical. Bees have flat and wide legs, and wasps have round and waxy legs.

Do you see how these last two stories—cup-and-ball and SOAR—are connected? First, in each case, students practiced weak strategies. Students practiced the cup-and-ball game every day for several weeks, but their practice routine was flawed. They tried swinging the ball up in a circular motion with a maximum circumference; that strategy simply did not work, as the ball struck the cup too hard to hold it in place. Meanwhile, untrained students in the SOAR experiment used faulty study strategies involving sketchy note-taking and rote memorization that they had practiced throughout their academic careers, strategies that proved ineffective in our study. Yes, there was practice in each case, but practice was flawed. Second, with just a small dose of instruction in how to do things right, in how to practice properly, performance skyrocketed. Cup-and-ball gamers tripled their success rate, and SOAR studiers raised their academic achievement 20% above that of traditional studiers. Wow!

The big message, of course, is that most of you reading this book are like the students I just described. You are trying hard, and you are practicing, but you are using weak strategies and practice routines that are not maximizing academic performance. We're going to change that now. In the coming chapters you'll learn and practice strategies—emphasizing SOAR methods—that really work, and that can maximize your performance in college and beyond.

The Motivation Story

Amadeus Mozart, Tiger Woods, and Bobby Fischer all acquired amazing skills thanks to strong instruction and a lot of proper practice. Fischer, for example, seemed to practice nonstop. As a child, he sat for hours at the board playing both sides of a game, tucked chess books inside his school books when he was supposed to be studying his subjects, and spent long evenings pushing pawns with grandmasters at local chess clubs, often forgetting to go home. If that wasn't enough dedication, Fischer quit school at age 16 to focus on chess full time. But what propels some people—like Fischer, Mozart, and Woods—to practice so hard and for so long? Why, motivation, of course. Motivation can propel people to great heights, to accomplish what might seem impossible.

Most psychologists believe that motivation is largely made, rather than born. People do things because they enjoy pursuing them, regardless of the outcome. They enjoy the path, enjoy the journey. Author Louis L'Amour (2003) said, "The trail is the thing, not the end of the trail." Speaking of trails, here is the story of Dick and Rick Hoyt.

Dick Hoyt was a sedentary man who had never run more than a mile, had never learned to swim, and had not ridden a bicycle since he was 6 years old. His high-school-aged son, Rick, was wheelchair bound and could not speak. Rick wanted to participate in a 5-mile charity run for a classmate paralyzed in an accident. He typed, "Dad, I want to do that." Dick, who was not fit, somehow mustered the strength to push Rick through the race, which left Dick fatigued and sore. Afterward, Rick typed, "Dad, when we were running, it felt like I wasn't disabled anymore" (Reilly, 2005). Those powerful words became Dick's motivation to learn to run, swim, and bike; get in shape; and eventually push, pull, and carry his son through hundreds of triathlons (including six Ironman Triathlons), dozens of marathons, and hundreds of shorter races. Dick Hoyt also pedaled his son on a bike across America and lifted him to mountain peaks. There is no stopping motivation.

Here's another motivation story. Joel Sartore is a famous nature photographer. His wildlife photos often adorn the covers of *National Geographic*. Today, Sartore is on a 20-year mission to photograph every one of the approximately 15,000 species living in zoos and wildlife sanctuaries around the world. Why? What's Sartore's motivation? He's using the power of photography to inspire people to save species before it's too late, before they become endangered or extinct like so many before them. Sartore's motivation to complete this photo ark project actually hatched as a child. He said:

> My mother had a set of *Time-Life* picture books. One was called *The Birds*. In that book was a look at several birds that have gone extinct. ... The very last passenger pigeon, a bird named Martha, was shown alive in a photo taken just before her death in the Cincinnati Zoo back in 1914. I was astounded. This was once the most numerous bird on Earth, with an estimated population of five billion, and here it was reduced to this single female, with no hope of saving it. I couldn't understand how anyone could tolerate this. I still feel the same way, and I work hard to prevent this from ever happening again. (Sartore, n.d.)

Sartore credits motivation for his ongoing success. He said: "My success comes from being ... very driven, never putting something off, do it right now, very energetic, very persistent, even aggressive about what I want and what I'm going to achieve. I never put off until tomorrow what I can achieve today."

In both of these stories, motivation was sparked by a single incident and fueled by a burning passion—the love of a child in one case, and the love of nature in the other.

Activity 1.4

Make a list of all the things that motivate you to succeed in college.

The Mindset Story

Your mindset is what you believe about the origins of talent and ability. Do you believe talent is inborn or made? Do you believe mathematical ability is predetermined at birth or is the product of one's actions? These are no small questions, because what you believe determines a great deal about the paths you choose and where you end up.

If you believe that talent or ability is inborn, you hold a fixed mindset: What you were born with is all you'll get. If you believe that talent or ability is modifiable, you hold a growth mindset: What you have can be improved through experience. Here's a story about how these two mindsets affected the paths students chose, and where they ended up, in an experiment reported by mindset guru Carol Dweck (2008).

In round 1 of the experiment, elementary school students were given a problem-solving test that was fairly easy and yielded high scores for all. Afterward, students were given their score and a single line of praise. Through random assignment, half were praised for their high intelligence (reflective of a fixed mindset): "You must be really smart." Half were praised for their hard work (reflective of a growth mindset): "You must have worked really hard." In round 2, students were given their choice of test: an easy test like the first one or a more difficult test they could learn from. Among those praised for high ability (fixed mindset), 67% chose the easy test; among those praised for hard work (growth mindset), 92% chose the difficult test. Dweck (2008) concluded that those praised for ability (fixed mindset) chose the easy test to continue looking smart and not risk making mistakes, whereas those praised for effort (growth mindset) chose the difficult test because they welcomed the challenge and the chance to learn and grow despite the likelihood of failure. In round 3, all students received a difficult test, and all failed as expected. Failure reactions, though, differed markedly. Those praised for their hard work at the start (growth mindset) tried hard, enjoyed the challenging test, and attributed failure to things like needing to learn more. Meanwhile, those praised for high ability at the start (fixed mindset) found test-taking miserable and attributed failure to not being smart. In the fourth and final round, all students were again given simple problems to solve, as in round 1. Those originally praised for hard work (growth mindset) improved their first-round scores by 30%, while those originally praised for high ability (fixed mindset) lowered their first-round scores by 20%, resulting in a 50% performance difference between groups. Table 1-6 summarizes the study methods and findings. To recap, those with fixed mindsets believe that ability is innate and unchangeable. They prefer simple tasks to challenging ones, and when challenged, they give up. Meanwhile, those with growth mindsets believe that ability is learned and modifiable. They prefer challenging tasks to simple ones, because they see challenging tasks and temporary failure as pathways to improvement (Dweck, 2008).

Table 1-6 SUMMARY OF DWECK'S FIXED VERSUS GROWTH MINDSET EXPERIMENT

Round	Fixed Mindset	Growth Mindset
1. Administered easy test	• High scores • Praised for intelligence	• High scores • Praised for effort
2. Given choice of test	67% chose easy test to look smart and avoid failure	92% chose difficult test because they welcomed the challenge to learn and grow
3. All given difficult test	Failed, were miserable, and attributed failure to not being smart	Failed, enjoyed experience, and attributed failure to needing to learn more
4. Administered easy test like in round 1	Round 1 score decreased 20%	Round 1 score increased 30%

Chess and martial arts champion Josh Waitzkin (2007) likens a person with a fixed mindset to an anorexic hermit crab. Hermit crabs, as you might know, outgrow their protective shells. When they do, they must leave them and find a larger shell to accommodate their larger size. During their search for a new shell, they are unprotected and vulnerable. A crab afraid to leave the comfort of its present shell might starve itself so that it does not grow. Those with a fixed mindset are much the same. They are afraid to risk, afraid to fail, and afraid to grow.

Activity 1.5

Describe how someone with a fixed mindset and someone with a growth mindset might react to each situation below:

- Meeting the goal of making 5 out of 10 free throws.
- Getting a C on a writing assignment and receiving lots of corrective feedback.
- Trying to learn how to play chess.
- Being told, "You're a natural athlete."

The Life- and Time-Management Story

Among the talented people I've studied are about 20 highly productive educational researchers—scholars who published hundreds of articles and books over their decades-long careers (e.g., Flanigan et al., 2018; Kiewra & Creswell, 2000; Patterson-Hazley & Kiewra, 2013). How did they do it? One key was developing life habits and routines that allowed them to maximize time. For example, they preserved the morning hours to write because they were fresher and more productive in the morning. They often spent morning hours at home, away from their universities and their many distractions. While working, they silenced their electronic notifications to maintain concentration. They pushed more perfunctory tasks like teaching, meetings, and correspondence to the afternoon. As to how they went about their work, they rarely conducted research on their own. They collaborated with colleagues and students because many hands make light work. Because they collaborated, they often worked on five to ten different projects at any one time. They were masters at maintaining focus. They worked almost exclusively in their scholarly interest area and applied those interests to all facets of their job—research, teaching, and professional service. They rarely wandered from their chosen paths. They often turned down opportunities and requests, so not to be spread too thin. They valued personal health and carved out ample time each day for exercise and leisure. To use a chess metaphor, they were kings and queens in control of their time and their lives, not helpless pawns pushed around by others.

I've also studied first-year college students who earned National Merit Scholarships and were top-of-the-class in high school. Like the productive scholars, they were life and time masters. In addition to completing a full school day, the young scholars spent several hours each day on homework or scholarly interests like physics or sports analytics. All were heavily involved in time-consuming extracurricular activities too, making time management crucial. Emma, for example, said, "I was busy all the time. On a normal day, I'd go to school. After that were the activities like soccer and debate. I'd go home and do schoolwork for [several] hours and practice my bass" (Kiewra and Rom, 2019). Lin's routine was similar. Lin spent 2–4 hours on schoolwork each day and 4–6 hours the day before a test. On top of this, Lin budgeted time for her many extracurricular activities such as figure skating, varsity tennis, being editor-in-chief of the school paper, DECA, two honor societies, and volunteer tennis

The Habits and Routines of Productive Scholars

- Did the most important work early in the morning, when the mind is freshest.
- Pushed less challenging tasks to the afternoon.
- Worked at home, when possible, for maximum concentration.
- Silenced electronic notifications when they worked, to avoid distractions.
- Collaborated with others on multiple projects, to accomplish more.
- Maintained focus by working almost exclusively on their scholarly interest and turning down opportunities outside their interest.
- Valued personal health and spent time each day on exercise and leisure.

Activity 1.6

As you think about your daily activities, in what ways are you are wasting time or being inefficient? How can you modify or add routines that make you more efficient and successful?

coaching. Although Lin was super busy, she found pleasure in all she did, saying, "I really enjoyed the things I did and wanted to keep doing them. I didn't consider what I did as work but as fun" (Kiewra and Rom, 2019).

So What's the Point of These Stories?

Benjamin Bloom concluded: What any person in the world can learn, almost all persons can learn if provided with the appropriate conditions of learning (Bloom, 1985). Having read the chapter stories, you now know those conditions: effective instruction, proper practice, SOAR strategies, motivation, a growth mindset, and effective life- and time-management. Table 1-7 summarizes the chapter stories. Hopefully, this chapter has laid out the importance of each success factor and convinced you that each is within your reach, in the palm of your hand, as you strive to become a more successful and powerful learner. You've witnessed how talent is made, not born. That should give you the growth mindset and motivation

Table 1-7 A SUMMARY OF CHAPTER 1 SUCCESS STORIES

	Talent	Cup-and-Ball	SOAR	Motivation	Mindset	Life- and Time-Management
Main Idea	Talent is made, not born, and is within your reach	Practice is not enough; you need proper practice	SOAR methods better than students' preferred study methods	Motivation propels people to practice a lot for a long time	Growth mindset (the belief that success is made) Is crucial to success	Success depends on life- and time-management
Key Ideas	Instruction and proper practice yield talent		Students use weak strategies such as rote review of notes	Motivation is made and can be sparked by single incident	Fixed mindset is the dangerous belief that talents are born and outside your control	Be goal-directed, say no to things outside your goals, use morning hours to do taxing work, avoid distractions, and collaborate
Examples	• Mozart in music • Tiger Woods in golf • Bobby Fischer in chess	Cup-and-ball practice did not yield improvement until students saw and practiced proper technique	SOAR training led to SOAR strategy use and 20% higher achievement	• Dick Hoyt's endurance exploits with disabled son Rick • Joel Sartore's motivation to photograph endangered species	Dweck's study: Growth mindset led to choosing challenging tasks, perseverance, and learning from failure	• Productive educational researchers • Merit Scholars budget life and time for academic and extra-curricular success

needed to tackle and apply what's in this book. You'll learn more about mindset and motivation in Chapter 8. You've seen the benefits of proper practice and the downsides of improper practice. That should also give you the motivation and mindset to practice long, hard, and smart, using effective methods like SOAR and avoiding ineffective methods like rote memorization. Chapters 2 through 7 focus on the SOAR method for college success and beyond. You'll need to manage your life and your time like both the seasoned and young scholars I studied. That's the topic of Chapter 9. Finally, you'll need proper instruction to learn, master, and apply all of this, and I'll certainly do my best to provide effective instruction within these pages. As an educational psychologist, this is what I'm trained and committed to do.

So, lets rock and roll. Let's SOAR to college success and beyond!

Answers to Focus Questions

1. Mozart displayed immense talent as a child, leading many to believe that talent is born, not made. Mozart's prodigious talent, though, is easily explained by his early training in a musical household, expert instruction, passion for music, and arduous practice.

2. Students practicing the cup-and-ball game didn't improve at first because they practiced using bad technique. Once they observed good technique and practiced in that way, their performance rose dramatically.

3. In the SOAR study, students reported that they record notes when they read but then use rote memory strategies such as rehearsal to study noted information. When students' actual study behaviors were assessed, it was found that most students took incomplete notes, did not make graphic organizers to organize notes, made no associations, and did not generate practice test questions.

4. SOAR's four components are select, organize, associate, and regulate. Select yields a complete set of notes. Organize yields an organized set of notes using graphic organizers, such as a matrix. Associate yields relationships among facts. Regulate yields practice test questions useful for assessing learning and understanding.

5. The cup-and-ball game story and the SOAR story are similar in that untrained students practiced ineffectively. Cup-and-ball players used poor technique; students studied text materials using weak strategies like repetition. But with effective instruction in how to swing the ball and how to study, students practiced properly and greatly improved their performance.

6. Students are not taught how to learn because most teachers focus on teaching content and rarely teach how to learn content, such as how to take complete notes or construct graphic organizers. As to why teachers rarely teach strategies, most erroneously believe that students naturally know how to learn and need not be taught.

7. In both the Hoyt and Sartore motivation stories, motivation was sparked by a specific event. Hoyt was motivated by his son not feeling disabled as the two raced. Sartore was motivated by the unexplainable and senseless extinction of a once-plentiful species. In each case, their passion fueled their motivation to accomplish amazing things—the completion of endurance events and the photographing of thousands of species.

8. The growth mindset is the belief that talent and abilities are made, not born, and under one's control. Those with growth mindsets outperform those with fixed mindsets who, in turn, believe talents and abilities are fixed. Those with growth mindsets excel because, unlike those with fixed mindsets, they choose difficult over simple tasks, enjoy challenging tasks, and are unafraid of failure. They don't give up. They see failure as temporary and as an opportunity for growth.

9. Productive scholars maximize time by doing their most taxing work, like writing, in the morning, when they are freshest. They postpone more mundane and less taxing tasks, like meetings and correspondence, until the afternoon. They silence mobile devices to limit distractions and aid concentration. They spend time doing work in line with their goals and turn down opportunities incompatible with their goals. They are also adept at focusing their teaching, research, and service efforts in a single area rather than being spread too thin. And they collaborate on multiple projects, as a way of accomplishing more than they could by working alone or working on just one project at a time.

10. The main point of all of the chapter stories is that success is not dependent on inborn qualities but is linked to environmental factors such as practice, instruction, motivation, and mindset. And the wonderful news is that all of these factors are under your control. You make success.

Figure Credit

CHAPTER 2

The SOAR Method for College Success

OVERVIEW

Objectives

1. Recognize ineffective learning strategies and identify effective learning strategies that help you SOAR to success.

2. Describe how information is processed in memory and how that process relates to SOAR strategies.

3. Make the argument that SOAR is an effective way to learn, based on research and on its link to memory processes.

Focus Questions

1. Describe the characteristics of most students' notes.

2. What are some redundant strategies students commonly use?

3. Describe the four SOAR components.

4. What is the evidence that SOAR works?

5. How many stimuli can be attended to at one time, and which stimuli are most likely to command attention?

6. In what ways is short-term memory limited? How can these limitations be overcome?

7. What does it mean to build internal and external connections?

8. What are the keys to retrieving information from long-term memory?

9. How are your memory system and SOAR linked?

s Euro history a mystery? Let's see what we can do about that.

Suppose you had to learn the information contained in the boxed passage on Romanesque and Gothic architecture. What would you do?

Romanesque and Gothic Architecture

Romanesque and Gothic architecture styles were prevalent in Europe between the 10th and 15th centuries, particularly in church buildings. The two styles have some similarities but many differences.

Romanesque architecture was prevalent during the 10th through 12th centuries. Its primary feature is the traditional Roman arch. Other characteristics include large internal spaces, heavy frames, and thick walls, which negated the need for buttresses. There were also rounded arches on windows and doors. Because of these arches, windows were typically small, which meant that rooms were dimly lit, and the mood was somber. Romanesque churches had towers with blunted shapes. Overall, Romanesque architecture was designed to convey the spiritual power of the church.

Gothic architecture was intended to make churches look like heaven. Consequently, they were bright, colorful, and soaring. This was accomplished by including features like highness, flying buttresses (wall and ceiling supports), and vertical lines. These buildings had a slender skeleton and tall, pointed spires reaching toward the heavens. Gothic structures had large windows covered in stained glass that offered a lot of light into their rooms. Gothic architecture was prevalent during the 12th through 15th centuries.

What Ineffective Learners Do

If you're like most students reading the passage, you'd typically record a set of incomplete and linear notes like that in Table 2-1 (the non-noted information is in red and italicized) and then study those notes one idea at a time by rehearsing each note over and over. Remember the experiment I recounted in Chapter 1? Those are the strategies that most students reported using to learn from school assignments, and the ones untrained students used in the experiment to learn about apes before scoring 20% lower than SOAR-trained students on a test covering the ape material.

Table 2-1 INCOMPLETE NOTES RECORDED FOR ARCHITECTURE PASSAGE (MISSING INFORMATION IN RED)

Romanesque	• *Prevalent* 10th–12th centuries • Roman arch *is primary feature* • Large *internal* spaces • *Thick* walls • No buttresses • Rounded arches—*windows and doors* • *Small windows* • Dim *lighting* • *Somber mood* • Blunted *towers* • *Convey* spiritual power of church
Gothic	• *Convey* heaven • Bright, *colorful, soaring* • *Featured* highness, *vertical* lines, flying buttresses *(supports)* • Slender skeleton • *Tall, pointed* spires • *Large* windows • Stained glass • Well lit • *Prevalent 12th–15th centuries*

The left side of Table 2-2 shows the ineffective strategies students commonly use. Students generally record incomplete notes from lectures and texts, usually just one third of important lesson ideas. Look back at the notes in Table 2-1, and you'll see the problem with incomplete notes. These notes are missing several important details, such as the Romanesque style's small windows and somber mood. The notes mention walls but fail to mention that they are thick. Imagine having only these notes to study three weeks later in preparation for a test. Incomplete note-taking is like asking someone for their phone number and then entering just three digits of their 10-digit number into your phone. Good luck ever texting them.

Table 2-2 STRATEGIES COMMONLY USED BY INEFFECTIVE AND EFFECTIVE LEARNERS

	Ineffective	Effective
Select	Incomplete notes	Complete notes
Organize	Linear notes	Graphic organizers
Associate	Piecemeal learning	Associative learning
Regulate	Redundant strategies	Self-testing

The notes students record are usually linear, list-like. The problem with linear notes is that they separate information that belongs together, thereby making it difficult to see and learn relationships between lesson ideas. Notice, for example, that information about each architectural style's time period in Table 2-1 is separated by intervening information and by a great deal of physical space. When related information is separated in this way, it is difficult to associate the information and form relationships. To better understand the detriment of linear notes, imagine that you wanted to compare the appearance of two Yorkshire terriers. To do so, you would certainly want them next to one another rather than in opposite corners of a room.

Most students learn information in a piecemeal fashion, one idea at a time, instead of associating information. Returning to Table 2-1, students might try to memorize the fact that Romanesque architecture was prevalent during the 10th through 12th centuries and then later try to memorize the fact that Gothic architecture was prevalent during the 12th through 15th centuries, rather than associating and learning these two facts together: *These architectural styles were prevalent during the 10th–15th centuries, with Romanesque coming first (10th–12th) and overlapping in the 12th century with Gothic, which came later (12th–15th).* The folly of piecemeal learning is akin to approaching a jigsaw puzzle one piece at a time. When you assemble a puzzle, you don't pick up a piece and describe its characteristics ("jagged piece with burnt orange color") and continue in that way piece by piece ("blue-colored edge piece with flecks of gray ..."). Instead, you join like pieces and seek the puzzle's completion, the big picture.

Most students study using redundant strategies like *rehearsing, rereading, rewriting, reciting, recopying,* and *regurgitating* ... *rediculous!* Students studying the notes in Table 2-1 might sound like a broken record or a defective iTunes clip: "Gothic: stained-glass windows, Gothic: stained-glass windows, Gothic: stained-glass windows ... ." You know from experience that mere repetition does not work. That's why you can't now draw the six-of-hearts playing card (shown in Figure 2-1) from memory even though you've seen it thousands of times, or reproduce the face of your smartphone (shown in Figure 2-2) even though you see that dozens of times every day. Repeated exposure and rote repetition do not ensure learning.

Activity 2.1

Examine your notes from a lesson for a class you are presently taking. Are they complete? Can you reconstruct the entire lesson from your notes? How could you improve these notes?

Figure 2-1 Playing Card Illustration

Figure 2-2 Smartphone Photo

Activity 2.2

Think of three other situations, in or out of school, where you relied on redundant strategies to learn and found that your efforts proved fruitless. What could you have done instead, to learn more effectively?

Effective Learners SOAR

The right side of Table 2-2 shows the SOAR strategies effective learners use. Rather than record incomplete and linear notes, effective learners *select* all the important lesson ideas and note them. When possible, they *organize* those notes using graphic organizers. The graphic organizer in Table 2-3 shows all the key ideas in the architecture passage in an organized form for easy comparison. Examination of that organizer reveals that effective learners make *associations* like the following:

(a) Romanesque has a thick, heavy, wide structure, whereas Gothic has a tall, slender structure;

(b) Romanesque has a somber tone, whereas Gothic has a rejoiceful tone;

(c) Romanesque conveys the church's power, whereas Gothic conveys heaven.

Table 2-3 GRAPHIC ORGANIZER FOR ARCHITECTURE PASSAGE

	Romanesque Architecture	Gothic Architecture
Prevalence	10th–12th century	12th–15th century
Primary Feature	Roman arch	Tall, pointed design
Structure	Wide internal spaces, heavy frames, thick walls	Slender
Buttresses	None	Flying buttress
Windows	Small with arches above	Large with stained glass
Lighting	Dim	Well lit
Mood	Somber	Rejoiceful
Conveys	Church's spiritual power	Heaven
Towers	Blunted shape	Has spires on top

Finally, effective learners *regulate* their understanding by self-testing. They test themselves so thoroughly, before the instructor does, that there is nothing the instructor can ask them come test time that they haven't already asked themselves. They construct and answer practice test questions like the following:

(a) Which style is well lit?

(b) Which style has arches?

(c) Compare the two styles in terms of structure and mood.

(d) Label each illustration in Figure 2-3 as Romanesque or Gothic.

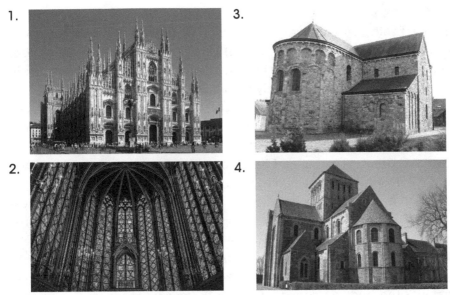

Figure 2-3 Practice Test Item for Architecture Styles

Activity 2.3

Below is a set of notes. Try to organize them better for easy comparison. Hint: Someone can be prejudiced or not prejudiced and can discriminate or not discriminate.

Prejudice and Discrimination

Discrimination: An unfair action or treatment toward someone

Prejudice: An attitude, prejudging

Sometimes prejudice and discrimination match or don't match.

1. All-weather bigot: is prejudiced and discriminates. One might say, "Of course I act harshly toward trilobites; they deserve it."

2. Fair-weather bigot: is prejudiced but does not discriminate. One might say, "I don't like trilobites, but I can't turn them away."

3. Fair-weather liberal: is not prejudiced but does discriminate. A server at a restaurant might be told by his boss to provide slower service to trilobites and remark, "What can I do? I don't want to get fired."

4. All-weather liberal: is not prejudiced and does not discriminate. One might say, "Everyone, including trilobites, should be treated equally. Anything less is immoral. I would never be part of that."

To recap, effective learners select, organize, and associate information and regulate their learning. They SOAR to success.

SOAR Works

In Chapter 1, I told you about an experiment I conducted that proved SOAR boosted achievement (Daher & Kiewra, 2016). Now examine the graphic organizer in Table 2-4, where four different SOAR studies, including the one described in Chapter 1, are summarized collectively (Daher & Kiewra, 2016; Jairam & Kiewra, 2009; Jairam & Kiewra, 2010; Jairam et al., 2013). Looking across the organizer's first row, you'll see that all the studies involved college students, just like you. In the next row, you'll see that three of the studies compared SOAR strategies to students' preferred strategies. One study, though, compared SOAR to the venerable SQ3R study method, which has been popular since the 1940s. SQ3R stands for survey, question, read, recite, and review. The next two rows reveal instructional support and student training. In two studies, students were provided with optimal SOAR materials but were untrained; in another, they were provided with optimal SOAR or SQ3R materials and were trained in their use; in the fourth, they were trained in SOAR but were not provided with SOAR materials (that was the study described in Chapter 1). The next three rows show that students learned from a variety of chapter-length text materials, presented in print or on computer. The final four rows reveal the impressive results as percentage scores. Across all four experiments, SOAR studiers achieved more than

Table 2-4 GRAPHIC ORGANIZER SUMMARIZING FOUR SOAR STUDIES

	2009	2010	2016	2013
Participants	College	College	College	College
Design	SOAR v. Preferred	SOAR v. Preferred	SOAR v. Preferred	SOAR v. SQ3R
SOAR Training	None	None	30 min	30 min
Instructional Support	SOAR Provided	SOAR Assisted	None	SOAR and SQ3R Provided
MATERIALS				
Topic	Wildcats	Wildcats	Apes	Reinforcement Schedules
Form	Printed Text	Computer Text	5 Computer Texts	Printed Text
Word length	1500	1500	1400	2100
RESULTS	SOAR>Preferred	SOAR>Preferred	SOAR>Preferred	SOAR>SQ3R
Facts	80 76	71 42	74 66	70 56
Relationships	94 46	84 21	70 39	72 51
Concepts	— —	— —	57 46	71 57

Source: Kenneth A. Kiewra, et al., from "Learning Strategies That Help Students SOAR to Success," *Oxford Research Encyclopedia of Education.* Copyright © 2020 by Oxford University Press.

those using preferred methods or SQ3R methods. This was true for all types of testing: facts (e.g., What are male gorillas called?), relationships (e.g., Which ape is the tallest?), and concepts (e.g., At the zoo, you notice a tiny ape high up in the trees moving quickly from branch to branch; what type is this?).

Of course, each of the four SOAR strategies has also proven effective on its own. Students recording lesson notes achieve more than students not recording lesson notes. Students studying graphic organizers achieve more than students studying linearly organized texts or outlines. Students using associative strategies that connect lesson ideas to one another or to prior knowledge achieve more than students studying single facts one at a time. And students who engage in practice testing achieve more than students who use rote memorization techniques like rehearsal. SOAR works.

Why SOAR Works

To understand why SOAR works, you must understand how your memory system works. That's because SOAR strategies are designed to make your memory system work optimally. Understanding how your memory system works is important in its own right as well because it controls learning. But forget memory for just a moment; let's talk about your computer. Your computer allows you to perform amazing tasks like creating a Word document or PowerPoint presentation. You can also edit documents and presentations and save them. You can email, Zoom, surf the internet, and much, much more—so long as you know that your computer is capable of such things and you know how to operate it. What a waste of resources it would be if you didn't know how to copy and paste, attach a file, download a document, research Gothic architecture, or play some Ariana Grande tunes. Okay, now back to memory.

The same is true of memory. Like a computer, it can do amazing things too. For example, it can focus attention on the tiny squiggles on the page you're reading, decipher one squiggle from another, make sense of them, link them with other page squiggles and things you've learned before, store them in memory for a lifetime, and retrieve them in an instant when needed. Amazing stuff, but only useful if you understand how memory operates and how to operate it.

You would think the study of memory would be central in the earliest of school curriculums, but as disclosed in Chapter 1, schools rarely teach students about learning or about how to learn. Instead, instructors sometimes toss out information about apes or architecture or other subjects and hope it sticks in a student's memory. It's mind-boggling to think that you've attended school for nearly two decades without properly studying your own memory system. That's changing now. It's time for a crash course in how memory operates and how to control it using SOAR strategies. Buckle up.

Your Amazing Memory System

Imagine this. You're seated in the back row of your European history class. Your instructor is droning on about Constantine the Great. You think, "I've never heard about this dude, how great can he be?" Other names surface: Armenia … Constantinople … Persians … "Blah, blah, blah," you hear. Your attention wanders from the lesson to classmates' muffled conversations, chesty coughs, and restless toe tapping. Your own laptop distracts as you skim the day's sports headlines or Google the latest fashions. Then you hear, "Alaric," and instantly return your attention to the lesson, wondering why the instructor is talking about a familiar gaming character. But no, this guy's for real, and he's more combative than any gaming character who's lit up your screen. You come to find out that Alaric, meaning ruler of all, was chief of the Visigoths and the leader of the army that sacked Rome in the year 410, an event that symbolized the fall of the Western Roman Empire. You're all ears now, and you hear that Alaric was first a Gothic soldier and later a Roman soldier. "That's a move up to the Major Leagues," you figure. You're also reminded that you recently studied Roman and Gothic architecture and that the architectural order was just the opposite: Roman then Gothic. Alaric led a winning battle for Rome, your instructor reports, where 10,000 of his men were lost. "Some win," you think. "Reminds me of the 50 million deaths stemming from World War II." You hear that Alaric received little recognition for his efforts from the Roman emperor. Because he was snubbed, the story continues, he became leader of the Visigoths and destroyed Corinth, Megara, Argos, and Sparta. "Talk about holding a grudge," you think. Finally, it's reported that when Roman soldiers massacred tens of thousands of Gothic civilians, 30,000 Gothic soldiers joined Alaric in his march on Rome to avenge their murdered families.

Now, let's break this instructional episode down in terms of your memory system, which is shown in Figure 2-4. Many stimuli in your European history classroom impinge upon your five senses, are held in your sensory memory for a few seconds, and compete for your selective attention. Stimuli such as muffled conversations, chesty coughs, toe-tapping movements, laptop headlines, and the teacher's lesson all enter sensory memory and compete for selective attention. Here's the problem: Contrary to popular belief, you can only pay attention

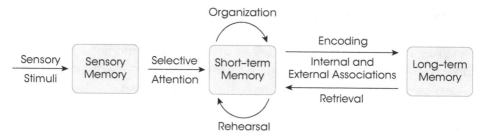

Figure 2-4 Memory System Illustration

to or select one stimulus at a time. Humans are serial processors. You can change processing channels quickly, but just like when you're channel surfing on your TV, you can focus on just one thing at a time. It is either the teacher, a muffled conversation, tapping toes, a chesty cough, or a computer headline to which you selectively attend in a given moment. Some stimuli, though, compete for selective attention better than others. When things are familiar, such as your name or the name of a gaming character, those stimuli go to the head of the class. So too do novel stimuli, such as the score of a soccer match where 10 goals were scored, or a leader as combative as Alaric. And so too do stimuli you are on the lookout for, perhaps the score of a particular soccer match or the instructor's next words after she calls out, "Listen up!" Stimuli that are familiar, novel, or on your radar tend to grab selective attention.

Information that is selectively attended to enters short-term memory. Short-term memory is aptly named because it is limited in space and time. It holds just seven or so items at a time, for approximately 15 seconds. In the European history class, items such as Alaric's name, its meaning, the Emperor's snub, and Alaric's conquest of Rome, among other details, occupied short-term memory at some point. Fortunately, the limits of short-term memory can be expanded, using two memory processes: rehearsal and organization. That's why short-term memory is also called working memory—because as you rehearse or organize information in short-term memory, you are also working on it. Rehearsal keeps information active in short-term memory beyond the 15-second time limit. So long as information is rehearsed, it remains in short-term memory. So as you repeat this information—Alaric destroyed Corinth, Megara, Argos, Sparta, and Rome—it remains active in short-term memory. There are two problems with rehearsal. The first is that while you rehearse information, you can't really do anything else with that information or take new information into short-term memory, because short-term memory is busy rehearsing. You're stuck in that rehearsal loop. The second problem, as mentioned in Chapter 1, is that rote rehearsal does not move information into long-term memory. Organization, meanwhile, condenses information and thereby allows more than 7 items to occupy

Activity 2.4

Let's try an activity from Dave Crenshaw's book, *The Myth of Multitasking: How Doing It All Gets Nothing Done*. First, do the following two tasks using multitasking. Write down the sentence, "Multitasking is worse than a lie," as many times as you can in 60 seconds. As you do this, complete a second task at the same time: Write down consecutive numbers beginning with 1 by writing one number after you write each letter. For example, M1, U2 ... Count how many letters and numbers you write. Next, try this activity without multitasking. Write out the sentence as many times as you can in 30 seconds and then write as many consecutive numbers as you can in 30 seconds. Count how many letters and numbers you wrote, and compare those findings with your earlier multitasking findings. What did you learn?

short-term memory at one time. For example, when the cities that Alaric conquered are placed on a single map such as that in Figure 2-5, that map organizes those five items into a single item that now occupies less short-term memory space.

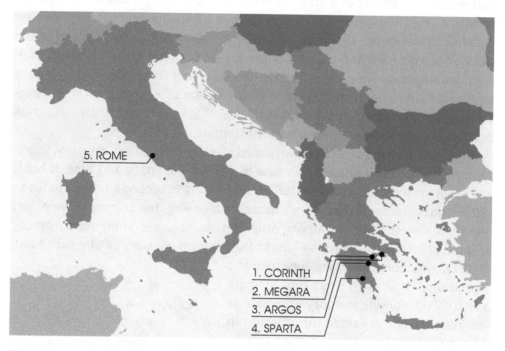

Figure 2-5 Geographic Organizer Showing Alaric's Conquests

Activity 2.5

Trigrams are three-consonant structures like BKF or MRL. Have a friend show you two trigrams at one time, for 5 seconds. After you study the two trigrams, have your friend remove them and ask you to recall them 20 seconds later. Do this activity a second time with new trigrams, but after studying the new trigrams for 5 seconds, count backwards from 75 to zero by threes. Then try recalling the trigrams. What happened? How does this activity simulate how information is lost in short-term memory?

The output of short-term memory enters long-term memory, which is everything short-term memory is not. Long-term memory is without limit. It has enormous space that can perhaps never be filled, and information can perhaps reside there permanently. Long-term storage depends on converting trivial information pieces in short-term memory into meaningful information packages through a process called encoding. There are two encoding processes: building internal associations and building external associations. Internal associations are those made among ideas within the lesson. For example, you might internally associate lesson pieces sequentially: Alaric was a Gothic, then a Roman, and then a Visigoth leader. You might also internally associate lesson ideas in terms of cause and effect: The emperor's snubbing caused Alaric to leave the Romans; the killing of Gothic civilians caused Gothic soldiers to join Alaric and the Visigoth army. External associations are those made between lesson ideas and ideas outside the lesson, ideas previously learned and stored in long-term memory. For example, you might link Alaric's movement from the Gothic army to the Roman army to a baseball player moving from the minor leagues to the Major Leagues. You might use the letter sequence GRV (for Gothic, Roman, Visigoth) to form the word "grave" and remember that Alaric sent soldiers to their grave, in this order, as a military leader. Or you might link the fall of the Roman Empire to the transition from Romanesque to Gothic architecture. It is these meaningful internal and external associations that store information purposefully and economically in long-term memory (much like books stored by subject or author in a library), allowing for easy access and retrieval.

Speaking of retrieval, it is never sufficient to simply store information in long-term memory; it must be retrieved when needed. But sometimes we have trouble retrieving even well-known information, such as when we make introductions: "I'd like you to meet … ah … um … my mom!" Fortunately, the keys to effective encoding—constructing meaningful internal and external associations—are also the keys to effective retrieval. Think of it this way. To lock valuables away in a safe deposit box requires a key. That same key also unlocks the box and allows you to retrieve your valuables. So the associations you make as you encode information into long-term memory when you learn are the same associations that

Activity 2.6

Returning to Activity 2-5, how could you have quickly moved the trigrams you studied into long-term memory using external associations? Using the trigrams I presented earlier, I might encode BKF as Burger King Fries and encode MRL as the name Myrl. In each case, I took non-meaningful information and made it meaningful by linking it to prior knowledge. I created external associations to quickly move the information into long-term memory. Now, you do the same for the trigrams you had to memorize. Also use external associations to remember these new trigrams: HRF and JLT.

A Recap of How Memory Works

1. Many stimuli impinge upon your senses and are held in sensory memory for a few seconds.
2. You selectively attend to a few of those stimuli (especially those that are familiar, novel, or on your radar) one at a time.
3. Attended stimuli enter short-term memory, which is limited in time (about 15 seconds) and amount (usually about seven items). Rehearsal activities can increase time; organization activities can increase amount.
4. Information in short-term memory can move to long-term memory, which is unlimited in the time or amount of information held, through the encoding process, which involves building internal (within the lesson) and external (outside the lesson) associations.
5. These same associations made during encoding help you retrieve information from long-term memory.

permit retrieval later. In this manner, the encoded association GRV helps you retrieve the order of armies Alaric led: Gothic, Roman, Visigoth. Similarly, your encoded association between European architecture and the toppling of Rome helps you retrieve the fact that Gothic soldiers helped topple Rome, much the way Gothic architecture supplanted Roman architecture.

A recap of how memory works is presented in the box above. In summary, environmental stimuli impinge on your five senses and are briefly stored in sensory memory. From this large array of information, you selectively attend to just a fraction of it, especially to things that are familiar, novel, or on your watch list. Selected information enters short-term memory, which is limited in time and space but can hold more information for a longer time using organization and rehearsal processes. However, if encoded by building internal and external associations, that information can move to long-term memory, which has no time and space limitations. Effective encoding not only stores information economically, but also offers the key to later retrieving that information. The takeaway message is that new information is not remembered automatically or without effort. Memory storage requires an effective operator who knows how to attend, hold, encode, and retrieve information. Just as the best computer can do nothing without an effective operator, the memory system is just a tangle of useless storage units and processes without a knowledgeable and skilled operator. Now that you know how your memory operates, let's see how SOAR makes it fire.

Memory and SOAR

Figure 2-6 again shows the memory system, but this time with the addition of SOAR strategies and the places where they impact memory. SOAR's first component is select, and it is linked to the memory system's selective attention process. As you'll see in Chapter 3, note-taking helps you avoid distractions and attend selectively to lesson ideas. In the European history lesson, a SOAR-trained student would not sit in the back of the classroom, a place rife with distractions, but in the front row—away from chatting, coughing, and foot-tapping

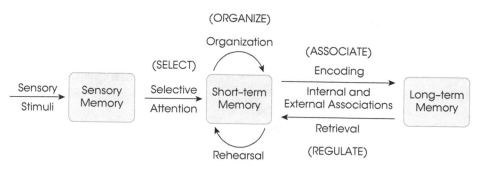

Figure 2-6 Memory System Illustration (With SOAR Strategies)

classmates—where attention is easily focused on what the instructor does and says. Moreover, the student would not use her laptop for nefarious, cyber-slacking purposes. It would be opened to course material and a page for note-taking. Recording a complete set of notes keeps students attentive and provides them with an excellent review source.

SOAR's second component, organize, is linked to the memory system's organization process in short-term memory. Organization strategies are the topic of Chapter 4. For the European history lesson, a SOAR-trained student might envision or create a graphic organizer, like that in Figure 2-5, that displays Alaric's conquests in an organized, easy-to-view fashion. The student might also envision or create the sequence organizer shown in Figure 2-7, which displays the sequence of military allegiances Alaric held.

Alaric's Military Allegiances

Gothic ⟶ *Roman* ⟶ *Visigoth*

Figure 2-7 Sequence Organizer Showing Alaric's Military Allegiances

SOAR's third component, associate, is linked to the memory system's encoding process (which moves information into long-term memory) and is the topic of Chapter 5. Constructing internal associations, within the lesson material, and external associations, outside the lesson material, is what gives information meaning, prompts efficient memory storage, and facilitates retrieval. Earlier, you saw examples of internal and external associations for the European history lesson that were reflective of SOAR's association strategy.

Internal Associations:
- The emperor's snubbing caused Alaric to leave the Romans.

- The killing of Gothic civilians caused Gothic soldiers to join Alaric and the Visigoth army.

External Associations:
- Alaric's movement from the Gothic to the Roman army is similar to a baseball player moving from the minor leagues to the Major Leagues.

- The word GRaVe helps you remember that Alaric sent soldiers to their grave in this order as a military leader: Gothic, Roman, Visigoth.

SOAR's fourth component, regulate, is linked to the memory system's retrieval

Activity 2.7

Returning to Activity 2-3, what associations can you make to remember the information about prejudice and discrimination?

process (which returns stored information to short-term memory for further use) and is the topic of Chapter 6. The SOAR strategy that best influences retrieval is self-testing. Self-testing is a form of retrieval practice and a means for establishing whether learning has occurred. A SOAR-trained student might generate practice test questions like the following:

1. What does the name Alaric mean?

2. What army did Alaric lead in his defeat of Rome?

3. What other soldiers joined Alaric in the conquering of Rome?

4. Why did Alaric leave the Roman army?

Putting It All Together

The evidence is in. SOAR works. Research confirms that it boosts achievement. And now you know why: SOAR supports and bolsters the memory processes that govern learning. Euro history, no more mystery. The next four chapters detail how you can select, organize, and associate information, and regulate learning. Let's keep SOARing.

Answers to Focus Questions

1. Most students record incomplete notes containing just one third of important lesson information. Students also record linear notes that obscure relationships between lesson ideas.

2. Students use a host of redundant strategies such as rehearsal, rereading, rewriting, and reciting. These are passive and rote strategies that do not work.

3. SOAR is an acronym for a package of strategies that help students learn. These include: select, organize, associate, and regulate. Select involves noting all important lesson ideas. Organize involves organizing notes using graphic organizers. Associate involves drawing relationships among lesson ideas and linking new information to prior knowledge. Regulate involves self-monitoring one's learning, usually through self-testing.

4. In a series of studies conducted by Kiewra and colleagues that employed test items measuring fact, relationship, and concept learning, college students using SOAR methods achieved more than students using their preferred study methods or methods from a competing study system (Daher & Kiewra, 2016; Jairam & Kiewra, 2009; Jairam & Kiewra, 2010; Jairam et al., 2013). Students were able to use SOAR effectively after as little as 30 minutes of SOAR training.

5. Humans are serial processors. That means we can pay attention to just one stimulus at a time, which runs counter to most people's multi-tasking beliefs and futile attempts. The type of stimuli most likely to command attention include: (a) familiar things, like the name Jean Piaget in human development; (b) novel things, like new information that Piaget worked at the Binet Institute developing an intelligence test; and (c) things one is looking for, such as an example of Piaget's concept of conservation.

6. Short-term memory is limited in two ways: in space and time. It can only hold about 7 items at one time in its limited space, and it can only hold information for about 15 seconds. These limitations can be overcome through the use of strategies. Rehearsal strategies can keep information active in short-term memory beyond the 15-second time limit. Organization strategies can condense or chunk information, thereby clearing space to hold more than 7 things at one time.

7. Building internal and external associations is the key to moving information from short-term memory to long-term memory. Internal associations are those linking lesson information. As you read about short-term and long-term memory, you might make the internal association that short-term memory is limited in time and space, whereas long-term memory is unlimited in time and space. External associations are those linking lesson information to ideas outside the lesson, to your prior knowledge. As you read about short-term memory limitations, you might link that to a prior experience where you were introduced to a room full of people and seconds later you remembered almost none of their names.

8. The keys to retrieving information from long-term memory are the same as the keys for encoding information into long-term memory: internal and external associations. That's because the associations you make while learning the material become the ideal cues for later retrieving that information. For example, if you remember a locker combination by thinking of the jersey numbers of famous basketball players—Bird, 33; Jordan, 23; and Wade, 3—thinking about those players will later help you retrieve the combination.

9. SOAR is based, in part, on the workings of the memory system. SOAR strategies can be used to help memory operate at its full capacity. Select strategies, such as note-taking, aid memory's selective attention process. Organize strategies, such as constructing graphic organizers, aid the organization of information in short-term memory. Associate strategies, such as building internal and external associations, aid the memory system's encoding process—the movement of information from short-term to long-term memory. Regulate strategies, such as self-testing, aid memory retrieval.

CHAPTER 3

Selection Strategies for Noting Lecture and Text Information

OVERVIEW

Objectives

1. Describe problems associated with student note-taking and methods for overcoming them.

2. Describe what you can do before, during, and after lectures to select and record lecture ideas.

3. Record effective notes from lectures and texts.

Focus Questions

1. What are the two reasons why note-taking is important?

2. How do students usually record notes?

3. Why is going to class important?

4. How can you be on the edge during lectures?

5. Explain why recording complete notes is difficult but important.

6. What are the benefits of provided notes?

7. What are the benefits of organizational cues?

8. How should you take notes when given PowerPoint slides?

9. What are the cyber-slacking dangers of laptops and smartphones?

10. What are the advantages of recording and replaying lectures?

11. What are the advantages and preferred methods for revising notes?

12. What problems are associated with highlighting?

A Note-Taking Nightmare

Isabelle glances nervously at her phone as she approaches Lecture Hall 334. "Fourteen minutes past 8. I'm way late for history class," she frets. Huffing and puffing from dashing across campus and high-stepping up three flights of stairs, Isabelle fills her lungs with oxygen and her heart with courage and slowly pulls open the room's old wooden door, which creaks and groans and publicizes her late arrival. Instantly, 200 sets of eyes turn her way, paralyzing her as though she were a frightened deer frozen in a car's headlights. Another gasp for air, and Isabelle shuffles across the room's crowded back row toward a vacant seat. She tramples toes, jostles desks, and leaves a string of dislodged power cords in her wake. Once seated, Isabelle fires up her laptop and opens a Word document for note-taking.

At last, Isabelle tunes into the instructor, who seems light-years away at the front of the cavernous room and who is barely audible amid the keyboard tapping, pen clicking, and conversations surrounding her. Worse yet, the guy next to her is wearing headphones and chomping handfuls of crunchy cereal. The rhythmic chomping leads Isabelle to suspect that he's listening to progressive rock. Meanwhile, the instructor describes several events leading up to the French Revolution, and Isabelle proudly types her first note: French Revolution. The next several minutes are abuzz with French Revolution names, places, and dates Isabelle's not heard before. "Perhaps they were introduced when I missed last class period because my sweatpants were in the dryer," she laments. Now Isabelle's brain drifts in and out, and her notes, like the lines on an electroencephalogram, reflect her mental lapses. She records only occasional and meaningless words—Napoleon ... 1786 ... King Louis the 16th ... 1791 ... Versailles ... Marie Antoinette ... Maximilien de Robespierre ... Austria ... Prussia—that capture the instructor's historical story the way a chain-link fence captures water.

Eventually, Isabelle gives up and opens her internet browser. First, she checks on airfare prices for her spring break trip. An ad for boots pops up, and soon Isabelle is knee-high in boot options. She bookmarks that page for later reference, perhaps during her afternoon algebra class. She next checks Facebook and grins at recently posted photos of her toddler niece. "What a sweetie," she muses. Her phone buzzes. She slips it from her pocket and thumbs her lunch preference reply to her roommate. Twelve messages later, they agree to meet at the Canteen, where they lunch together most every day, for mac and cheese and a chat.

The instructor projects a map on the room's front screen, and Isabelle glances up to see a distorted image. She tilts her glasses nearer her eyes to try to bring the image into focus. She searches for a notepad from her backpack, eventually locates one, and then hurriedly tries to draw the map. As she does, her brain becomes immune to what the instructor is saying about the map. Suddenly, the image flickers and goes black like a falling star in the night sky. In the end, Isabelle has a partial sketch but has no idea what it means.

Isabelle's anguish and frustration with the lecture, though, are quickly buoyed by the closing bell. She inspects her lesson notations, which amount to about half a page of notes—mostly discrete names and terms she does not understand—and proudly closes her laptop. As she leaves, she notices a group of students huddled together discussing the lecture and revising their notes. "No time for that," Isabelle muses. "Sociology begins in 15 minutes, and I need to stop by the coffee shop and pick up a little pick-me-up. And, at this time of day, a 20-minute line would be a welcomed sight."

Why Note-Taking Is Important

Isabelle's fictional lecture hall nightmare is, unfortunately, a harsh reality series for many students who fail to learn from lectures because, like Isabelle, they fail to select and note important lecture ideas for further study. How can they when they miss class or show up late, lack background knowledge about the topic, sit in the rear of the room beyond their visual and auditory range amid distractions, cyber-slack using digital devices like laptops and phones, and record sketchy notes? They can't. You can't. Learning does not work that way. It only works when you work. And learning work begins with selecting and noting key lesson ideas.

Note-taking is the key to information selection for two reasons. First, the act of taking notes makes you more attentive during lectures. When you are busy taking notes, you are not busy daydreaming, surfing the net, or being bored. And, when focused on note-taking, you are less likely to be distracted by other sights and sounds. Students who record lecture notes achieve more than students who simply listen to the lecture without recording notes.

Second, note-taking creates a permanent record of selected ideas—a record that can be reviewed weeks or months later when it's time to prepare for a test. Some students shun note-taking, believing they'll remember what they hear or read. Not so. Humans quickly forget much of what they experience, even when they make a mental note to remember it. Mental notes fade quickly; written notes endure. Students who review lecture notes achieve more than students who do not review lecture notes.

Recording and reviewing notes, then, is certainly a great plan, but it's a plan many students don't follow well. As mentioned in Chapter 2, students often record sketchy notes—a paltry one third of lesson ideas—when they should, instead, be recording complete notes. Meanwhile, the probability of recalling non-noted information on a test is just 5%. That means: not noted, not learned. When it comes to reviewing notes, most students veer off course there too. As also mentioned in Chapter 2, students usually study one idea at a time and in redundant fashion, when they should organize and associate noted ideas and regulate learning instead.

The bulk of this chapter describes how to select and note lecture information. Doing so is crucial because lecture information is fleeting, gone in an instant. Note it now, or never. The last part of the chapter addresses how to select and note text information. Chapters 4–6 pertain to the learning or studying of what's noted.

Selecting and Noting Lecture Information

There are things you can do before, during, and after a lecture to improve the selection and notation of information. Let's take a look.

Before the Lecture

There are four simple things you can do to improve note-taking before the lecture even starts. I call these the four BEs: BE there, BE on time, BE up front, and BE on the edge of your seat.

1. BE There!

It's been said that 80% of success in life is just showing up. A Harvard Business School professor delivering a TED Talk on six vital lessons for success made showing up number one. "If you don't show up," she said, "nothing happens" (Kanter, 2016). I'll add: Learning certainly doesn't happen.

When you miss class, you miss all the presented information. Without information selection, there are no notes to study, and the other SOAR factors cannot fire. Some of this information can perhaps be recouped if you examine classmates' notes, the text, or class handouts and postings. But those sources usually offer just snippets and secondhand accounts of what happened, much like reading a movie review instead of seeing the movie firsthand.

When you miss class, you also forfeit any opportunity to ask questions and contribute to class discussions. Classes should be experienced, not just attended. Learning is a constructive two-way process, and you are part of that process.

When you miss class, you also miss out on the joys of classroom learning. Don't laugh. Hopefully, you're in school not only to get gym access and graduate but also to enjoy the learning process. You might not realize it now, but college is likely the most intellectually fueled time of your life, a time when passionate students learn from one another and from domain experts standing before you.

You're thinking, "Okay, going to class is important, but sometimes I simply can't make it. I got places to go (like a job interview), things to do (like picking up my parents at the airport), and people to see (like my advisor). And, other times, things just happen. You know, dead car battery and a sore throat." First off, if tomorrow you were getting married, dining with the college president, or going to see the hottest new play, would you let any of these reasons stop you? Of course not; that's because they are not reasons for absenteeism but excuses well within your control. Let's see.

- Job interview: Your job is school. Who scheduled this interview, the attorney general? Schedule the interview for another time.

- Picking up parents: Let them take a cab or Uber. Let them enjoy a lovely meal at the airport until you can swing by after class.

- Seeing advisor: It's doubtful your advisor would advise you to miss class. Schedule an appointment outside class time.

- Dead battery: Walk, run, skip, hop. Ride a bike. Call a friend. Use that Uber app you recommended to your parents.

- Illness: Are you so sick that you'd miss your wedding? If you can attend the wedding, you can attend class. But if you are too sick: Stay home, heal quickly, and arrange to Zoom in or have someone record the class for you. Use technology to your advantage.

Two more things. First, don't be under the false assumption that missing the first class doesn't matter, because "Nothing ever happens the first day." Not true. In my 100-point learning strategies class, students who are absent the first day can find themselves in the hole quickly. When they miss day 1, they lose 2 points for attendance and 2 points for not completing an in-class assignment. When they show up the second day of class, most lose 3 more points for not having the out-of-class assignment from day 1 completed, and they are likely to fail the 3-point quiz covering day 1 material. Do the math. That's 10 percentage points squandered, a full letter grade, due to one early absence.

Second, beware the absolution delusion. Perhaps your instructor says it's okay to miss class any time or to miss class some number of times per semester. Or perhaps your instructor gives you special permission to be absent while you attend a campus event or have your dog groomed. In each case, the instructor is absolving you from your class-missing sin. Don't buy it. Even though you have the green light to skip class, don't be deluded into thinking your absence won't hurt you. When you miss class, you miss vital information, the opportunity to contribute, and the joy of learning. BE there.

2. BE on Time!

Being late does not play well in the real world. Imagine being late for work, late picking up your child from pre-school, or late for reveille in the military. All unacceptable with harsh repercussions. Tardiness can doom you in the classroom too. If you're late for class, you're not there, so all the same issues linked to missing class apply: You're not learning, contributing to learning, or enjoying learning. And you have no notes to review. To curtail late behavior, some instructors, like me, start right on time and often begin with a pop quiz that students cannot begin late. Furthermore, slipping into class late is inconsiderate to classmates and the instructor, who are hard at work.

There's really no excuse for being late. "I'm not a morning person" doesn't fly when you saunter into your 7:30 class still wearing pajama bottoms. Counter the early-morning blahs by getting up at 6:00, exercising, showering, and eating a healthy breakfast—all before class. "I couldn't find a parking space" is a feeble excuse too. Arrive early, when spaces are plentiful. Or explore other means of transportation such as walking, running, biking, and ride sharing. For every problem, there's a solution.

A college baseball coach tells his team, "If you're on time, you're late." He wants them at practices early to warm up, stretch, and get their heads in the game. You should do the same: Arrive early to class, grab a good seat, ready your materials, and review previous notes. BE on time and ready to work.

3. BE up Front!

You have the opportunity to purchase concert tickets to hear your favorite group, football tickets to cheer on your favorite football team, or theater tickets to watch a new smash play. Where would you choose to sit if all seats were available? Likely down front, close to the action, where you can watch the musicians strum difficult licks, the actors spit, and the players collide. Why then do most students scurry to the rear of the classroom, leaving the front seats unoccupied? Some want to hide in the back behind tall people, so they can text and surf the net. Most, though, simply want to don an invisibility cloak and be left alone because they perceive education as a passive, one-way information transfer. But it's not.

True education is an active, multi-directional information exchange involving students and teacher. So come out of the stands onto the field, out from the wings onto the stage, up from the back of the classroom to the front. In the front of the classroom, you can see well and hear well and are less likely to be distracted by slacking students. You're more likely to pay attention, take copious notes, and participate. You're also more likely to be looked upon favorably by instructors—and that's no small matter when they evaluate your work. Whatever the reason, students who sit toward the front tend to achieve more than students who sit toward the back. Don't be on the outside looking in. Don't be a spectator. Be a player. Be up front.

4. BE on the Edge!

It does no good to go to class early, grab a front-row seat, and then sit there passively like a zombie. Don't just show up and hope your instructors fill your mind the way bakers fill a cake mold. That's not happening. You've got to reach out and grab knowledge. Instead of being passive, be perched on the edge of your seat as if watching a World Cup shoot-out or the final heart-wrenching scene in *Romeo and Juliet*. Lean into the lecture as if you were trying to hear Romeo's dying words. Eye the instructor as intently as the outstretched keeper diving to make the save. Hang on every word, every slide, and every raised eyebrow or exuberant head nod that signal something important is coming your way. Be completely in the moment.

Maintain concentration throughout the lecture. It is common for students to take fewer notes in the second half of lectures because they tire, slack off, and await the closing bell. Stave off fatigue by being physically prepared to go the distance. Stay fresh by getting plenty of sleep and aerobic exercise. Don't go to class hungry and become distracted by your rumbling tummy. Don't go to class overly full and become sleepy.

Like a surgeon about to operate, have all the necessary tools on hand before class begins. Fire up your laptop and set it to course material. Have your textbook, notebook, and writing utensils at hand. Turn off your phone and put it in your backpack where it won't distract. I am always shocked when I observe students begin class with nothing on their desk. Only when the instructor begins lecturing do they casually search for what they need. By the time they're ready, the instructor is 10 ideas deep into the lesson—10 ideas those slow-moving students miss.

Finally, part of being on the edge involves being mentally prepared and up-to-date. Before the lecture, read assigned chapters and review lecture notes from the previous week. Acquiring new knowledge depends on associating it to previous knowledge in long-term memory, as you learned in Chapter 2. Lectures are fleeting and fast. And your ability to keep pace depends on your level of understanding going in. If the gap between your knowledge and the instructor's presentation is too wide, you'll be left in the dust. Read, review, be on the edge, and be ready to roll.

During the Lecture

During the lecture, one primary goal is to acquire a complete set of notes. Complete note-taking helps you pay attention and learn during the lecture, and it provides you with useful notes for later review. Students, though, are incomplete notetakers. As you'll see in the many research studies reviewed throughout this chapter, students commonly record just one third of important lecture information. Why is this? One reason is that students foolishly believe they'll remember what they hear. That's wrong. Human memory is fallible, and students are likely to later recall only 5% of non-noted lecture information. Did you write that down? Another reason is that students mistakenly believe they should note only those things they do not understand. That's wrong too. If you do that, you'll naturally end up with a bunch of notes you don't understand. Your notes should provide a complete and comprehensible record of important lecture ideas. Finally, our own physical limitations make complete note-taking difficult. Most lectures are paced at about 120–180 words per minute, but most people can only type at about 33 words per minute and write at about 22 words per minute. Those limitations make it hard to keep up with fast-talking speakers.

In this section, we'll cover four points aimed at helping you derive complete and useful notes: (a) use what's given, (b) beware the laptop and other mobile devices, (c) note these things, and (d) get it all.

Activity 3.1

Let's see just how fast you can write and type the following sentence: Taking complete notes is likely hampered by our physical limitations.

1. Set a timer for 1 minute and write this sentence by hand as many times as you can.

2. Set a timer for 1 minute and type this sentence as many times as you can.

3. Count the number of words you produced in each case; that represents your words-per-minute results.

4. Which was faster and by how much?

5. Keep this limitation in mind as you strive to take complete lecture notes in your classes.

Use What's Given

While I was a first-year graduate student at Florida State University, I took a statistics course from Professor Fletcher, who forbade note-taking. His reasoning was that if students were busy taking notes, they weren't fully thinking about the lecture ideas. To compensate for their not having notes to review, Dr. Fletcher gave students a complete set of notes following each lecture. Most students were delighted with this arrangement, as they could kick back, simply listen to the lecture, and still have a complete set of notes to review. I was not among the enamored. I was a voracious notetaker who commonly filled pages with lesson points and personal elaborations. Small wonder I was twice named Notetaker of the Year Runner-up in college. Because I could not overtly record notes in Fletcher's class, I retreated to the rear of the room and hid in the shadow of a former Seminole lineman, concealed by his bulk. There I huddled over a tiny notepad and wrote feverishly whenever Fletcher glanced away. I was a clandestine notetaker. One day, as I scribbled, Fletcher crept up from behind and caught me pen-handed. "Mr. Kiewra, are you taking notes in my class?" he chided. "Ah, no," I fibbed, "I'm writing a letter to a friend back home." Staring at the exposed notepad, Fletcher retorted, "Well, how nice of you to tell your friend about omnibus testing."

It turns out Fletcher knew what he was doing, as I later proved in a study I conducted with Steve Benton (Kiewra & Benton, 1987). In that study, college students in education watched a recorded 20-minute lesson on learning hierarchies, with one group recording notes while the other group did not. Later, notetakers reviewed their notes, and non-notetakers reviewed a set of provided notes. Following the 25-minute review period, all students were tested on the lesson. Those reviewing the provided notes scored 17% higher than those reviewing their own notes. Not surprising given that the provided notes contained all lesson ideas, whereas students' own notes contained just 38% of lesson ideas on average. This study confirmed that students are sketchy notetakers, recording just one third of important lesson ideas, and that they benefit from having a complete set of notes to review, even when those notes are provided by some other source.

Another study I conducted went so far as to show that reviewing a complete set of provided notes can even compensate for missing a lesson (Kiewra, 1985b). College students attended the 20-minute lesson on learning hierarchies and either took notes or simply listened. Another group did not attend the lesson at all. Later, students reviewed either no notes, their own notes, provided notes, or both their own notes and provided notes, resulting in the seven groups shown on the left side of Table 3-1.

Table 3-1 THE BENEFITS OF RECEIVING PROVIDED NOTES

Groups	Test Results
Take notes/Review own + provided	71%
Not attend/Review provided	69%
Listen/Review provided	63%
Take notes/Review own	51%
Take notes/Review no notes	44%
Listen/Review no notes	43%
Not attend/Review no notes	33%

Source: Adapted from Kenneth A. Kiewra, *Teaching How to Learn: The Teacher's Guide to Student Success*, p. 28. Copyright © 2009 by Corwin Press.

The right side shows the findings. Notice that the highest-achieving groups all studied the provided notes, the lowest-achieving groups all studied without notes, and the middle-most group took their own notes and studied only those. These findings make sense because self-recorded notes contained just 35% of the lesson ideas, whereas provided notes contained all lesson ideas. This study confirmed that note-taking's primary value lies in the review of complete notes and that a student's tried-and-true method, of recording and reviewing sketchy notes, is less than optimal. Students should certainly take advantage of complete notes when provided.

Another instructor-provided gift horse you should not look in the mouth is partial notes, which provide the lesson's main ideas or structure, with spaces to note lesson details. In a study I conducted with several colleagues, college students attended a recorded lesson on the topic of creativity and recorded notes—either from scratch or using the partial notes framework in Table 3-2 (Kiewra et al., 1995). Those taking notes on their own recorded 38% of the lesson ideas, whereas those recording notes on the partial notes framework recorded 56% of lesson ideas. This note-taking boost led to higher achievement by the partial notes group.

Table 3-2 PARTIAL NOTES FRAMEWORK FOR CREATIVITY LECTURE

	Creativity		
	Adaptive Creativity	Innovative Creativity	Emergent Creativity
Outcome			
Motivation			
Time Demands			
Example			

When students are given partial notes to help them learn from computer-provided text, some students make the mistake of copying and pasting large verbatim chunks of text information—sometimes entire paragraphs—into their notes. When they do, they are just filling space instead of thinking about what they are noting. A research study by Brent Igo and I showed that restricting the amount of information college students copy and paste into notes made them more selective and boosted achievement. The restricted copy-and-paste notetakers out-achieved the non-restricted copy-and-paste notetakers by 12% on idea recall, 20% on classification of new examples, and 28% on idea comparisons (Igo & Kiewra, 2007). Notes need to be complete but not a word-for-word restatement of the lesson.

You should also tune in to the signals instructors give regarding what's worth noting. An instructor might not-so-subtly say, "This point is noteworthy/imperative/absolutely critical/likely to be on the test." You had better be scribing then. Sometimes, it's not what instructors say but how they say it. Listen for variations in voice pitch, cadence, volume, or rate that signal noteworthy ideas. Repeating something is also an importance cue or a sign of failing memory. Be on the lookout for nonverbal cues, too, such as pointing, clapping, finger snapping, hand waving, a piercing glance, or a rap on the table. Silence can also be a cue, as your instructor is providing additional time for you to note something important. My favorite university professor used to provide a cue medley when making a particularly important point. He'd put his foot up on the table, cross his arms and rest them on his knee, squint his eyes, jut out his lower lip, arch his eyebrows, and nod vehemently. Eventually, we recognized this as a time to write feverishly rather than seek medical attention.

One of the best cues is writing something on the board, and students know it. They write down nearly 90% of what's written on the board, including notes left from the room's previous instructor. Another effective cue is pre-questions. In one research study, students listened to a lecture divided into 16 sections. One group received a pre-question before each section, while another group did not. The pre-question group recorded 10 times the number of notes and later recalled 25% more lecture ideas than the non-question group (Rickards and McCormick, 1988).

The cues described above all signal importance. There is another sort of cue you should watch for: organizational cues, which signal the lesson's organizational structure. In a study I conducted with Scott Titsworth (Titsworth & Kiewra, 2004), college students listened to one of two versions of a lecture on communication theories: cued and un-cued. Both were well organized and identical, with one exception: The cued lesson signaled the lesson's organization by emphasizing the four lesson topics (the names of the communication theories) and five lesson categories common to each topic (such as definition, example, and application). For instance, one cue was, "Next, we examine an *application* of *general systems theory."* Another was, "Here is the *definition* of *mass media theory."* There were 20 organizational cues in total. During the lesson, students recorded notes. After that, they reviewed notes and were tested. Results showed that the un-cued group recorded 37% of lesson ideas, whereas the cued group recorded 80% of lesson ideas, a staggering difference. In terms of achievement, the cued group outscored the un-cued group by 45% on a test measuring recall of the lesson's organization and by 16% on a test measuring recall of the lesson's details. Following are some other examples of organizational cues and the types of notes you should prepare to record. Chapter 4 covers organizational cues in greater depth.

- "Atoms have three parts." Listen for and note the three parts.

- "I'll next compare the four theories in terms of origin, evidence, and limitations." Listen for and note the names of the four theories and the details for each regarding their origin, evidence, and limitations.

- "Now, we'll describe the surface features of Mars." Listen for and note Mars's surface features. Also be on the lookout for the surface features of other planets.

- "Let's look at how blood flows through the heart's four chambers." Listen for and note the names of the four chambers and the order in which blood flows through them.

Activity 3.2

Underline the organizational cues in the following lecture snippets:

1. The nine main phyla of the animal kingdom are described.

2. To test a food for the presence of simple sugar, place the food in a test tube, then add enough clear Benedict's solution to cover it. Next, heat it until it boils.

3. In this section, we consider growth hormones and their role in regulation. Two types of growth hormones are auxins and gibberellins.

4. Methods for the transfer of food energy in a food chain fall within three categories—predation, scavenging, and symbiosis. Symbiosis can be defined as a nutritive relationship between two organisms. There are three types of symbiosis.

PowerPoint slides have become omnipresent in education, pushing aside the likes of chalk and overheads. Do they help students record or establish complete notes? Students believe so. Researchers examined student perceptions of PowerPoint presentations and found that 69% of students believed such presentations held their attention, and 80% believed printed PowerPoint handouts helped them take notes. Perceptions were reality in another study, where half the lectures were delivered with PowerPoint slides and half in traditional fashion without PowerPoint slides. Students who experienced both formats reported that note-taking was easier, more extensive, and more organized for the PowerPoint lectures than for traditional lectures (Frey and Birnbaum, 2002).

PowerPoint slides are especially effective when they are posted online for students to download prior to lectures. One semester-long study confirmed that downloading PowerPoint slides before classes had large and positive effects on students' exam performances throughout the semester (Nouri & Shahis, 2008). My own recommendation is for students to view PowerPoint slides during lectures, either as printed copies or online, and record notes right near corresponding slides, as shown in Figure 3-1. By doing so, you avoid duplication; you need not write down information or recreate figures already appearing on the slide. Instead, your notes contain lecture details, examples, personal thoughts, and associations absent from the slides. You also now have newly recorded information where it belongs—right next to related information—instead of on a faraway document stored elsewhere.

There are two types of NT cues—importance and organizational.
This is an example of importance cue.

Figure 3-1 Lecture Notes Taken Below PowerPoint Slide

Beware the Laptop and Other Mobile Devices

Warning! Warning! Warning! Cyber-slacking is the unwarranted use of mobile technology in the classroom for non-learning purposes, such as Isabelle's net surfing and text messaging, and it happens a lot. Laptops and other mobile devices are ubiquitous in college classrooms and prove costly as they pull students off task, limit note-taking, and reduce achievement. Here's how bad things are in college classrooms, based on research data (Fried, 2008). When students were asked how they used their laptops in class, 81% reported checking email,

43% reported surfing the web, 25% reported playing games, and 35% reported other activities unrelated to course material. Overall, students reported spending more than half a typical class period using laptops for non-class purposes. It's no surprise, then, that students who use laptops tend to have about a half-grade lower GPA than students who record longhand notes.

I've seen plenty of inappropriate laptop use firsthand. I often observe graduate teaching assistants teaching sections of our college's study skills class. In one recent observation, 22 of 30 students were using laptops, and only four of those laptops (18%) were being used to observe class slides or take notes. This is crazy—and in a study skills class, no less, where students are taught the dangers of cyber-slacking and where strict policies about unwarranted use are in play. And it's not just laptops. It's been reported that 70% of students send text messages via their phones during class, and they send or receive 20 text messages per class on average (Dietz and Henrich, 2014; Emanuel, 2013; Kornhauser et al., 2016). The box below recaps students' inappropriate technology use during class.

One study cleverly examined the effects of students' phone usage on note-taking and recall (Kuznekoff & Titsworth, 2013). Table 3-3 summarizes that study. College students watched a 12-minute video about communication theories with no phone distractions (received no text messages), low phone distractions (received a text message every 60 seconds), or high phone distractions (received a text message every 30 seconds). Students in the distraction groups had to respond to the messages when they occurred. Students were told to record notes during the lecture and were tested following the lecture. Text distractions lowered note-taking: The no-distraction group recorded 33% of lesson ideas, compared to 27% for the low-distraction group and 20% for the high-distraction group. Text distractions also lowered recall. The no-distraction group recalled about 50% more lesson ideas than the low-distraction group and about 100% more lesson ideas than the high-distraction group. Students clearly have unhealthy mobile technology addictions that negatively impact note-taking and achievement. Beware.

Recap of Inappropriate Technology Use During Class

- 18% of laptops were used for class activities.
- 81% of students report using laptops to check mail.
- 25% use laptops to play games.
- 35% use laptops for other non-class activities.
- 70% send/receive text messages, 20 messages per class.

Table 3-3 SUMMARY OF EXPERIMENT ON TEXT MESSAGING DURING CLASS

	No Distraction	**Low Distraction**	**High Distraction**
Text Messages Received and Answered	None	1 Per Minute	2 Per Minute
Percentage of Lesson Ideas in Notes	33	27	20
Lesson Ideas Recalled	—	50% Fewer	100% Fewer

Here's a strategy that might help: Cut it out. Leave laptops and cell phones off and in your backpack. Studies show that even having one's phone accessible, such as in one's pocket, is distracting because it vibrates or because students simply mull over its use.

Meanwhile, even when laptops are used legitimately to record lecture notes, laptop note-taking might be less effective than longhand (pen-and-paper) note-taking. In a study I conducted with Linlin Luo and others (Luo et al., 2018), college students watched a 23-minute, narrated PowerPoint lesson about educational measurement that contained 23 slides with text and images. Half the students recorded laptop notes, and half recorded longhand notes using pen and paper. Half the students in each note-taking group took immediate tests without reviewing notes. The other halves reviewed notes for 15 minutes and then took the same tests, which measured text and image learning. The major finding occurred when notes were reviewed. Longhand notetakers achieved more than laptop notetakers on both the image-based and text-based tests. The longhand notetakers' superior performance was likely due to their superior notes. Laptop and longhand notetakers recorded equal amounts of notes—about one third of lesson ideas. But laptop notes were wordier and less efficient, using more words to express ideas. Laptop notes were also qualitatively inferior. They contained more verbatim phrases taken directly from the lesson, compared to longhand notes, which contained more paraphrasing of lecture ideas. In other words, laptop notetakers were not thinking as they typed. They were not paraphrasing what the lecturer said, putting things in their own words. Instead, they were mindlessly typing what they heard. In contrast, longhand notetakers' paraphrased notes were more reflective of meaningful thinking and understanding.

Activity 3.3

Conduct your own informal study. Sit in the back of the classroom one day, and take a couple of minutes to observe your classmates. What percentage are using laptops? What percentage of laptops are set on non-course material? How many students are checking smartphones during class? Try not to scream. Now get back to work, and never return to the nefarious back-of-the-classroom hinterlands again.

Knowing that laptop notetakers tend to record verbatim notes, you might think: "Good to know—I won't do this." Don't be so sure. Other researchers actually warned laptop notetakers about verbatim note-taking and told them not to do it (Mueller & Oppenheimer, 2014). Turns out, they couldn't help themselves. Their laptop notes were still brimming with verbatim phrases and sentences. Returning to my own study, there was one more difference. Longhand notetakers recorded more images, such as graphs and figures, in their notes than laptop notetakers, who recorded none of these. Evidently, it is difficult to quickly sketch out images using a laptop. Table 3-4 summarizes my laptop versus longhand study (Luo et al., 2018).

Table 3-4 SUMMARY OF LAPTOP VERSUS LONGHAND NOTE-TAKING STUDY

	Laptop	Longhand
Notes		
Ideas	One third	One third
Words	Wordier, less efficient	Less wordy, more efficient
Quality	Low, verbatim	High, paraphrased
Images	None	Some
Achievement		
Text-Based	Lower	Higher
Image-Based	Lower	Higher

So beware the laptop and other digital devices. They distract, and the laptop might lead to inferior note-taking compared to longhand note-taking. Still, I believe there is perhaps a place for judicious laptop and smartphone use in class. When your instructors make PowerPoint slides available to you in advance of the lecture, open the presentation on your laptop in class and set the presentation to the add notes mode, so you can record notes below each slide. This way, you need not duplicate in notes what is already on the slides, and slides and notes are in close proximity, where they belong for best organization and association. When instructors display additional images, such as drawings and graphs, outside the PowerPoint, capture these with your phone camera ... and then put it away.

Note These Things

I was in my university office one day, and the office phone rang. The caller identified himself as an attorney from a large Texas energy company. He explained that the company was accused by a government agency of making false and misleading statements to potential investors and that a trial date had been set.

The evidence for these false statements, according to the government agency, was the handwritten notes recorded by potential investors during investment meetings with the company's executive officer. The attorney asked if I would perhaps cast doubt on the veracity of recorded notes. "Not interested," I said. "I'm an educational psychologist concerned solely with educational issues." "It pays gobs of money," he replied. I said, "Well, this certainly sounds educational to me." And, with that, note-taking was about to go on trial for the very first time. When I told this story to my students, they couldn't believe it: "The university still uses landlines?" and "You were in your office?" they asked.

I was able to easily make a few points for the defense about the shoddy notes people usually take.

1. *Notes are incomplete.* Across 16 experiments I conducted, individuals, on average, noted just 35% of presented information.

2. *Notes omit details.* Notetakers record most of a presentation's main ideas but omit most details supporting those main ideas. In one study I conducted (Kiewra, Benton, & Lewis, 1987), presented information was classified into level 1–4 ideas. Level 1 ideas were most superordinate; levels 2–4 were successively more subordinate and detailed. Consider these notes, for example:

   Note-taking increases achievement (level 1) *through the process and product functions* (level 2). *The process function involves the activity of note-taking* (level 3) *and is measured by comparing the achievement of notetakers and listeners* (level 4).

   Students, on average, recorded 37% of all presentation ideas. In terms of idea levels, they captured 91% of level 1 ideas, 60% of level 2 ideas, 35% of level 3 ideas, and 11% of level 4 ideas.

3. *Notes omit context.* In one study I conducted (Titsworth & Kiewra, 2004), students listening to a presentation on communication theories recorded just 15% of contextual details that specified where noted ideas fit in the scheme of things. For example, a student might have noted that "self-disclosure is at the core of relationship development," without noting that this is an assumption of social penetration theory.

4. *Notes omit essential qualifiers.* In one study (Maddox & Hoole, 1975), a presenter spoke about "western coastal areas," but most notetakers only recorded "coastal areas." When the presenter stated that "Malaria influences the distribution of population in South Vietnam," the qualifying phrase "South Vietnam" was commonly omitted.

5. *Notes contain vague or inaccurate statements.* In one note-taking study (Crawford, 1925), 53% of noted information was correct, 45% was vague, and 2% was inaccurate. In another study (Maddox & Hoole, 1975), 61% of notetakers made one or more errors in their notes, and most errors involved the recording of numerals, diagrams, figures, and equations.

Now that you see the types of things commonly missing from notes, let's focus on what notes should contain. To do so, we'll look at the text below, pretending that it's a spoken lecture, and illustrate how the Table 3-5 notes were recorded.

Schedules of Reinforcement Lecture

Okay, class, we've just covered reinforcement. Now, we'll see that there are different schedules one might use in delivering reinforcement.

Suppose you have a pigeon, and you want to train it to peck a key. To train the pigeon, you give it food pellets for pecking the correct keys. There are four main schedules you can use to deliver the reinforcement. The type of schedule used determines several things about the animal's behavior.

Fixed-interval schedules deliver reinforcement following the first response after a fixed time interval. The pigeon, for example, might receive food for its first peck after a 10-second interval. Fixed-interval schedules produce slow response rates that contain pauses in responding. It is relatively easy to extinguish (eliminate) behaviors learned on this schedule.

Variable-interval schedules deliver reinforcement following the first response after a predetermined but variable time interval. The pigeon, for example, might receive food following intervals of 5, 15, 2, and 18 seconds for an average interval of 10 seconds. Variable-interval schedules produce slow but steady response rates. It is difficult to extinguish behaviors learned on this schedule.

Fixed-ratio schedules deliver reinforcement following a fixed number of responses. The pigeon, for example, might receive food following every 10 key pecks. Fixed-ratio schedules produce rapid responding, although the animal pauses briefly following reinforcement. It is relatively easy to extinguish behaviors learned on this schedule.

Variable-ratio schedules deliver reinforcement after a predetermined but variable number of responses. The pigeon, for example, might receive food after making 5, 15, 2, and 18 pecks for an average ratio of 10 pecks. Variable-ratio schedules produce rapid and steady responding. It is difficult to extinguish behaviors learned on this schedule.

Table 3-5 SCHEDULES OF REINFORCEMENT NOTES

Schedules of Reinforcement	
Fixed Interval	Reinforcement: 1st response after fixed time interval Exp: pigeon fed for 1st response after 10 sec Response rate: slow Response pattern: pause after rein Extinction: easy to eliminate behavior
Variable Int	Rein: 1st res after predetermined but var time int Exp: pigeon fed after 5, 15, 2, 18 sec intervals Res rate: slow Res pat: steady Ext: difficult
Fixed Ratio	Rein: 1st response after fixed # of res Exp: pigeon fed after 10 pecks Res rate: rapid Res pat: brief pause after rein Extinction: EZ
Variable Ratio	Rein: after predetermined but var # responses Exp: pigeon fed after 5, 15, 2, 18 pecks Res rate: rapid Res pat: steady Ext: difficult

Notes should contain a *title* that captures the overall focus of the lesson. *Schedules of Reinforcement* is an obvious and appropriate title here. An expanded and more descriptive title such as *How Schedules of Reinforcement Affect Behavior* would be a solid option too. A best-fit title might not become apparent until the lecture is complete.

Notes should contain *topics* that capture the lesson's main features. Here, the topics are the four types of schedules: fixed interval, variable interval, fixed ratio, and variable ratio. Topics are usually described along certain *categories*. In most any lesson, you can count on two of those categories being definitions and examples. In this lesson, definitions pertain to when reinforcement is delivered, and examples illustrate reinforcement delivery following some pattern of pigeon pecks. When I gave my own students this material to note, most omitted the examples. When I tell an illustrative story in class, students often drop their pens, sit back, smile, and enjoy the story. But the story is the vital example needed to understand lesson points. All examples should be recorded. You'll notice that there are three other categories in this lesson: response rate, response pattern, and extinction. The last item that notes contain is *details*. For instance, the detail *rapid* fits with the fixed-ratio topic and the response rate category.

Four more things. One, notice that details are brief. Notes can and should be complete, but brief. Two, notice that details do not float. They are hinged to certain topics and categories. They have context. The detail rapid is hinged to fixed ratio and response rate. Three, notice that abbreviations are used. You can write faster and write more when you abbreviate. Four, notice that spacing is used throughout the notes to show the superordinate topics and the subordinate categories and details. Of course, your notes might not be this well organized as you strain to keep up with a fast-talking lecturer, but you can always revise and improve your notes following the lecture.

Activity 3.4

The box below is another brief "lecture" on memory. Try taking notes from that lecture, making sure to include title, topics, categories, and details. Once you're done, check your notes against mine in Table 3-6.

Memory Lecture

Psychologists believe there are three different types of memory stores: sensory, short-term, and long-term. Sensory memory has a large capacity. It holds all the sights, sounds, and other sensations in the environment. It holds all these things for just a second or so to allow you time to decide what to pay attention to. While your attention is focused on the pitcher at a ball game, all other sensations—crowd noise, the smell of popcorn, a bird flying overhead—are briefly recorded in your sensory memory to allow you time to quickly consider them and perhaps shift attention. You quickly forget all the information in sensory memory, though, as it is pushed out by new incoming information.

Short-term memory has a brief duration too—15 to 20 seconds. It also has a limited capacity. It only holds about seven things at a time. Short-term memory is like a work bench. It can't hold a lot of things, but whatever you're working on at the time—or thinking about—is present in short-term memory. Forgetting occurs when old information fades or is pushed out by new information entering short-term memory.

Long-term memory is indeed that. Some believe its duration is infinite and that people never truly forget. Forgetting occurs because people simply can't locate the "missing" information stored in long-term memory. Regarding capacity, long-term memory has no limits. It can store more than any computer. If short-term memory is the work bench, then long-term memory is the shelves used to store all the tools and supplies.

Table 3-6 MEMORY NOTES

3 Types of Memory	Sensory (S) Short-term (STM) Long-term (LTM)
Sensory Memory	Capacity—large (all input from senses) Duration—sec or so Purpose—provides time to consider stimuli and shift attention Ex.—Focus on baseball pitcher but other stimuli in envir (noise, smells) recorded in S Forgetting—pushed out by incoming information

STM	Duration—brief, 15–20 sec
	Capacity—limited, ≈ 7 items
	Ex.—work bench
	    Holds only a few items
	    What you are working on (thinking about)
	Forgetting—info fades or displaced

LTM	Duration—infinite Forgetting—none or can't locate it Capacity—no limit, more than computer Ex.—storage shelves around work bench

Get It All

To get it all, you'll first need to be an assertive student. I remember lecturing one time and showing a PowerPoint slide with tiny text. My bad. But what happened next was interesting. Most students just squinted, jotted a few sketchy notes, and then gave up. Not Kyle. He marched to the front of the room with notebook in hand and plopped down on the floor just in front of the screen and took his notes there. Way to go, Kyle. Way to be a lecture player instead of a lecture spectator. Too often, students are lecture complacent, satisfied to jot just a few lines of notes now and then. Change that attitude. Make it your mission to record a complete set of notes. Obtain a fast-moving pen, and scribe with purpose and alacrity.

Use abbreviations and notations to help get it all. Table 3-7 shows some common abbreviations and notations you might use. In addition, when terms repeat themselves in a lesson, establish your own abbreviations. Based on the two boxed lecture examples presented earlier, here are some abbreviations you might establish: FI, fixed interval; VR, variable ratio; EX, extinction; STM, short-term memory; Cap, capacity; and Dur, duration.

Table 3-7 COMMON ABBREVIATIONS AND NOTATIONS

Abbreviation/Notation	Translation
cf.	compare
e.g.	for example
ex.	for example
i.e.	that is
vs	versus
et al.	and others
w/	with
w/out	without
approx.	approximately
cm	centimeter
s	second
min	minute
lb	pound
=	equal
≈	approximately
<	less than
↑	increase
ψ	psychology

Use technology to help get it all. As mentioned earlier, you can use your smartphone camera to photograph displays shown on the classroom board or screen. I was recently at a major conference, and as speakers presented, dozens of cell phones were held aloft, snapping photos of their slides. So even your professors are doing this.

You can also use those phones to record lectures, if permitted. Once it's recorded, you can replay the lecture in its entirety or access and replay difficult sections where note-taking lagged. In one study I conducted (Kiewra, Mayer, et al., 1991), college students viewed a lesson once, twice, or three times. A fourth, free-viewing group could replay the lesson as they pleased: in full, or with pausing, rewinding, and fast-forwarding. All students recorded lecture notes as they viewed the lesson. In turned out that all groups recorded about

Activity 3.5

List some other common abbreviations and notations you can use while recording notes. Consider another class you're presently taking and find course-specific abbreviations and notations you can use for that class.

80% of the lesson's main ideas. That's great. When it came to recording lesson details, though, the groups differed markedly: the group with one viewing noted 35% of the lesson details; two viewings, 50%; three viewings, 60%, and free viewing, 65%. By the way, achievement results mirrored note-taking findings: The more details students recorded, the higher their achievement. Recording and replaying lectures is an effective means to boost note-taking and achievement.

After the Lecture

After the lecture, notes can still be improved through a process called revision. Linlin Luo, Lydia Samuelson, and I investigated revision over two experiments (Luo, Kiewra, & Samuelson, 2016). In the first, college students recorded notes as they listened to a 14-minute audio-recorded lecture. Following the lecture, half of them recopied their notes, as many students are apt to do, and the other half revised their notes. Revisers were instructed to add as much additional lecture information to their notes as possible from memory. Next, all students were tested. Both groups recorded 38% of lesson ideas during the lecture. Following the lecture, the revision group added three more ideas to notes, and re-copiers naturally added none. Although the note increase was modest, revisers outscored re-copiers by 12% on a test assessing relationship learning.

The second experiment investigated how best to carry out revision. College students recorded notes while listening to the same lecture as in Experiment 1, but this time students revised once for 15 minutes at the end of the lecture or revised during three 5-minute pauses spaced throughout the lecture. In addition, students either revised alone or with a partner. Results showed that revising during lecture pauses and with a partner was most effective. That group produced the most complete notes and attained higher test scores than those revising just once and alone.

Revision works because students can use their existing notes to retrieve other lesson ideas from memory that were not originally noted. Suppose you originally record the main idea that short-term memory is limited. That notation might help you to retrieve related lecture ideas during revision, such as short-term memory's 7-digit capacity, that were not noted originally. Pauses work because revision occurs more often and with less delay compared to revising just once at the end of the lecture. Revising with a partner is especially effective because two heads are better than one. Partners can share notes and collaborate on revisions. The adjacent box summarizes what you should know about note revision.

Note Revision Findings and Tips

- Revisers add lesson ideas to notes following the lesson.
- Revision should also be carried out during lesson pauses.
- Revision should be carried out with a partner when possible.
- Revisers learn more lesson relationships than non-revisers.

Activity 3.6

Here is a set of incomplete notes on the *After the Lecture* section. Try now to revise these notes and make them more complete.

After

— Revision

— 2 Experiments

— Revisers

— Copiers

— Revisers Better

— Pauses & Partners

So look to revise your notes when there are breaks in the lecture and certainly soon after the lecture. Whenever possible, revise with a serious partner also seeking to create a complete set of notes.

Selecting and Noting Text Information

Although lectures and texts might say the same thing, they are different animals. Lectures are fleeting, like a frightened rabbit. Texts are stationary, like a pet dog in a sunbeam. Lectures are demanding. They demand that you be in a certain place, at a certain time, and that you rapidly select vital information as the lecture speeds by. Texts are flexible. You can read them anywhere, anytime, and at your own pace. Whether you are learning from lecture or text, if you are going to SOAR to success, you must first select ideas for further study. Let's examine how that's best done for text.

First, a warning. Most students select text ideas using highlighting. Some highlight by underlining key text ideas with a pen; most do it by drawing a line through key text ideas with a translucent, colored marker. Either way, highlighting fails to boost learning. Here's why. Most students highlight too much information. Thumb through a previously owned book at the campus bookstore and you'll see what I mean. Some pages look like they were spray-painted yellow because there is so much highlighting. Students often mindlessly highlight most everything, falsely believing that highlighting equals understanding. It does not. Mere highlighting is a passive learning process. Moving your hand across a printed page is not helpful. Moreover, when students return to the highlighted page to study, the non-highlighted information sometimes stands out more because there is less of it. Research confirms that highlighting has little to no utility as a learning strategy (Dunlosky et al., 2013).

If highlighting is not the ticket for selecting text information, what is? The answer is a familiar one. Just as was true for lecture information, readers should record complete notes that contain titles, topics, categories, and details, with special attention paid to definitions and examples. Moreover, readers should be certain to paraphrase text ideas rather than mindlessly copy them verbatim. Paraphrasing forces you to think about text ideas and make them your own.

You can record text notes from scratch on paper or in a computer document, like the notes appearing in Table 3-5 on reinforcement schedules and in Table 3-6 on memory. Alternatively, you can record notes in the text itself, assuming you're permitted to do so, as in Figure 3-2 on memory. Notice that these notes mostly involve marking the text to show the text's topics, categories, and details. The text-marking system for doing this is simple: Boxes are drawn around topics, circles are drawn around categories, and details are underlined. Additional notes are made in the text's margins. It would be impossible to mark a text this way with a highlighter. That's why the pen is mightier than the highlighter.

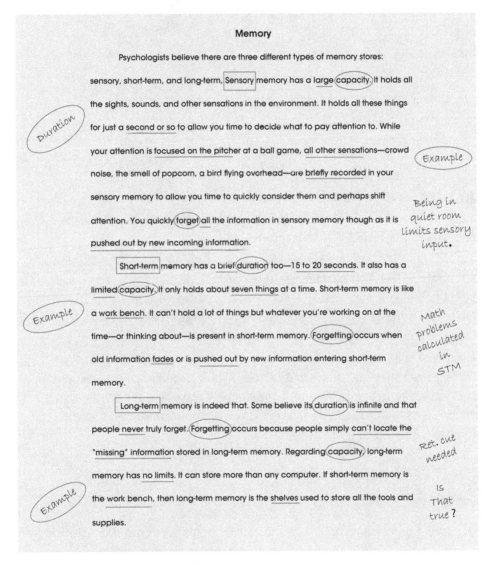

Figure 3-2 Text Notes for Memory Text

If the text you're reading is on a computer screen instead of paper, you can alter the text-marking system in this way: Bold the topics, italicize the categories, underline the details, and use the comment function to make additional notes. Table 3-8 shows the suggested text-marking system for paper and computer text.

Table 3-8 TEXT-MARKING SYSTEM FOR PAPER AND COMPUTER TEXT

	Paper Text	Computer Text
Topics	Box	Bold
Categories	Circle	Italics
Details	Underline	Underline
Additional Notes	Add in margins	Add using comments function

You'll learn more about text learning in Chapter 7.

Activity 3.7

Try taking text-marking notes in this text on faults.

A fault in the brittle layer of the earth's crust is a result of a sudden yielding under unequal stresses. There are several types.

A normal fault has a steep fault plane. The displacing movement is predominantly in a vertical direction. A normal fault results in a steep fault scarp. Fault scarps range in height from a few meters to several hundred meters. An example of a normal fault is the fault that was formed during the Hebgen Lake earthquake in Gallatin County, Montana in August 1959. The possibility of landslide is generally low.

In a reverse fault, the fault plane is such that one side rides up over the other. Reverse faults produce steep fault scarps, but the possibility of land sliding is great because an overhanging scarp tends to be formed. The displacing movement of a reverse fault is vertical. The site of the 1971 earthquake in San Fernando, California is an example of a reverse fault.

Answers to Focus Questions

1. Note-taking is important because it (a) helps students pay attention and (b) creates a permanent record of the lesson to be reviewed.

2. Students usually record incomplete notes containing just one third of important lesson ideas. Moreover, students' notes usually lack details, context, and essential qualifiers, and contain vague or inaccurate information.

3. Going to class gives students access to lesson information and hand-outs crucial for learning. When missing class, students also forfeit the joys of learning and the opportunity to contribute, participate, and clarify information.

4. Students should be on the edge of their seats during lectures by being active and engaged learners who are completely in the moment. Students should be physically prepared with necessary materials at hand, and be mentally prepared with previous material mastered and activated.

5. Recording complete notes is difficult because most lectures are paced much faster than students can write or type. Recording complete notes is important because note completeness is linked to high achievement.

6. Provided notes are likely to be complete, and having complete notes boosts achievement, as shown in Table 3-1. Provided notes can also be partial, and partial notes prompt student note-taking and result in more complete notes than conventional note-taking without note-taking prompts.

7. Lessons containing organizational cues, like "Next, we examine the fate of germ layers," lead to greater student note-taking (students record 80% of lesson details) and higher achievement than do lessons without organizational cues.

8. Students should download PowerPoint slides before lectures and should have electronic or paper copies on hand during lectures. Notes should be taken directly on or near to corresponding slides. This way, provided slide information need not be duplicated in notes, and noted information is in close proximity to the slide information to which it relates.

9. Mobile devices like laptops and smartphones are distracting and set the stage for student cyber-slacking. Research is staggering. For example, 81% of students use their laptops during class to check email, while 43% surf the web and 25% play games. Laptop use lowers student achievement by a half a letter grade. Meanwhile, 70% of students send text messages during class and send or receive about 20 messages per class period. The more students text, the lower their note-taking and achievement.

10. Students who record and replay lectures can increase the number of noted details from 35% to 65% and increase achievement too.

11. Revising notes leads to a more complete set of notes and to higher achievement than recopying notes. When possible, students are advised to revise notes throughout and following the lecture and to do so with a partner.

12. Highlighting text is a passive process that often results in too much material being selected and highlighted. Students should be more active when they study text by recording notes apart from the text or by marking the text in terms of topics, categories, and details.

CHAPTER 4

Organization Strategies Let You See Relationships in a Glance

Objectives

1. Engage an organizational mindset when approaching information.

2. Explain why graphic organizers are superior to linear displays.

3. Create effective graphic organizers—hierarchy, sequence, matrix, and illustration—based on organization methods described in this chapter.

Focus Questions

1. What does it mean to have an organizational mindset?

2. Why are graphic organizers superior to linear displays?

3. What are the four types of graphic organizers and the relationships each reveals?

4. What are the three tips for constructing hierarchies?

5. What are the four tips for creating sequences?

6. Why should hierarchies be created top down and sequences left to right?

7. What are the four tips for constructing matrices?

8. What are some sample words that alert you to a comparative relationship and to creating a matrix?

9. What guidelines should be followed when creating an illustration?

10. When are multiple organizers useful?

Suppose you were presented with the operant conditioning lesson in the box below in your psychology class. Chapter 3 advocated selecting key ideas and creating a set of notes like those in Table 4-1 as the lesson unfolds. These are pretty good notes and a good start toward learning. The notes are complete and fairly well organized. But they are not optimal. The Table 4-1 notes are

Operant Conditioning Lesson

Operant conditioning is a method for controlling behavior developed by behavioral psychologists. Although there are several operant methods, this lesson covers the four most popular methods: positive reinforcement, negative reinforcement, positive punishment, and negative punishment. Let's look at each in turn.

In positive reinforcement, a stimulus is presented following a behavior that works to increase that behavior. Suppose a rat is in a cage and there is a lever in the cage. When the rat presses the lever, a food pellet is dispensed. Receiving this pellet will likely result in increasing the rat's lever-pressing behavior.

In negative reinforcement, a stimulus is removed following a behavior that works to increase that behavior. Again, let's suppose a rat is in a cage and there is a lever in the cage. This time, there is also a mild shock shocking the rat. When the rat presses the lever, though, the shock stops temporarily. The rat is likely to continue pressing the lever to avoid the shock.

In positive punishment, a stimulus is presented following a behavior that works to decrease that behavior. Suppose a student is surfing the internet during a lesson (when he is not supposed to) and the teacher notices this. The teacher yells at the student in front of the entire class. As a result, the student does not repeat this off-task behavior in the future.

In negative punishment, a stimulus is removed following a behavior that works to decrease that behavior. In this case, a teacher might remove points from a student's grade after spotting him surfing the internet during a lesson. This should work to decrease future internet surfing during lessons.

linear, list-like. They present one operant conditioning technique after another. The notes are piecemeal and do not lend themselves to comparing the four techniques meaningfully and learning how they are alike and different.

Table 4-1 LINEAR NOTES FOR OPERANT CONDITIONING LESSON

Positive Reinforcement	Stimulus presented following behavior works to increase behavior Rat presses lever and receives food and presses lever more
Neg. Rein.	Stimulus removed following behavior increases behavior Rat presses lever to avoid shock
Pos. Punishment	Stimulus presented following behavior decreases behavior Teacher yelling decreases internet surfing during lesson
Neg. Pun.	Stimulus removed following behavior decreases behavior Removing points from student's grade decreases internet surfing

Developing an Organizational Mindset

Before showing you a better way to note these operant concepts, I want to convey that most any information can be made meaningful when it is approached with an organizational mindset. That is: How is this information related? How is it best organized? Returning to the operant conditioning concepts, let's just think about them for a minute based on their names. We see there are two types of reinforcement: positive and negative. Seeing this, we know these two types must be alike in some way because they are both types of reinforcement. Yet they must be different in some way because each has a different first name (positive or negative). Now read the definitions for each and see how the two types of reinforcement are alike and different ... That's right: They are alike in that both types of *reinforcement increase* behavior; they are different in that *positive* reinforcement involves the *presentation* of a stimulus, whereas *negative* reinforcement involves the *removal* of a stimulus.

Now let's make predictions about punishment. How do you suppose punishment differs from reinforcement? That's right: If *reinforcement increases* behavior, *punishment* likely *decreases* behavior. Now what do you predict about the two types of punishment? Based on what you know about positive and negative reinforcement, you likely predicted that *positive* punishment involves the *presentation* of a stimulus, whereas *negative* punishment involves the *removal* of a stimulus. Exactly right on all counts. Putting this all together, we learned these simple but important relationships:

- Reinforcement increases behavior, whereas punishment decreases behavior.

- Positive techniques involve the presentation of a stimulus, whereas negative techniques involve the removal of a stimulus.

See what an organizational mindset, some organizational thinking, can do?

Notice, though, that the operant conditioning lesson and the Table 4-1 linear notes did not make these relationships apparent. That's because they presented information in a piecemeal fashion, one idea at a time. Unfortunately, this is the status quo with much of education: Information is presented in a disjoined, one-idea-at-a-time, piecemeal fashion that conceals important relationships. Historical periods are presented one after another without being connected. Ditto for musical styles, developmental theories, and mathematical formulae. What's needed, then, are learners who approach learning with a more organizational mindset, as we just did with the operant conditioning lesson. Rather than approach the operant terms as four distinct concepts, we sought to understand how they were related—alike and different.

The key to uncovering and understanding relationships is organization, the second step in the SOAR method. When information is optimally organized in graphic, visual ways, relationships are apparent with just a glance. They pop. They are not concealed, as they are with linearly organized materials like paragraphs, outlines, or lists. Take a look at the graphic organizer for operant conditioning in Figure 4-1, and notice how quickly and easily it reveals the important relationships just mentioned above.

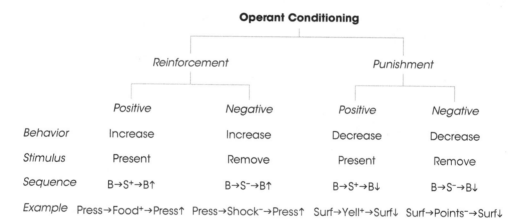

Figure 4-1 Operant Conditioning Graphic Organizer

Let's see one more example of organizational thinking and graphic organization before addressing why graphic organizers are effective and how to create them. You'll remember from Chapter 3 that linear notes were created for material on reinforcement schedules (Table 3-5 and now Table 4-2). Those notes were great because the goal during lectures is quickly recording notes that are as complete as possible. Looking at those linear notes, though, relationships are not immediately apparent. Using our organizational mindsets, we should ask: How are ratio and interval schedules different? How are fixed and variable schedules different?

Table 4-2 SCHEDULES OF REINFORCEMENT LINEAR NOTES

Fixed Interval	Reinforcement: 1st response after fixed time interval Exp: pigeon fed for 1st response after 10 sec Response rate: slow Response pattern: pause after rein Extinction: easy to eliminate behavior
Variable Int	Rein: 1st res after predetermined but var time int Exp: pigeon fed after 5, 15, 2, 18 sec intervals Res rate: slow Res pat: steady Ext: difficult
Fixed Ratio	Rein: 1st response after fixed # of res Exp: pigeon fed after 10 pecks Res rate: rapid Res pat: brief pause after rein Extinction: EZ
Variable Ratio	Rein: after predetermined but var # responses Exp: pigeon fed after 5, 15, 2, 18 pecks Res rate: rapid Res pat: steady Ext: difficult

After the lecture, we can transform those linear notes into the schedules of reinforcement graphic organizer in Figure 4-2. Notice how relationships pop. You can see in a glance that:

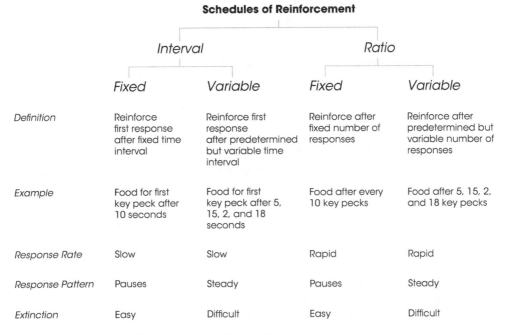

Schedules of Reinforcement

	Interval		Ratio	
	Fixed	*Variable*	*Fixed*	*Variable*
Definition	Reinforce first response after fixed time interval	Reinforce first response after predetermined but variable time interval	Reinforce after fixed number of responses	Reinforce after predetermined but variable number of responses
Example	Food for first key peck after 10 seconds	Food for first key peck after 5, 15, 2, and 18 seconds	Food after every 10 key pecks	Food after 5, 15, 2, and 18 key pecks
Response Rate	Slow	Slow	Rapid	Rapid
Response Pattern	Pauses	Steady	Pauses	Steady
Extinction	Easy	Difficult	Easy	Difficult

Figure 4-2 Schedules of Reinforcement Graphic Organizer

- Ratio schedules are based on the number of responses, whereas interval schedules are based on time passage.

- Ratio schedules produce rapid responding, whereas interval schedules produce slow responding.

- Fixed schedules produce paused responding, whereas variable schedules produce steady responding.

- Fixed schedules are easy to extinguish, whereas variable schedules are difficult to extinguish.

Just as was true for the operant conditioning material, none of these vital relationships were presented in the lesson. It was up to you to employ an organizational mindset and to construct a graphic organizer that made these relationships apparent and learnable.

Activity 4.1

Describe how you can approach the symbiosis material below with an organizational mindset.

Symbiosis: A situation in which two living organisms live together in a close nutritional relationship.

Commensalism: A type of symbiosis where one organism benefits and the other is unaffected.

Mutualism: A type of symbiosis where both organisms benefit.

Parasitism: A type of symbiosis where one organism benefits and the other is harmed.

Now try to organize the symbiosis material in an optimal way.

Why Graphic Organizers Are Effective

Before explaining why graphic organizers are effective, let me first prove to you that they are indeed effective. In one study I conducted with Daniel Robinson, we had college students study a long text about atypical behaviors under one of three conditions: text only, text plus seven outlines, or text plus seven graphic organizers. The outlines and organizers contained identical information but were naturally arranged in different formats. Results revealed that those in the graphic organizer group learned the most relationships and wrote essays containing more relationship statements (Robinson & Kiewra, 1995).

In another study I conducted with Doug Kauffman, college students studied information about six types of wildcats displayed in text, outline, or graphic organizer form. The three displays contained identical information but expressed the information in progressively fewer words: text (2,000), outline (367), and graphic organizer (244). After displays were studied for 15 minutes, all students took tests measuring fact learning (e.g., What does a tiger weigh?), local relationship learning pertaining to one wildcat characteristic (e.g., Which wildcat has the largest range?), and global relationship learning pertaining to multiple wildcat characteristics (e.g., What is the relationship between a wildcat's range and weight?). Results revealed that the graphic organizer group learned the most facts, local relationships, and global relationships (Kauffman & Kiewra, 2010).

Finally, Matt McCrudden and colleagues had college students study a brief text about how astronauts develop kidney stones. Students either studied the text alone, the text plus a list of key ideas, or the text plus a graphic organizer of key ideas. The list and graphic organizer contained the same information. Results revealed that the graphic organizer group achieved the most on a relationship test (McCrudden et al., 2009). Table 4-3 is a graphic organizer summarizing the three graphic organizer studies.

Table 4-3 GRAPHIC ORGANIZER SHOWING THREE GRAPHIC ORGANIZER (GO) STUDIES

	Robinson & Kiewra	Kauffman & Kiewra	McCrudden et al.
Students:	College	College	College
Topic Studied	Atypical behaviors	Six types of wildcats	Astronauts and kidney stones
Groups	• Text only • Text + 7 outlines • Text + 7 GOs	• Text • Outline • GO	• Text only • Text + List • Text + GO
Results	GO best • Learned most relationships • Wrote more relational essays	GO best • Learned most facts • Learned most local relationships • Learned most global relationships	GO best • Learned most relationships

Doug Kauffman and I investigated why graphic organizers are more effective than linear displays such as text, outlines, and lists and determined that their superiority is mostly due to superior localization (Kauffman & Kiewra, 2010). This means that graphic organizers are better at displaying related information in close proximity, where it is more easily compared. As an example, revisit the schedules of reinforcement linear notes in Table 4-2 and the corresponding graphic organizer notes in Figure 4-2. Notice that information about response rate, for example, appears on four different lines separated by intervening information in the linear notes but appears on just one line with no intervening information in the graphic organizer notes. The graphic organizer reveals in a glance an important relationship: interval schedules produce slow response rates while ratio schedules produce rapid response rates. This same relationship information is dispersed throughout the linear notes and is more difficult and time consuming to spot.

How to Create Graphic Organizers

Time for another story from my educational annals. My college days began a bit like the classic film *Animal House*. Although I was never placed on double secret probation, my grade-point average was barely divisible by one. To give you a sense of how bad things were, I remember going into a meteorology final with a B average and ending up with a final grade of D. I asked the instructor how this could happen, and he smartly remarked, "You had an F minus, minus, minus on the final. Perhaps you were under the weather." Yeah, like meteorologists are always right. Anyway, something transformative happened toward the end of my college career—year 7, I believe—and it wasn't a toga party. It was taking an educational psychology course taught by Professor Nelson DuBois and learning about learning. The material was delicious and infectious, and best of all, it taught me how to learn. After that, the remainder of college and my graduate school careers were a snap. As it turns out, I remained in contact with Professor DuBois, and together he and I developed the graphic organizer system I'm about to show you.

First, you should know that I've taught this system to thousands of students, many of whom say it is the single most important thing they learned in my classes. Second, you should know that this is a simple system as it only includes four types of graphic organizers. Having only four types makes our system powerful and easy to learn. You'll be able to create graphic organizers today. Third, and most importantly, you should know that there is one primary reason to create graphic organizers: to display and reveal informational relationships. Remember, I said earlier that I want you to have an organizational mindset. I want you to seek and understand the organization and relationships within information, such as the capacity limitations across memory stores, the order and locations of Alaric's conquests, the structural differences between Romanesque and Gothic architecture, and the effects of various reinforcement schedules on behavior. True learning is not piecemeal learning—one disjoined fact at a time. True learning involves learning meaningful relationships, and that's exactly what graphic organizers help you do.

Figure 4-3 is a graphic organizer displaying our system's four types of organizers: hierarchy, sequence, matrix, and illustration. Notice that each has a unique organization perfectly suited for displaying a unique relationship. Hierarchies are organized top to bottom and display superordinate-subordinate relationships. In the example, *insects* is superordinate to its two types: moth and butterfly.

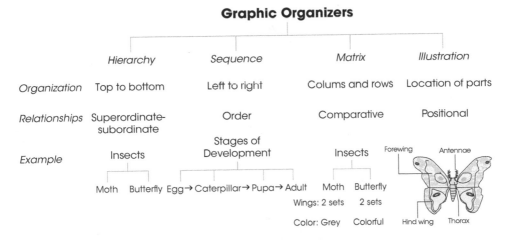

Figure 4-3 Graphic Organizer Displaying Four Organizer Types

Sequences are organized left to right and display order relationships. In the example, the four stages of development appear in order going from left to right. Matrices are organized in columns and rows and display comparative relationships. In the example, moths and butterflies are compared with respect to wings and color. Illustrations are organized according to the locations of the illustrated parts and display positional relationships. In the example, the relative locations of several moth parts are displayed.

Here is another example of the graphic organizer system. The next four figures show a series of graphic organizers pertaining to the planets. Figure 4-4 shows the five-step sequence for planetary formation. Figure 4-5 shows a planet hierarchy. There are two superordinate planet types: inner and outer, with each connected to its subordinate planets below. Figure 4-6 is a matrix. It is actually an extension of the Figure 4-5 hierarchy. It displays planet topics (Mercury, Venus, Earth...) across the top row, categories (diameter, surface, moons...) down the left side, and details (such as Venus's rocky surface) within matrix cells. Figure 4-7 is an illustration displaying the solar system's eight planets and their relative sizes and locations. Let's next examine the four organizer types in more detail and with more examples.

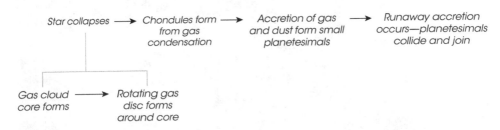

Figure 4-4 Sequence for Planetary Formation

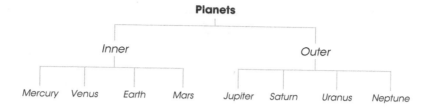

Figure 4-5 Planet Hierarchy

	Mercury	Venus	Earth	Mars	Jupiter	Saturn	Uranus	Neptune
Miles from the Sun	36 million	67 million	93 million	142 million	483 million	886 million	2 billion	3 billion
Revolution Time Around the Sun	3 months	8 months	1 year	2 years	12 years	30 years	84 years	165 years
Orbit Speed (Miles/Second)	30	22	19	15	8	6	4	3
Diameter (Miles)	3,000	8,000	8,000	4,000	89,000	75,000	32,000	31,000
Surface	Rocky	Rocky	Rocky	Rocky	Slushy	Slushy	Slushy	Slushy
Moons	0	0	1	2	17	22	15	6
Rotation Time	59 days	243 days	24 hours	25 hours	10 hours	11 hours	16 hours	19 hours

(Planets — Inner: Mercury, Venus, Earth, Mars; Outer: Jupiter, Saturn, Uranus, Neptune)

Figure 4-6 Planet Matrix

Figure 4-7 Planet Illustration

Hierarchy

A hierarchy organizes information from top to bottom and uses downward lines to reveal superordinate-subordinate relationships. A lot of information has a hierarchical structure. At most universities, there is a chancellor overseeing vice chancellors who oversee deans who oversee department chairs who oversee the 11–12 faculty who actually do the work. In biology, organisms are hierarchically classified. From top down: domain, kingdom, phylum, class, order, family, genus, and species. In American baseball, there are the American and National Leagues. Each league has an East, Central, and West division. Each division has five teams. In astronomy, the universe is comprised of galaxies, which are comprised of solar systems, which are comprised of stars, planets, and moons. And some material in this text is hierarchically organized. For example, there are the four types of graphic organizers, the three types of memory, and, of course, the four components of SOAR, as shown in Figure 4-8.

Activity 4.2

Now that you know about the four types of organizers (hierarchy, sequence, matrix, and illustration), create an example of each from a course you are presently taking or have taken in the past.

Figure 4-8 A SOAR Hierarchy

Here are three tips for creating hierarchies:

1. Always construct hierarchies top to bottom so that the superordinate-subordinate relationships are clear. Later, you'll see why this is especially important when combining hierarchies with other types of organizers.

   Do this:

   Not this:

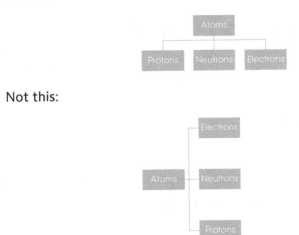

2. Include all levels. A hierarchy is more accurate and informative when it displays all important levels of information. Figure 4-9 is a poorly constructed hierarchy because it has just one level. It displays the seven types of real numbers as if they were all comparable. It fails to show the hierarchical relationships among those seven types. Figure 4-10 is much more informative and accurate. It is a multilevel hierarchy showing all the superordinate-subordinate relationships among the seven number types. Other examples of hierarchies with a missing level that are improved when a level is added are shown in Figure 4-11 (planets), Figure 4-12 (abnormal behaviors), and Figure 4-13 (clouds).

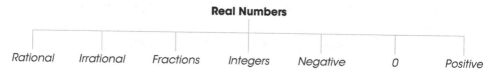

Figure 4-9 Poorly Constructed Single-Level Hierarchy

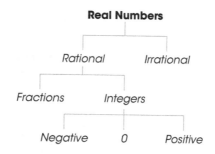

Figure 4-10 Well-Constructed Multilevel Hierarchy

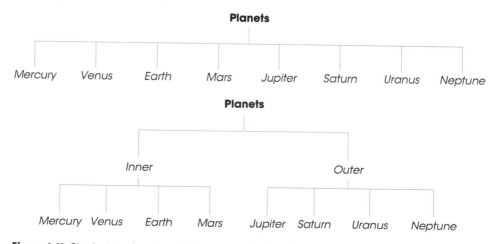

Figure 4-11 Single-Level and Multilevel Planet Hierarchies

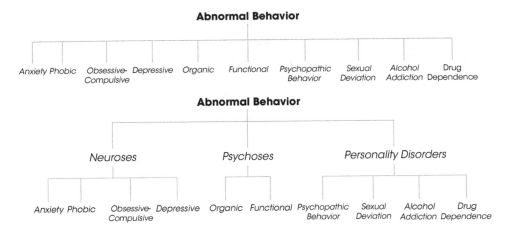

Figure 4-12 Single-Level and Multilevel Abnormal Behavior Hierarchies

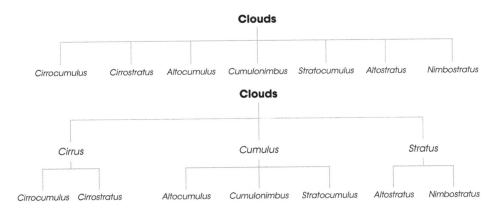

Figure 4-13 Single-Level and Multilevel Clouds Hierarchies

Activity 4.3

- Create a multilevel hierarchy for these tree types: pine, birch, deciduous, spruce, maple, conifer, fir, oak, and cedar.

- Create a multilevel hierarchy from these biology terms: liver, stomach, esophagus, respiratory system, kidneys, small intestine, trachea, digestive system, nostrils, excretory system, and skin.

3. Be alert for certain words (alert words, I call them) that signal a hierarchical organization. When you see or hear these or similar words, you should create a hierarchy: types, parts, levels, groups, kinds, elements, sets, categories, and contains. Here are some examples of alert words and resulting hierarchies.

■ There are three *types* of central tendency: mean, median, and mode.

■ There are six *kinds* of simple machines: lever, wheel, pulley, inclined plane, wedge, and screw.

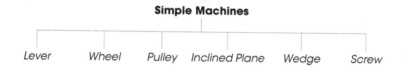

■ All insects have three body *parts*: head, thorax, and abdomen.

■ An orchestra is *comprised of* string, wind, brass, and percussion instruments.

■ Students were divided into three note-taking *groups*.

Sequence

A sequence organizes information left to right to reveal order relationships—what comes first, second, third, and so on—with left-to-right arrows connecting the sequence steps. A lot of information has a sequential structure. There are sequences of historical periods such as Bronze Age, Iron Age, Middle Ages, and Early Modern Period. A symphony has four sequential movements: opening sonata, slow movement, minuet, and allegro. Human digestion involves five sequential locations: mouth, esophagus, stomach, small intestine, and large intestine. Piaget recognizes four stages of development: sensorimotor, preoperational, concrete, and formal. In addition, there are eight phases of the moon, seven steps for administering CPR, seven stages in the water cycle, twelve days of Christmas, four actions in executing a tennis serve, and, obviously, five courses in the five-course meal, as shown in Figure 4-14. All sequential.

Five-Course Meal

Hors-d'oeuvres   Appetizer   Salad   Main course   Dessert

Figure 4-14 Sequence Showing Five-Course Meal

Here are three tips for creating sequences:

1. Always construct sequences left to right, with arrows placed between the steps. As was true with hierarchies, this configuration is necessary for combining sequences with other types of organizers.

Do this:

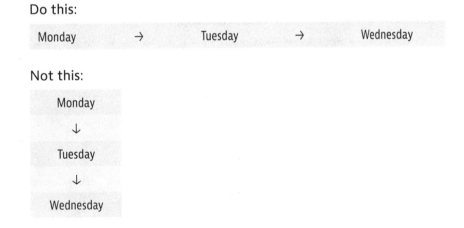

2. **Include all levels.** Just as some hierarchies have multiple levels, some sequences do too. Figure 4-15 is a single-level sequence showing periods of art history. Although it is informative, this sequence can be improved by the addition of a level above showing that the seven art periods fit into three more general periods, as shown in Figure 4-16. Similarly, the six stages of moral development shown in Figure 4-17 can be partitioned into three more general periods, as shown in Figure 4-18. Figures 4-19 (experimental procedure) and 4-20 (adding mixed fractions) also show sequences with multiple levels. Just as was true for hierarchies, sequences are more accurate and informative when they display all of the important levels of information.

Figure 4-15 Single-Level Sequence Showing Art History Periods

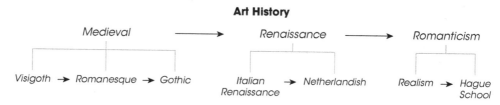

Figure 4-16 Multilevel Sequence Showing Art History Periods

Moral Development

Obedience → Self-interest → Conformity → Authority → Social Contract → Universal Ethics

Figure 4-17 Single-Level Sequence for Moral Development

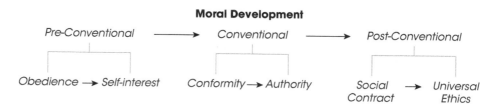

Figure 4-18 Multilevel Sequence for Moral Development

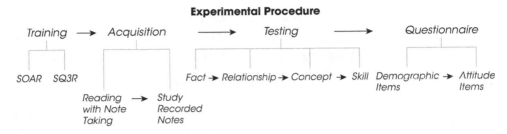

Figure 4-19 Multilevel Experimental Procedure Sequence

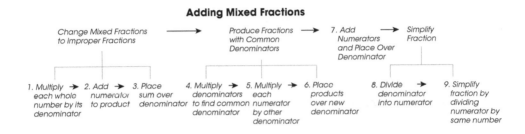

Figure 4-20 Multilevel Sequence for Adding Mixed Fractions

3. Be on the alert for words that signal order relationships, telling you that a sequence organizer is appropriate. When you see or hear these or similar words, you should create a sequence: steps, stages, phases, periods, cycle, next, before, after, develop, first, later, process, trend, and causes. Here are some examples of alert words and resulting sequences:

- In positive reinforcement, a stimulus is presented *following* a behavior that *yields* a behavior increase.

Positive Reinforcement

Behavior ⟶ Stimulus Presented ⟶ Behavior Increase

- Information *proceeds from* sensory memory *to* short-term memory *to* long-term memory.

Information Flow

Sensory Memory ⟶ Short-term Memory ⟶ Long-term Memory

- A butterfly goes through four *stages* of *development*: egg, caterpillar, pupa, and adult.

Butterfly Development

Egg ⟶ Caterpillar ⟶ Pupa ⟶ Adult

- *Calculating* standard deviation involves five *steps*: calculating deviation scores, squaring them, summing squared deviations, dividing sum by number of scores, and calculating square root.

Calculating Standard Deviation

Calculate Deviation Scores → Square Deviation Scores → Sum Squared Deviations → Divide Sum by Number of Scores → Calculate Square Root

- Smoking can *lead to* diabetes.

Smoking ⟶ Diabetes

Activity 4.4

Identify the alert words and create simple sequences for the following statements:

- Under-inflated tires cause excessive tread wear.
- After striking the ball, follow through.
- Nutrients travel from the roots to the stem to the leaves.
- First, elevate the head.

4. Combine sequences and hierarchies when appropriate. Hierarchies and sequences can certainly be combined, as shown in the Figure 4-19 organizer displaying an experimental procedure and the Figure 4-21 organizer showing the procedure for creating oxygen.

Creating Oxygen

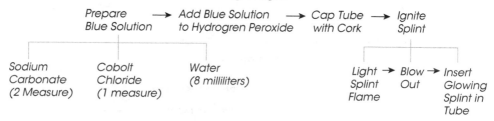

Figure 4-21 Graphic Organizer Combining Sequence and Hierarchy

Matrix

A matrix organizes information into columns and rows to reveal comparative relationships. That is, it compares two or more things. Take a look at the wildcat matrix in Figure 4-22, and you'll see how easy it is to compare the various wildcats because of their close proximity. With just a glance, several important relationships are apparent, such as:

- The louder the call, the heavier the cat, and the longer the lifespan.

- Jungle cats have smaller ranges than plains cats.

- Jungle cats are solitary and hunt at night, whereas plains cats live in groups and hunt by day.

- A cat's distinct trait determines its hunting method (e.g., the cheetah has speed to run down prey).

Wildcats

	Tiger	Lion	Jaguar	Leopard	Cheetah	Bobcat
Call	Roar	Roar	Growl	Growl	Hiss	Hiss
Weight (lbs)	450	400	200	150	125	30
Lifespan (years)	25	25	20	10	8	6
Habitat	Jungle	Plains	Jungle	Jungle	Plains	Jungle
Social Behavior	Solitary	Groups	Solitary	Solitary	Groups	Solitary
Range (sq.m)	30	150	5	15	50	30
Time of Hunt	Night	Day	Night	Night	Day	Night
Distinct Trait	Powerful upper body	Keen sense of smell	Powerful Jaws	Skilled climber	Speed	Keen eyes and ears
Method of Hunt	Knocks prey over	Scavenges for dead animals	Bites prey on neck	Hides leftovers in trees	Chases down prey	Ambushes prey

Figure 4-22 Wildcats Matrix

A lot of information has a comparative structure. You've already seen several matrices throughout the book, such as those comparing: apes (Table 1-3), ineffective and effective learners (Table 2-2), architecture styles (Table 2-3), SOAR research studies (Table 2-4), operant conditioning concepts (Figure 4-1), schedules of reinforcement (Figure 4-2), types of graphic organizers (Table 4-3), and planets (Figure 4-6). Other examples might include matrices comparing whole and rational numbers, types of raptors, central and peripheral nervous systems, structures and functions of roots and stems, modern and impressionistic art, mutual fund investments, comma versus semicolon usage, Kings of England, and birth rates by country. In fact, try to think of a single instance when a comparison is not possible. If you're studying Greek gods, you'll likely want to compare them with one another and with Roman gods. If you're studying perimeter, how does that compare with area? Speaking of area, as you learn the formula for calculating the area of rectangles, you might wonder how that compares to calculating the area of triangles and rhombuses. Igneous rock: sedimentary rock. Cumulus clouds: stratus clouds. Near-sightedness: far-sightedness. Hundred-year war: 30-year war. London: Paris. Abbott: Costello. Ford: Chevy. Coke: Pepsi. Matrices can be used when comparing anything, and much of what you learn involves comparisons.

Here are four tips for creating matrices:

1. Develop matrices from hierarchies and sequences. All hierarchies and sequences can be extended downward to form a matrix. That's what makes matrices the most prominent and powerful graphic organizer of all. Look at Figure 4-23. This is the clouds hierarchy from Figure 4-13 extended into a matrix. This was accomplished by adding the categories appearance, elevation, and weather patterns down the left side and then adding details in the matrix cells. Look at Figure 4-24. This is the moral development sequence from Figure 4-18 extended into a matrix. This was accomplished by adding the categories description, age, and example down the left side and adding details in the matrix cells.

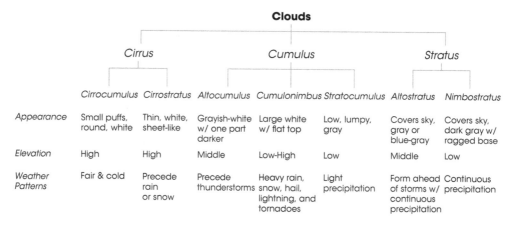

Figure 4-23 Cloud Hierarchy Extended Into a Matrix

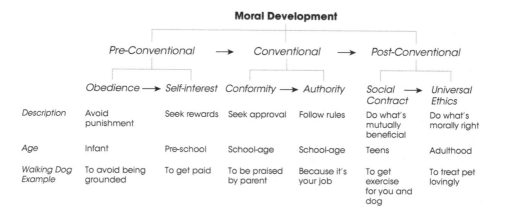

Figure 4-24 Moral Development Sequence Extended Into a Matrix

Because you are gaining an organizational mindset, always be thinking about the prospect of extending hierarchies and sequences into matrices. Your instructor says, "There are four levels of measurement." Right away, you're thinking, "Boom! Hierarchy! Levels of measurement subsumed by its four types." But you don't stop there. You listen for the eventual categories—like definition, example, and limitations—that you'll use to extend the hierarchy into a matrix. Same thing in music class. Your instructor says, "There are three major musical periods: Baroque, classical, and romantic." "Boom! Sequence!" you think. And now you listen for the categories common to these musical periods—like rhythm, melody, and composers—that you'll use to extend the sequence into a matrix.

2. Construct matrices with three parts. Matrices have topics on top, categories down the left side, and details in the intersecting matrix cells. Figure 4-25 is a matrix summarizing the matrix parts according to their location and description. Figure 4-26 shows a matrix about atoms with the three matrix parts labelled.

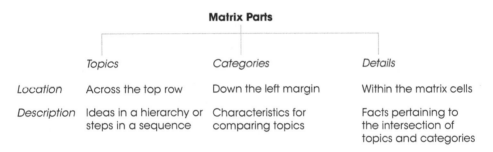

	Topics	Categories	Details
Location	Across the top row	Down the left margin	Within the matrix cells
Description	Ideas in a hierarchy or steps in a sequence	Characteristics for comparing topics	Facts pertaining to the intersection of topics and categories

Figure 4-25 Matrix Summarizing Matrix Parts

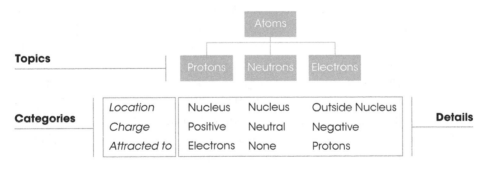

Figure 4-26 Atoms Matrix With Three Parts Labeled

3. Order topics and categories. Take another look at the Figure 4-6 planet matrix. It is organized so that planetary relationships are apparent with just a glance. You can see immediately that as planets' distance from the sun increases, their revolution times increase and their orbit speeds

decrease. You also see that inner planets have smaller diameters, rockier surfaces, fewer moons, and longer rotation times compared to outer planets. Now examine the planets matrix in Figure 4-27, which includes the identical planet information with topics and categories arranged alphabetically. This matrix is rubbish. It yields none of those same relationships easily if at all. The lesson here is that not all matrices are created equal. You want to arrange topics and categories in optimal ways that allow patterns and trends to easily emerge. The planets should be arranged in their natural order, and the categories (like revolution time and orbit speed) that belong together should be together.

Planets

	Earth	Jupiter	Mars	Mercury	Neptune	Saturn	Uranus	Venus
Diameter (Miles)	8,000	89,000	4,000	3,000	31,000	75,000	32,000	8,000
Miles from the Sun	93 million	483 million	142 million	36 million	3 billion	886 million	2 billion	67 million
Moons	1	17	2	0	6	22	15	0
Orbit Speed (Miles/Second)	19	8	15	30	3	6	4	22
Revolution Time Around the Sun	1 year	12 years	2 years	3 months	165 years	30 years	84 years	8 months
Rotation Time	24 hours	10 hours	25 hours	59 days	19 hours	11 hours	16 hours	243 days
Surface	Rocky	Slushy	Rocky	Rocky	Slushy	Slushy	Slushy	Rocky

Figure 4-27 Ineffective Planets Matrix With Topics and Categories Ordered Alphabetically

4. Be on the alert for words that signal comparative relationships, telling you that a matrix organizer is appropriate. You should create a matrix when you see or hear these or similar words: compare, contrast, whereas, however, similar, different, and alternative. Also be on the lookout for other modifying words. *Early* settlers suggest a potential comparison with *late* settlers, *domestic* laws with *international* laws, *organic* molecules with *inorganic* molecules, *liberal* viewpoints with *conservative* viewpoints, and *migratory* birds with *non-migratory* birds. Here are some examples of alert words and potentially resulting matrix frameworks:

- Let's *compare* the three wars in terms of combatants, causes, and outcomes.

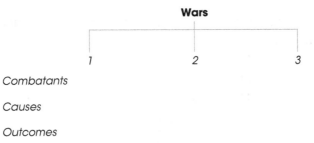

- Let's examine the characteristics of *rational* numbers.

- Poe's style, in *contrast* to Hemingway's, is more sombre.

- There are *advantages* to *surgical* procedures.

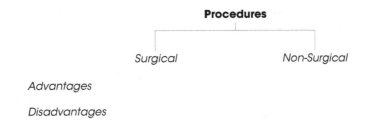

- SOAR has proven *superior* to *other* study systems.

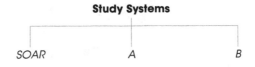

Activity 4.5

- **Create a matrix that would help a patient adhere to the prescription schedule listed below.**

    - **Inderal:**   1 tablet 3 times a day with meals
    - **Lanoxin:**   1 tablet every morning
    - **Carafate:**   1 tablet with meals and at bedtime
    - **Zantac:**   1 tablet midday and night
    - **Quinaglute:** 1 tablet 4 times a day
    - **Coumadin:**   1 tablet at bedtime

- **Create a matrix comparing the location, food, atmosphere, price, and service of three restaurants you've eaten at.**

Illustration

An illustration displays information pictorially and reveals positional relationships. It shows what something looks like, its parts, the relative position of those parts, and perhaps how those parts move. Figure 4-28 shows an illustration of a flower. Figure 4-29 shows an illustration of how radar works. Illustrations are helpful for displaying information in any subject area. In science, they can display the body parts of the hydra, the location of glands in the human body, the layers of the earth's core, or the appearance of cumulonimbus clouds. In social studies, they can display the structure of Gothic architecture, the appearance of inlets and

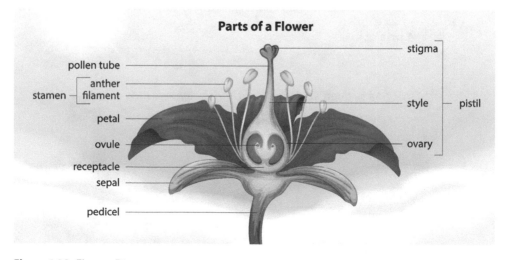

Figure 4-28 Flower Diagram

Radar waves are emitted by a transmitter. They strike an object, like a plane, and reflected waves return to the receiver.

reflected wave

Sender/
Receiver

Object

original wave

distance

Figure 4-29 How Radar Works

islets, military weaponry, or religious artifacts. In mathematics, they can display geometric figures like scalene triangles or quadrilaterals. In physical education, they can display a 4-3-3 alignment on a soccer pitch or the steps in a golf swing.

Illustrations can stand alone or be used in conjunction with other organizers. An architecture matrix could include the category *appearance* and an illustration of each architecture type. A polygon matrix could include the category *example* and an illustration of each polygon type, such as triangle and rhombus, in the cells. Figure 4-30 shows a fish matrix that includes illustrations. Those illustrations are important for depicting fish appearances and for clarifying the relationship between fish appearance and habitat (fish live where they cannot be easily seen). Figure 4-31 shows a levers matrix with illustrations depicting the force, fulcrum, and load positioning for each lever type.

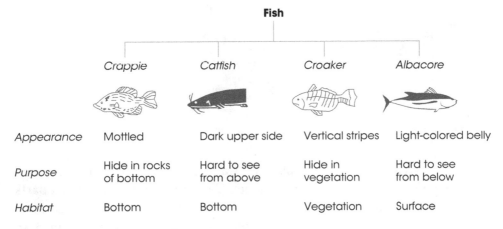

Fish			
Crappie	Catfish	Croaker	Albacore
Appearance			
Mottled	Dark upper side	Vertical stripes	Light-colored belly
Purpose			
Hide in rocks of bottom	Hard to see from above	Hide in vegetation	Hard to see from below
Habitat			
Bottom	Bottom	Vegetation	Surface

Figure 4-30 Fish Matrix With Illustrations

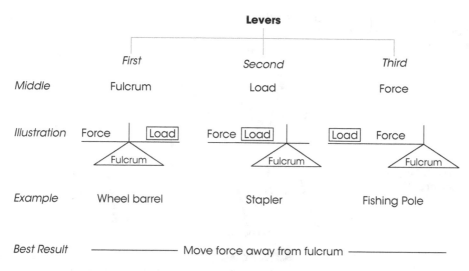

		Levers	
	First	*Second*	*Third*
Middle	Fulcrum	Load	Force
Illustration	Force | Load	Force Load |	Load | Force
	Fulcrum	Fulcrum	Fulcrum
Example	Wheel barrel	Stapler	Fishing Pole
Best Result		Move force away from fulcrum	

Figure 4-31 Levers Matrix With Illustrations

Here are three tips for creating illustrations:

1. Keep it simple. You don't need to be an artist to create illustrations. Although illustrations show what things look like, they need not be exact replicas to be effective. Don't worry about how realistic something looks. Include only the necessary parts, and omit unneeded details. The flower and radar illustrations in Figures 4-28 and 4-29, respectively, are simple but effective illustrations showing the general appearance and placement of important parts. Figure 4-32 is a simple illustration displaying hand bones.

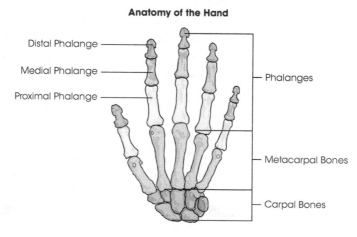

Figure 4-32 Illustration of Hand Bones

2. Use labels and captions to explain illustrations. Notice how the flower, radar, and hand illustrations all contain labels showing where the different parts are located and how the radar illustration contains a caption explaining the radar process. Whenever possible, place labels and captions in close

proximity to their referents, so that relationships are easily drawn between words and pictures. As is true with all displays, place things that belong together in close proximity.

3. Be on the alert for words that signal positional relationships, telling you that an illustration organizer is appropriate. When you see or hear these or similar words, you should create an illustration:

Activity 4.6

Construct simple illustrations of a hammer, a chair, and a plant. Be sure to label the parts for each.

- Part words—wheel, wing, seat, strap, filament, spool, flange

- Appearance words—grey, cylindrical, calloused, pointed, smooth, tilted

- Position words—near, below, alongside, over, left, between, top

- Movement words—clockwise, diagonally, forward, spinning, swooping, sliding

Here are some alert words and resulting illustrations:

- Spiders have a *head, body,* and *eight symmetrical legs.*

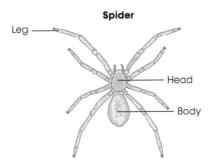

- Flexor muscles are in the *top, inner* portion of the arm; extensor muscles are in the *top, outer* portion of the arm.

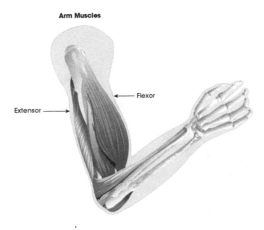

- In chess, a knight *moves two squares in one direction and then one square in a perpendicular direction.*

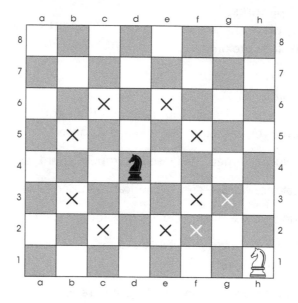

- A scalene triangle has *three closed sides* of *unequal length.*

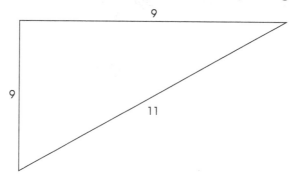

- Spermatozoon has an *oblong head*, a long, *thin tail*, and *a middle part.*

Spermatozoon

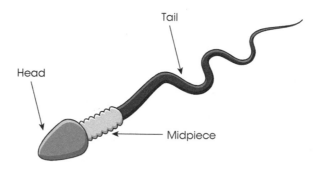

Table 4-4 compiles sample alert words for all four graphic organizer types.

Table 4-4 SAMPLE ALERT WORDS SIGNALING THE FOUR TYPES OF GRAPHIC ORGANIZERS

Hierarchy	Sequence	Matrix	Illustration
• types	• steps	• compare	Part
• parts	• stages	• contrast	• wheel
• levels	• phases	• whereas	• wing
• groups	• periods	• however	• seat strap
• kinds	• cycle	• similar	
• elements	• next	• different	Appearance
• sets	• before	• alternative	• grey
• categories	• after	• early	• cylindrical
• contains	• develop	• domestic	• calloused
	• first	• international	
	• later	• organic	Position
	• process	• liberal	• near
	• trend	• migratory	• below
	• causes		• alongside
			Movement
			• clockwise
			• diagonally
			• forward

Multiple Organizers

You've seen that the various organizers can be combined. Hierarchies and sequences can be combined into a single organizer, and each can be extended into a matrix. Matrices can also contain illustrations. You've seen tips for creating organizers, the most important of which are adding levels when helpful and ordering topics and categories in optimal ways. Now there is one more thing to cover: multiple organizers.

Sometimes one organizer is not enough. Sometimes you need more. Figure 4-33 shows how all four types of graphic organizers might be useful for learning about the ladybug. There is a sequence for lifecycle, a hierarchy for types, a matrix comparing those types, and an illustration of parts. Figure 4-34 shows how multiple organizers aid in the learning of imaginative literature. There is a multi-level hierarchy showing all types and subtypes (A), followed by matrices for comparing the prose subtypes (B), the poetry subtypes (C), and drama subtypes (D). The reason a single matrix cannot accomplish this is because the categories vary for the three types of imaginative literature. For example, length, number of pages, and complexity are the categories for comparing types of prose, whereas tone and ending are the categories for comparing types of

Ladybug Life Cycle

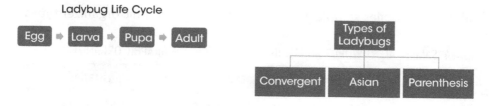

Types of Ladybugs		
	Convergent	Asian	Parenthesis
Location:	California	East Coast	All over the U.S.
Distinct Trait:	Wings separated by a white line	Large and rounded	Only two or four black marks on the wings
Dwelling:	Fields/ gardens	Fields/ gardens	Fields/ gardens

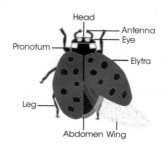

Figure 4-33 Multiple Ladybug Graphic Organizers

drama. One more example. While learning about measurement, you might create a matrix comparing levels of measurement (nominal, ordinal, interval, and ratio), a matrix comparing types of central tendency (mode, median, and mean), a matrix comparing types of dispersion (range, variance, and standard deviation), and a matrix comparing types of distributions (normal, skewed, and bimodal—including illustrations of each).

Activity 4.7

Construct multiple organizers related to a school topic you are studying presently or studied previously.

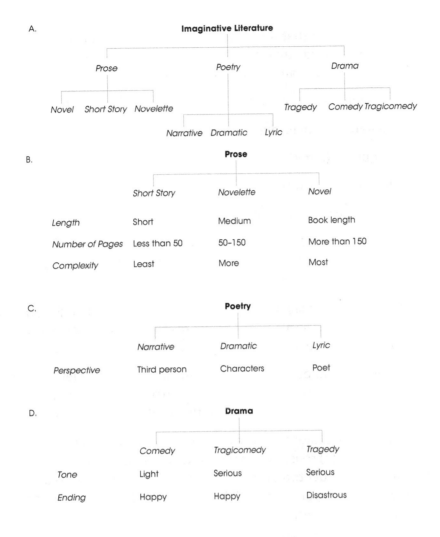

Figure 4-34 Multiple Graphic Organizers for Imaginative Literature

Answers to Focus Questions

1. Having an organizational mindset means that you seek the underlying or optimal organization of information. You seek to uncover relationships, such as the order among things or comparisons between things. You are not satisfied with piecemeal learning and instead seek the organization and association of those pieces. You use your organizational tools—hierarchy, sequence, matrix, and illustration—to guide your organizational thinking and to create graphic organizers that reveal relationships with just a glance.

2. Graphic organizers are superior to linear displays because graphic organizers are better at positioning related information in close proximity, where it is easily compared. Graphic organizers reveal patterns and relationships

with just a glance that linear displays obscure. Graphic organizers also contain fewer words than comparable linear displays and lead to higher achievement on fact and relationship tests.

3. The four types of graphic organizers (and the relationships they reveal) are:

   - Hierarchy (superordinate-subordinate)

   - Sequence (order)

   - Matrix (comparative)

   - Illustration (positional)

4. The three tips for creating hierarchies are: (a) construct top to bottom, (b) include all levels, and (c) be on the alert for alert words that signal super-ordinate-subordinate relationships.

5. The four tips for creating sequences are: (a) construct left to right, (b) include all levels, (c) be on the alert for alert words that signal order relationships, and (d) combine sequences and hierarchies when appropriate.

6. Hierarchies should be created top down, and sequences left to right, so that each can be extended easily into a matrix by adding categories down the left side and by adding details in the resulting matrix cells.

7. The four tips for creating matrices are: (a) develop matrices from hierarchies and sequences, (b) construct matrices with three parts—topics, categories, and details, (c) order topics and categories in logical ways so that relation-ships are easily apparent, and (d) be on the alert for alert words signalling comparative relationships.

8. Some sample matrix alert words signalling comparison include: compare, different, similar, whereas, and however. Modifying words can signal com-parative relationships too. Early settlers suggest a potential comparison with late settlers, and fountain pen suggests a potential comparison with other pen types such as ballpoint.

9. When creating an illustration, follow these guidelines: (a) keep it simple, (b) use labels and captions to explain illustrations, and (c) be on the alert for certain words that signal positional relationships—words that pertain to an object's parts, including their appearance, relative position, and movement.

10. Multiple organizers are useful when a single organizer just won't do. A subject you're studying might contain superordinate-subordinate relation-ships requiring a hierarchy, order relationships requiring a sequence, and comparative relationships requiring a matrix. Or you might need to create multiple matrices, each with its own unique categories.

CHAPTER 5

Association Strategies for Meaningful Learning

OVERVIEW

Objectives

Focus Questions

The Power of Association

Two Types of Associations
Internal Associations
External Associations

Answers to Focus Questions

Objectives

1. Make the argument that a great memory is made, not born.

2. Recognize examples of internal and external associations.

3. Create internal and external associations when given new material to learn.

Focus Questions

1. How can memory experts remember so much, and can the average Joe do the same?

2. What's the difference between internal and external associations?

3. What internal association questions are associated with information organized (a) hierarchically, (b) sequentially, and (c) comparatively?

4. Differentiate among within-topic, across-topic, and global relationships using an example where three baseball teams are compared in terms of winning percentage (WP), batting average (BA), and earned run average (ERA).

5. Why can a chess master who sees a chess position for a few seconds remember it better than a chess novice?

6. When you are learning new terms and definitions, how can examples help?

7. Which mnemonic techniques are effective for learning lists?

8. Which mnemonic technique works well for learning pairs?

9. Which mnemonic technique works well for learning several related facts?

The Power of Association

Here is a list of 12 digits: 4, 2, 5, 1, 0, 6, 6, 9, 3, 5, 3, 2. Say them to yourself at a rate of about one per second. Now, without looking, how many digits can you recall accurately in order?

If you're like most people, your limit is about seven digits, which as you learned in Chapter 2 is the capacity of short-term memory. After that, numbers stack up and fall off like luggage at an airport baggage claim. How, then, can dozens of people recall more than 100 digits, some recall 300 digits, and the world record holder recall 432 digits? (Yes, there are world records for everything!) The answer, of course, is association.

Memory researcher Anders Ericsson got the memory arms race started in the 1970s when he worked with a few typical college students, trying to get them to improve their memory performance on this digit-remembering task (Ericsson & Pool, 2016). Before then, little attention was paid to such memory performance, and the scant research done on the topic reported on two students in the 1920s who improved their memory performance to about 15 digits after four months of practice. Ericsson's memory subjects fared much better. With several months of practice, one student topped out at 82 digits, while another topped 100.

How did Ericsson's students become the world's best memorizers? Well, neither one had unusual ability. Just like you, their original digit spans were around seven digits. And neither could simply memorize so many random digits, one at a time, in a piecemeal fashion. Short-term memory doesn't hold more than about seven things, and long-term memory doesn't readily open its doors to non-meaningful information. Instead, both happened to be long distance runners and running enthusiasts who could meaningfully associate digit segments with running. For example, the digit series 9, 0, 7 was associated with "a pretty good 2-mile time." The digit series 3, 4, 9, 2 was associated with "3 minutes and 49.2 seconds, near world-record time in the mile." The students also made some associations between digit series and other familiar patterns, such as dates in history. The series 1, 9, 4, 4 was associated with "near the end of World War II." Making meaningful associations allowed the students to store the digits in long-term memory.

Since the pioneering achievements of Ericsson's students, memory competitors (yes, there are memory competitions) have found ways to extend memory performance even further—using association strategies, of course (Casper, 2007). To do so, most use a well-established technique that sounds complex at first but becomes quick and automatic with practice. In this system, each digit is given a code letter based on its associated sound or appearance. Letters can be associated more meaningfully than digits. For instance, 0 is a z because of its z sound; 1 is d because the letter d has one downstroke; 2 is n because the letter n has two downstrokes; 3 is m because the letter 3 has three downstrokes; 4 is r because the number four ends with an r sound; and 5 is L because L is the Roman Numeral symbol for fifty.... Codes that can be used for all 10 digits are shown in Table 5-1.

Table 5-1 LETTER CODES FOR REMEMBERING DIGITS

Digit	Letter Used	Rationale for Letter
0	Z	zero begins with z
1	D	d has 1 downstroke
2	N	n has 2 downstrokes
3	M	m has 3 downstrokes
4	R	four ends with r
5	L	L is Roman Numeral for 50
6	G	G looks like 6
7	K	k looks like two 7s on their side
8	F	cursive f has upper and lower loops like 8
9	P	p looks like 9 flipped horizontally

When a memorizer is learning a long list of digits, the digits are combined into two-digit units, and an image is produced for that unit based on the code letters. Returning to our list of 12 digits at the beginning of this chapter, the first four digits were 4, 2, 5, 1. For the unit 42, the code letters are r for 4 and n for 2, which can be combined to form the word rain and its image. For the next unit, 51, the word lid and its image can be formed based on the code letters L for 5 and d for 1.

Activity 5.1

Using the technique just described, create one combined image for the last four digits presented at the start of the chapter: 3, 5, 3, 2.

These two images are then combined into a single image, so that one image is enough to remember four digits. The image might be rain falling on someone covering his head with a garbage can lid. In this way, a single image, like that in Figure 5-1, is created for every four digits. But that's not all.

Memory competitors also have several "memory palaces" in mind to house the constructed images. A memory palace contains a series of about 20 spatial locations, all in a familiar place. These could be rooms in a house, towns along a highway, or buildings on a college campus. Figure 5-2 shows a simple memory palace. If the first memory palace location in a house setting is the bathroom, that location is associated with the first image. Imagine rain from the bathroom shower pouring down on someone as the rain is deflected with a garbage can lid. And on it goes. Each series of four digits is combined into an image and associated with a subsequent memory palace location. This process continues until the memory palace's 20 or so locations are filled, and then it's on to the next memory palace. To retrieve the digits, the memorizer simply

Figure 5-1 Single Image for Remembering the Digits: 4, 2, 5, 1

retraces steps through the memory palaces and deconstructs the images back into digits.

"Woo! That seems hard," you're thinking. "I could never do that." It is hard, at first, but with practice it is hardly impossible and quite doable. Consider the tale of Josh Foer, chronicled in his book *Moonwalking with Einstein: The Art and Science of Remembering Everything*. Foer was a journalist who one day wondered who the smartest person in the world was. His quest to find the smartest person led him to Ben Pridmore, who once memorized over 1,500 digits in an hour. Tantalized by Pridmore's prodigious memory, Foer began to study the methods of

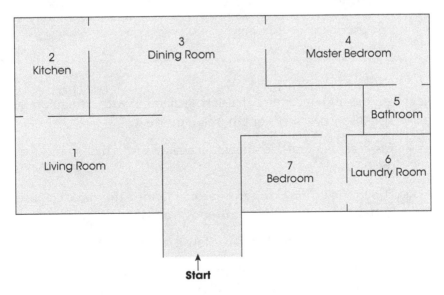

Figure 5-2 A Simple Memory Palace Using Rooms in a House

competitive memory experts (Foer, 2011). That study led him to train his own memory, which he described as "average at best," and to compete just one year later in the 2006 U.S. Memory Championship, which he won! Another national memory champion, Tatiana Cooley, also admitted to having no special talents. She said, "I'm just like everybody else. Anybody can do this" (Ericsson, 2007).

What makes average people super memorizers? Association. What makes average students super students? Association. Just as memory experts learn a series of rapidly presented digits by associating digits with letters, letters with words, words with images, images with images, and images with locations, super students rely on associations too.

As an example, let's revisit the Figure 5-3 matrix about fish, which we saw in Chapter 4. An average student tries to learn this information in a piecemeal fashion, one disjointed idea after another: "The crappie has a mottled appearance ... It hides in rocks at the bottom ... The catfish has a dark upper side ..." The super student, meanwhile, creates meaningful associations like the following.

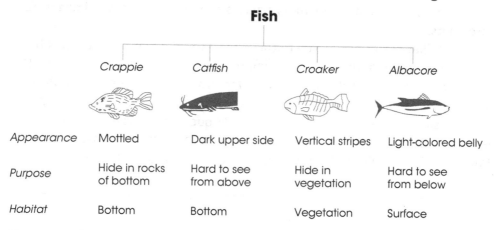

Figure 5-3 A Matrix About Fish

1. Each fish has an appearance that lets it blend in with its habitat so that other fish (likely predators or prey) cannot see it.

   ▪ The crappie's mottled appearance allows it to hide in rocks at the bottom.

   ▪ The catfish's dark upper side blends into the dark colored bottom, making it difficult to spot from above.

   ▪ The croaker's vertical stripes allow it to blend into vegetation.

   ▪ The albacore's light-colored underbelly blends into the light-colored surface, making it difficult to spot from below.

2. I'll also remember that crappie live at the bottom because there is a lot of crap (sounds like crappie) at the bottom of the ocean.

3. I'll also remember that catfish have a dark upper side because my cat, Twinkles, has a dark upper side.

4. I'll also remember that croakers live in vegetation because I'd rather croak (die) than eat sea vegetation like seaweed and kelp.

5. I know that albacore is the highest grade of tuna and is used to make solid white tuna. That helps me remember that albacore are light colored.

In the remainder of this chapter, you'll learn about two types of association—internal and external—and strategies for creating them. Association strategies help you learn information faster, understand it better, and remember it longer than the typical and ineffective piecemeal (one idea at a time) and rehearsal (repeating information over and over) methods most students use, as was described in Chapter 2. To get started, read the passage below about levels of measurement, and then take the quiz covering that material in the subsequent box.

A Passage About Levels of Measurement

Levels of Measurement
There are many different things that can be measured. We can, for example, measure someone's religious preference, class rank, intelligence, or height. Measuring different things not only requires different measuring tools (such as an IQ test for intelligence and a ruler for height) but also requires different levels of measurement. The four levels of measurement are nominal, ordinal, interval, and ratio.

Nominal Measurement
Nominal measurement is defined as categorizing people or things into classes or sets. For example, you have probably filled out forms where you marked 1 if you were male and 2 if you were female. Or maybe you indicated your religious preference by marking 3 if you were Methodist and 5 if you were Catholic. Such numerical codes for gender and religious preference would be nominal measurement.

A characteristic of nominal measurement is that the assignment of numbers to categories is arbitrary. For example, it would make no difference in our previous examples if we assigned females as 1 and males as 2, and Methodists as 5 and Catholics as 3. Its limitation is that it provides no quantitative information. It is considered measurement in name only (that is, nominal). To capture more than just categorical classification, a higher measurement level is needed.

Ordinal Measurement

Ordinal measurement provides more information than nominal measurement. By definition, it tells the relative position, order, or rank of people or things. Class rankings and percentile ranks on standardized tests are examples of ordinal measurement.

A characteristic of an ordinal measure is that it provides certain quantitative information (for example, Sue scored higher than Tom on a science test). Its limitation, though, is that it does not tell the distance between scores. We only know that Sue scored higher than Tom. How much higher she scored, or how much more science knowledge she has, is unknown. Similarly, looking only at class rank in high school, we might learn that Bernice ranks 10th and Phillip 15th. This ordinal information, though, tells us nothing about their actual GPAs and the magnitude of their differences. For that, we need a higher level of measurement.

Interval Measurement

By definition, interval measurement specifies the distance between scores. Thus, interval measurement not only reveals that one score is higher than another; it also reveals how much higher. For example, with an interval test, we cannot only say that Sue's score was higher than Tom's, but also say that it was 5 points higher. A characteristic of interval measurement is consistency. With interval measurement, a difference of 5 points is consistent; it means the same whether the scores being compared are 28 and 23, or 88 and 83.

Interval measurement has two limitations. First, there is no true zero point, where zero designates a total absence of something. If someone scored zero on an intelligence test or even a math test, the zero score would probably not indicate the absence of any intelligence or math knowledge. Second, interval measurement does not provide realistic ratio information. If Bernice scores 80 on a math test and Phillip scores 40, we cannot assume that Bernice knows twice as much math as Phillip. Such comparisons depend on ratio measurement.

Ratio Measurement

Ratio scores are defined as those where the ratio between scores is meaningful. For example, a score of 80 really means twice as much as a score of 40. Another characteristic is that a score of zero really indicates the absence of the attribute being measured. It is possible, for example, for something to have zero height.

Although there are many examples of ratio measurement (e.g., height, weight, volume, speed, or distance), there are few instances of ratio measurement in education. This limitation comes about because educators simply do not have yardsticks to measure students' abilities or achievements with the same accuracy as those used to measure height or weight.

A Quiz Covering Levels of Measurement

1. Which level of measurement has a true zero point?
   a. Ordinal
   b. Ratio
   c. Interval
   d. Nominal

2. Which level of measurement is rarely used in education?
   a. Ordinal
   b. Ratio
   c. Interval
   d. Nominal

3. Which level of measurement provides no quantitative information?
   a. Ordinal
   b. Ratio
   c. Interval
   d. Nominal

4. Which levels of measurement allow for an understanding of the distance between scores?
   a. Ordinal and interval
   b. Interval and ratio
   c. Interval only
   d. Ratio only
   e. Ordinal only

5. On an interest inventory, students checked 1 if they were interested in the arts, 2 for athletics, and 3 for science. These data best fit with which level of measurement?
   a. Ordinal
   b. Interval
   c. Nominal
   d. Ratio

6. In the latest football poll, Manchester United was ranked 3rd and Arsenal was ranked 6th. These data best fit with which level of measurement?
   a. Ordinal
   b. Interval
   c. Nominal
   d. Ratio

Two Types of Associations

Was the levels of measurement material hard to learn? Was the quiz difficult? I bet things would have been easier had you created Table 5-3 and made associations.

Table 5-3 LEVELS OF MEASUREMENT MATRIX ORGANIZER

	Nominal	Ordinal	Interval	Ratio
Definition	Categorizing into classes	Relative order or rank of things	Specifies distance between scores	Provides meaningful ratio between scores
Example	Male = 1 Female = 2	Class rankings	Sue scored 5 points higher than Tom	Height and weight
Characteristic	Number assignment is arbitrary	Provides some quantitative information	Consistency	Zero means absence of something
Limitation	No quantitative information	Does not tell distance between scores	No zero point or ratio information	Few instances of ratio measurement in education

There are two types of associations you can make when learning new material—internal and external. As shown in Figure 5-4, internal associations are those made within the material being learned. The Xs in Figure 5-4 represent ideas a reader has selected from a text, and the broken lines represent internal associations the reader has made by joining those text ideas. The solid lines joining the text ideas (the Xs) and information previously stored in the reader's memory (the triangles) represent external associations. To remember this, remember this association: *Internal* associations are *within* the material being learned, and *external* associations go *outside* the material being learned. Here are some internal and external associations stemming from the levels of measurement material.

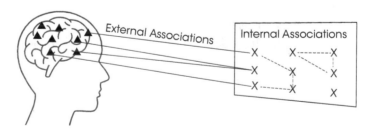

Figure 5-4 Internal and External Associations

Internal Associations

- The four levels increase in sophistication. Nominal simply categorizes things (e.g., male-female). Ordinal ranks things (e.g., class rank). Interval makes clear the distance between things (e.g., 5 points). And ratio reveals the ratio of scores (e.g., 80 is twice 40).

- Each level has a limitation. Nominal contains no quantitative information. Ratio does not reveal distance between scores. Interval has no zero point or ratio information. Ratio measurement is rare in education.

External Associations

- An example of nominal measurement is assigning numbers to countries, such as 1 for Serbia, 2 for Spain, and 3 for Switzerland.

- An example of ordinal measurement is tennis rankings, such as: Novak Djokovic is 1, Rafael Nadal is 2, and Roger Federer is 3.

- An example of interval measurement is the number of points each tennis player has accumulated: Djokovic, 9,865; Nadal, 9,225; and Federer, 7,130.

- An example of ratio measurement is the height of the three players: Djokovic, 6 ft 2 in; Federer, 6 ft 1 in; and Nadal, 6 ft 0 in.

- I'll also remember the order of levels by remembering the sentence: *No, I run*, which uses the first letters of the levels—*No* (nominal and ordinal), *I* (interval), and *run* (ratio).

- I'll also remember that nominal pertains to the names of things because *nominal* sounds like *names*. I'll also remember that nominal provides the least information because nominal also means very small.

Activity 5.2

Here is a matrix about eating disorders. Create 3 internal and 3 external associations to help you learn and remember this information.

Table 5-2 EATING DISORDER MATRIX

	Anorexia Nervosa	Bulimia Nervosa	Binge Eating Disorder
What happens?	People restrict calories and do not sustain a healthy body weight	People binge (eat a lot) and then purge (vomit)	People binge but do not purge
How common is it?	9 in 1,000 women 3 in 1,000 men	15 in 1,000 women 5 in 1,000 men	35 in 1,000 women 20 in 1,000 men
Average Age of Onset	Early, mid, or late adolescence	Adolescence, young adulthood	Adulthood

Internal Associations

Creating internal associations involves finding relationships among the ideas being learned. First, organizing ideas, as was taught in Chapter 4, helps you find those relationships. The internal associations just provided for levels of measurement are easy to create when the information is first represented in the matrix organizer found in Table 5-3. As another example, examine the matrix about black and white rhinos found in Table 5-4. It is easy to create the following internal associations when examining that matrix:

- Twigs are in jungles.

- Hooked lips grasp twigs.

- Grass is in the plains.

- Square lips scoop grass.

- Habitat, food, and lips are all associated because the food is plentiful in the habitat where it's found, and the rhinos' lips are well suited to eating that food.

Table 5-4 RHINOS MATRIX ORGANIZER

	Black	White
Habitat	Jungle	Plains
Food	Twigs	Grass
Lips	Hooked	Square

There are four questions you can ask yourself to help find and form internal associations. You'll notice that these questions are tied to the various graphic organizers presented in Chapter 4.

1. What's Above, Below, and Alongside?

This is a question that helps you discern hierarchical relationships. Suppose you're in a psychology class, learning about forgetting, and you learn that one type of forgetting is interference. Ask yourself: What's above, below, and alongside? As shown in the top portion of the Figure 5-5 hierarchy, you'll come to learn that interference is a type of forgetting (that's what's above), that there are two types of interference, proactive and retroactive (that's what's below), and that there are other types of forgetting, namely decay and distortion (that's what's alongside). Asking and answering the question of what's above, below, and alongside helps you learn how some information is linked hierarchically.

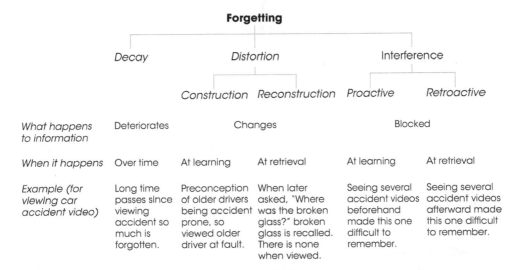

Figure 5-5 Forgetting Organizer

As another example, suppose you were learning about classical conditioning theory in your psychology class. How does that fit with other theoretical concepts? To find out, ask and answer the question of what's above, below, and alongside. As you'll see in the top portion of the Figure 5-6 hierarchy, classical conditioning is a behavioral theory (what's above?). There are types of classical conditioning methods, such as simultaneous, trace, and delayed (what's below?). And there are other types of behavioral theories, namely operant and social learning (what's alongside?). Of course, you can continue this line of questioning to learn other hierarchical relationships, such as that behavioral theory is a type of learning theory (what's above?), and that there are other learning theories in addition to behavioral, such as cognitive and developmental (what's alongside?).

Learning Theories

Behavioral | *Cognitive* | *Developmental*

	Operant Conditioning	*Classical Conditioning*	*Social Learning*
Definition	An association is made between a certain response (R) and a stimulus (S) that strengthens or weakens that response.	A stimulus (S) that elicits a response (R) is paired with a neutral stimulus (NS) such that the neutral stimulus eventually elicits the response.	A response (R1) is modeled by one person and observed and performed (R2) by another person.
Example	Perform trick → Food	1. Meat → Salivate 2. Meat + Bell → Salivate 3. Bell → Salivate	Observe reading → Read

	Simultaneous	*Trace*	Delayed
Stimulus Relationship	S and NS presented at same time.	NS presented first; S presented after NS ends.	NS presented first but is overlapped by the presentation of S.
Example	Food and bell presented simultaneously	Bell rings and ends and then food is presented	Bell rings first and then food is presented while bell is still sounding

Figure 5-6 Learning Theories Organizer

2. What's Before and After?

This is a question that helps you discern sequential relationships. Suppose, in a biology class, you are learning about the human heart and how it circulates blood. The question of what's before and after helps you understand the blood circulation sequence, as shown in the top portion of Figure 5-7. From this sequence, it is easy to see what is before and after each blood-flow step.

As another example from biology, your instructor is discussing the Mesozoic era of the Earth's evolution. The what's before and after question would reveal

Blood Circulation

	Right Atrium →	*Right Ventricle* →	*Pulmonary Arteries* →	*Lungs* →	*Pulmonary Veins* →	*Left Atrium* →	*Left Ventricle* →	*Aorta* →	*Body*
Structure	Upper heart soft-walled	Lower heart tough-walled	Tube-like		Tube-like	Upper heart soft-walled	Lower heart tough-walled	Tube-like	
Function	Receive blood	Pump blood to lungs	Carry deoxygenized blood away from heart to lungs	Supply blood with oxygen	Carry oxygen-rich blood from lungs to heart	Receive oxygenized blood	Pump blood to body	Carry oxygenated blood to body	

Figure 5-7 Blood Circulation Organizer

that the Mesozoic era was preceded by the Azoic, Precambrian, and Paleozoic eras and followed by the Cenozoic era, as shown in the top portion of the Figure 5-8 sequence.

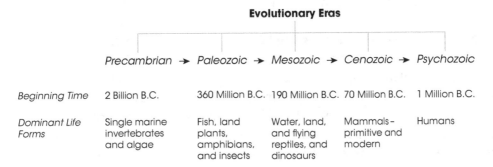

	Precambrian →	Paleozoic →	Mesozoic →	Cenozoic →	Psychozoic
Beginning Time	2 Billion B.C.	360 Million B.C.	190 Million B.C.	70 Million B.C.	1 Million B.C.
Dominant Life Forms	Single marine invertebrates and algae	Fish, land plants, amphibians, and insects	Water, land, and flying reptiles, and dinosaurs	Mammals – primitive and modern	Humans

Figure 5-8 Evolutionary Eras Organizer

3. What Categories Cut Across These Topics?

This is a question that helps you discern comparative relationships found in a matrix. Remember from Chapter 4 that any time you have multiple topics (such as theories of forgetting, behavioral theories, steps in blood circulation, and evolutional eras), you should determine the categories that cut across those topics. Oftentimes, your instructors and your textbooks do not make these categories obvious or even evident, so you'll need to be a careful listener, reader, and thinker to uncover them.

Also know that some areas have a set of common categories that your teachers and textbooks have likely never told you about. For instance, what cuts across most scientific concepts? The answer is structure, function, and location. Think about the body parts involved in digestion (mouth, esophagus, stomach, and intestines). Each has a structure, function, and location. Think about the three germ layers (ectoderm, mesoderm, and endoderm). Each has a structure, function, and location. What cuts across historical events like wars or elections? All have a who (was involved), where (did it happen), when (did it happen), what (happened), why (did it happen), and so what (does it matter) component. Think about literature. All stories have characters, setting, plot, conflict, and resolution. Then there's music. Music has melody, rhythm, tempo, harmony, dynamics, and timbre. Get the picture? Speaking of pictures, they have symmetry, texture, depth, and lines.

Returning to Figures 5-5 through 5-8, you'll see along the figures' left sides some categories you're likely to uncover. Cutting across the forgetting topics in Figure 5-5 are the categories what happens to information, when it happens, and example. Cutting across the learning theories topics in Figure 5-6 are the categories definition and example, while below that, the categories stimulus relationship and example cut across the classical conditioning topics. Cutting across the blood circulation steps in Figure 5-7 are the categories structure and function. And cutting across the evolutionary eras in Figure 5-8 are the categories beginning time and dominant life forms. When topics and categories and their resulting details are apparent, associations are ripe for the picking.

4. What Internal Associations Are Within and Across Topics?

This is the big question to ask when learning. At the heart of any learning task is discerning relationships within and across topics. Within-topic relationships are gleaned when an organizer is examined vertically; across-topic relationships are gleaned when an organizer is examined horizontally. Let's revisit Figures 5-5 and 5-6 and see what associations they reveal. Some of these associations might seem complex as you've not seriously studied this information, but look closely and see just how important each association is for mastering these topics.

Starting with Figure 5-5 on forgetting, the following are among the internal associations that are apparent:

- Forgetting can occur because information deteriorates (decay), changes (distortion), or is blocked (interference). (Across topic.)

- There are two types of distortion: construction and reconstruction. (Within topic.) Construction occurs at the time of learning, whereas reconstruction occurs at the time of retrieval. (Across topic.)

- There are two types of interference: proactive and retroactive. (Within topic). Proactive occurs at the time of learning, whereas retroactive occurs at the time of retrieval. (Across topic.)

- Decay is information deterioration over time, such as when you view a car accident and cannot recall what happened weeks later. (Within topic.)

- Forgetting can occur at the time of learning, such as with constructive distortion and proactive interference. In each case, previously learned information inhibits new learning. (Across topic.)

- Forgetting can occur at the time of retrieval, such as with reconstructive distortion and retroactive interference. In each case, subsequently learned information inhibits retrieval of previously acquired information. (Across topic.)

- Bringing the preconception that older drivers are accident prone to the viewing of an accident, and having that preconception shape your perception of the accident, is an example of how memories can be altered at the time of learning. (Within topic.)

- When an accident video is shown, accident videos seen previously can block learning of the target video (proactive interference), and accident videos shown after the target video can also block recall of the target video (retroactive interference). (Across topic.)

Here are some internal associations revealed from Figure 5-6 on learning theories:

- Behavioral, cognitive, and developmental theory are all learning theories. (Within topic.)

- There are three behavioral theories: classical, operant, and social learning. (Within topic.)

- All three behavioral theories involve responding: classical conditioning focuses on the stimuli that elicit (come before) a response (S-R); operant conditioning focuses on the stimuli that follow a response and strengthen or weaken that response (R-S); and social learning theory focuses on a response being modelled (R1) by one person and performed by an observer (R2). (Across topic.)

- In classical conditioning, meat is a stimulus (S) that naturally elicits salivation (R). Meat and a bell (NS) are paired and elicit salivation (R). Eventually the bell (NS) elicits salivation (R). (Within topic.)

- In operant conditioning, performing a trick is a response (R) that can be strengthened by receiving a food stimulus (S) following the response. (Within topic.)

- In social learning, observing a reading response (R1) can prompt someone to emit a reading response (R2). (Within topic.)

- There are three types of classical conditioning: simultaneous, trace, and delayed. (Within topic.) These differ in their NS-S timing. Simultaneous: NS and S occur at the same time. Trace: NS first and S after NS ends. Delayed: NS is presented and stays on while S is presented. (Across topic.)

- An example of delayed conditioning is: (1) bell rings (NS); (2) while bell is sounding, meat (S) is presented. (Within topic.)

There is a third type of internal association I call global. Global associations occur across multiple organizer rows and are the most powerful association of all. Here's one global association from Figure 5-9 to get you acquainted: The louder a wildcat's call, the heavier the wildcat. Notice that this one association incorporated 12 wildcat facts (the six calls and the six weights). See how many other global associations you can find in Figure 5-9 before checking my list.

	Tiger	Lion	Jaguar	Leopard	Cheetah	Bobcat
Call	Roar	Roar	Growl	Growl	Hiss	Hiss
Weight (lbs)	450	400	200	150	125	30
Lifespan (years)	25	25	20	10	8	6
Habitat	Jungle	Plains	Jungle	Jungle	Plains	Jungle
Social Behavior	Solitary	Groups	Solitary	Solitary	Groups	Solitary
Range (sq. miles)	30	150	5	15	50	30
Time of Hunt	Night	Day	Night	Night	Day	Night
Distinct Trait	Powerful upper body	Keen sense of smell	Powerful jaws	Skilled climber	Speed	Keen eyes and ears
Method of Hunt	Knocks prey over	Scavenges for dead animals	Bites prey on neck	Hides leftovers in trees	Chases down prey	Ambushes prey

Figure 5-9 Wildcat Matrix

- The louder the call, the heavier the wildcat, and the longer the lifespan (18 facts).

- Jungle cats are solitary, have small ranges, and hunt at night, whereas plains cats live in groups, have large ranges, and hunt by day (24 facts).

- A wildcat's distinct trait is linked to its hunting method: The tiger uses its powerful upper body to knock prey over; the lion uses its keen sense of smell to scavenge for dead animals; the jaguar uses its powerful jaws to bite prey on the neck; the leopard is a skilled climber, which allows it to hide leftovers in trees; the cheetah uses its speed to chase down prey; and the bobcat uses its keen eyes and ears to ambush prey (12 facts).

Activity 5.3

Here is a matrix about skin cancers. Make within-topic, across-topic, and global internal associations.

Table 5-5 SKIN CANCER MATRIX

	Basal Cell Carcinoma	Squamous Cell Carcinoma	Malignant Melanoma
Prevalence	Most common	Middle	Least common
Severity	Least	Middle	Most
Cause	Many years of sun exposure	Many years of sun exposure	Many years of sun exposure
Prevention	Sun block, clothing	Sun block, clothing	Sun block, clothing
Development	Underlying skin cells damaged, tumor, ulcer	Underlying skin cells damaged, tumor, ulcer	Underlying skin cells damaged, tumor, ulcer
Symptoms	Small, flesh-colored lump	Firm lump	Flat spot or bump w/ dark pigment and other colors. Jagged edges, asymmetrical
Common Sites	Ears, hands	Ears, hands	Any skin surface
Outlook	Good, rarely metastasizes, causes local tissue damage if neglected	Good w/ early detection, otherwise bad—metastasizes	Early detection essential, otherwise metastasizes quickly
Follow-Up	Check for 2 yrs.	Check for 5 yrs.	Check for lifetime

External Associations

Learning depends on linking new information to previous information. And creating external associations does just that. It involves finding relationships between the information to be learned and existing knowledge. As a learner, you bring considerable information already stored in memory to any learning task. Remember from Chapter 2 that you cannot simply toss information haphazardly into long-term memory and expect to retrieve it later. Retrieval depends on storing new things with similar things. A new weather fact should be stored with existing weather information, and news of a football trade should be stored with existing football information or perhaps with deals-gone-bad information. Think about a closet. If you toss new things in haphazardly, you'll have trouble finding them or even remembering you have them. You want to store new dress shirts with other dress shirts and new shoes with other shoes. Libraries (remember them?) do this, of course. New biographies are stored with existing biographies, and a new book on the Supreme Court is stored with existing books on American government. Below are three questions you can ask yourself to help find and form external associations. Table 5-6 shows the questions to be asked and answered for internal and external associations.

Table 5-6 INTERNAL AND EXTERNAL ASSOCIATION QUESTIONS TO BE ASKED AND ANSWERED

Internal	External
1. What's above, below, and alongside?	1. What do I know about this?
2. What's before and after?	2. What new examples can I provide?
3. What categories cut across these topics?	3. What mnemonics can I create?
4. What internal associations are within and across topics?	

1. What Do I Know About This?

Use your existing knowledge to help you understand and remember new information. Some psychologists call this elaboration because you are going beyond to-be-learned information by linking it to prior knowledge. Returning to Figure 5-7 about blood circulation, try to associate the new information with things you know or think you know that help make the new information make sense. Here are some helpful external associations:

- The atriums are soft walled because their function is to receive blood. A catcher's mitt is soft too because it receives pitches.

- The ventricles are tough walled because they must be tough to pump blood. Similarly, a tire pump must be tough to pump air.

- I know that pulmonary has to do with respiration, so it makes sense that the pulmonary arteries carry blood to the lungs and that pulmonary veins carry blood from the lungs.

- Arteries carry blood away from the heart. *Arteries* and *away* both begin with the letter *A*.

- Arteries are red colored because they carry blood rich in oxygen, which gives them their rich red color.

- An atrium is a place where people enter and gather. Atriums in the heart are where blood enters and gathers.

- The blood says, "I aorta get back to the body." This is how I'll remember that the aorta carries blood to the body.

Here is another example of using existing knowledge to understand and remember new information. Consider two chess players—one a novice and one an expert—trying to memorize the position shown in Figure 5-10. A novice player tries to learn the position in a piecemeal fashion: "White has a queen on the e2 square. White has a king on g1. White has a rook on b7 and on f1 ..." This approach leaves the novice trying to memorize the placement of 22 discrete pieces. Not going to happen. An expert player, though, uses her prior chess knowledge to understand and remember new positions, like this:

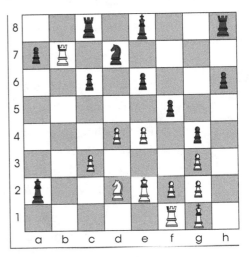

Figure 5-10 A Chess Position

White has castled his king to the kingside and is safely tucked behind his castle of pawns, although the h-pawn is doubled on the g-file, and that can become a weakness. Black has failed to castle his king, which lies vulnerable in the center. The Black king is flanked by his rooks, but neither is powerful because both rest on closed files. There is tension in the center. White is threatening to capture Black's f-pawn, which is unprotected because Black's e-pawn cannot recapture, because it is pinned to the king by White's queen...

You probably have no idea what all of this means, but the chess expert does. The expert player understands and remembers the placement of the pieces because she is linking the new position to past knowledge about chess positions. The chess expert can easily remember a few meaningful chunks, while the novice struggles to learn nearly two dozen isolated bits of information. To do this, of course, the expert must have accumulated previous chess knowledge. The rich get richer. The more one knows, the easier it is to learn more, as new information is linked to past knowledge through the creation of external associations.

Activity 5.4

Returning to the skin cancer material in Activity 5-3, use the "What do I know about this?" question to create external associations helpful for learning and remembering that material.

2. What New Examples Can I Provide?

Here is the definition of positive reinforcement: A stimulus presented following a response increases that response. Clear, right? Not really. Now let's make things murkier. Here is the definition of negative reinforcement: A stimulus removed following a response increases that response. Making internal associations helps some.

- Both increase a response.

- Both follow the same sequence: response—stimulus—response.

- The difference is that the stimulus is presented for positive and removed for negative.

Still, it is difficult to really know what positive and negative reinforcement are like. You might be able to recite the definitions, but could you identify new examples? Below are four behavior change examples. See if you can identify which are positive reinforcement and which are negative reinforcement.

1. Every time Murphy comes into the house when called, the Preston family gives her a treat from the treat dish. Now, Murphy always comes right away when called, even when there are squirrels in sight.

2. Ms. Sharp used a token economy. She took tokens away when students earned low grades. As a result, students earned fewer low grades.

3. The heat outside was excruciating all week long. Dallas stayed inside more that week, to avoid the heat.

4. Coach pushed Sam's hands lower each time he raised his bat too high during batting drills. In time, Sam rarely raised his bat too high.

Not so easy, huh? Number 1 was an example of positive reinforcement, and Number 3 was negative reinforcement. The other two examples were types of punishment.

What is needed when learning new terms and definitions are examples. Examples help you understand and remember new terms, and they help you identify new examples when needed. So let's supply some examples when learning about reinforcement, as shown in Figure 5-11. These new examples make clear that both techniques increase desired behaviors, but they go about it in different ways. Positive reinforcement involves making a response to attain something desirable such as food, praise, or a new game jersey, whereas negative reinforcement involves making the same response to avoid something aversive such as failing a course, being shocked, or running stairs. This makes me think of yet another example, shown in Figure 5-12: a horse moving forward to get the carrot dangling on the stick in front of him (positive reinforcement), versus moving forward to avoid the whip (negative reinforcement).

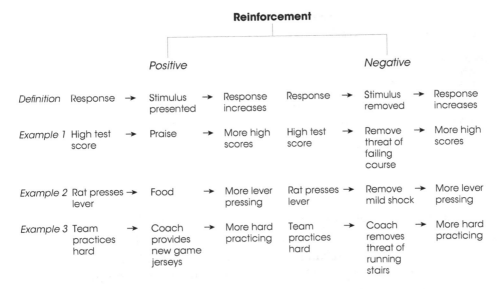

Reinforcement

	Positive			Negative		
Definition	Response →	Stimulus presented →	Response increases	Response →	Stimulus removed →	Response increases
Example 1	High test score →	Praise →	More high scores	High test score →	Remove threat of failing course →	More high scores
Example 2	Rat presses lever →	Food →	More lever pressing	Rat presses lever →	Remove mild shock →	More lever pressing
Example 3	Team practices hard →	Coach provides new game jerseys →	More hard practicing	Team practices hard →	Coach removes threat of running stairs →	More hard practicing

Figure 5-11 Reinforcement Examples

Figure 5-12 Example of Positive and Negative Reinforcement

Returning to the classical conditioning material introduced earlier, you'll see that adding new examples aids understanding and memory, as shown in Figure 5-13. Notice that the new examples and their parts are placed near the term's definition and its parts just above. Setting up examples in this way makes it easy to connect them to their definitions. With just a glance at Figure 5-13, we can see, among other things, that music is a stimulus that can elicit a good-feelings response. An advertised product can be a neutral stimulus, paired with music, that eventually elicits a good-feelings response on its own.

Classical Conditioning

Definition	S → R		NS + S → R		NS → R	
Familiar Example	Meat → Salivate		Bell + Meat → Salivate		Bell → Salivate	
Example 1	Music → Good feelings		Slogan + Music → Good feelings		Slogan → Good feelings	
Example 2	Thunder → Fear		Rain + Thunder → Fear		Rain → Fear	
Example 3	Bed → Sleep		School work + Bed → Sleep		School work → Sleep	

Figure 5-13 New Classical Conditioning Examples

Another example. Suppose you were learning about the defense mechanisms posited by psychologist Sigmund Freud. The top portion of Figure 5-14 shows some of those defense mechanisms and their definitions. The bottom portion shows examples you might create to better understand and remember the definitions. Having all the examples pertain to the same situation (in this case an ill parent), instead of varying situations, makes it easier to compare the examples.

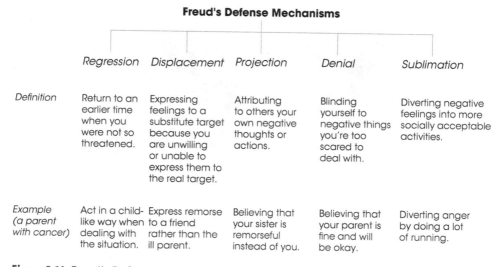

Freud's Defense Mechanisms

	Regression	Displacement	Projection	Denial	Sublimation
Definition	Return to an earlier time when you were not so threatened.	Expressing feelings to a substitute target because you are unwilling or unable to express them to the real target.	Attributing to others your own negative thoughts or actions.	Blinding yourself to negative things you're too scared to deal with.	Diverting negative feelings into more socially acceptable activities.
Example (a parent with cancer)	Act in a child-like way when dealing with the situation.	Express remorse to a friend rather than the ill parent.	Believing that your sister is remorseful instead of you.	Believing that your parent is fine and will be okay.	Diverting anger by doing a lot of running.

Figure 5-14 Freud's Defense Mechanism Examples

One last example. This time, you'll see how you can make both internal and external associations to help you learn and remember. Look at Table 5-7, which provides definitions for three types of symbiosis. Again, most students are apt to learn these three terms in a piecemeal and rote fashion, as if the three symbiosis terms have no link to one another (internal associations) or to their prior knowledge (external associations).

Table 5-7 SYMBIOSIS TERMS AND DEFINITIONS

Commensalism	A type of symbiosis where one organism benefits and the other is unaffected.
Mutualism	A type of symbiosis where both organisms benefit.
Parasitism	A type of symbiosis where one organism benefits and the other is harmed.

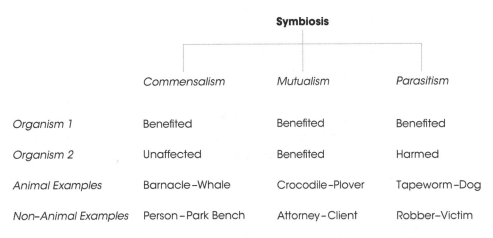

	Commensalism	Mutualism	Parasitism
Organism 1	Benefited	Benefited	Benefited
Organism 2	Unaffected	Benefited	Harmed
Animal Examples	Barnacle–Whale	Crocodile–Plover	Tapeworm–Dog
Non-Animal Examples	Person–Park Bench	Attorney–Client	Robber–Victim

Figure 5-15 Symbiosis Matrix With Examples

Now look at Figure 5-15, a matrix ideal for making internal and external associations. In terms of internal associations, just a glance at Figure 5-15 makes the following internal associations evident:

- Symbiosis involves two organisms in a nutritional relationship.

- One organism always benefits (that's how the three types are alike).

- The three types are different in what happens to the second organism, which can be unaffected (commensalism), benefited (mutualism), or harmed (parasitism).

By adding animal examples to the matrix, we are making external associations that help us understand and remember the three symbiosis types. For instance, the commensalism example of barnacles latching onto whales, and the knowledge that barnacles are fed (benefited) while whales are unaffected, helps us understand and remember commensalism. So too does adding familiar examples beyond the animal kingdom, such as a person benefiting from a park bench (commensalism) and a robber stealing money from a victim (parasitism).

Activity 5.5

Try adding your own new examples to the materials presented in this section on reinforcement, classical conditioning, defense mechanisms, and symbiosis.

3. What Mnemonics Can I Create?

Sometimes it is difficult to link information to prior knowledge, or to generate meaningful examples, if you know little about the topic at hand and the information to be learned seems arbitrary. Consider this seemingly arbitrary information from a geology lesson on fault planes:

- Dip-slip faults are created when two or more fault blocks move in a vertical direction relative to each other.

- Strike-slip faults are created when two or more fault blocks move in a horizontal direction relative to each other.

How can you remember how each fault is created? Perhaps you can remember that dip faults are created vertically because when you take a dip in a pool you dive in vertically, and perhaps you can remember that strike faults are created horizontally because when you strike a baseball you do so horizontally. This is an example of using mnemonics.

Mnemonics are contrived or artificial associations that boost memory when more meaningful external associations are not easily made. Although it is best to create meaningful associations, mnemonic associations are quite powerful and often act as the icing on the cake for remembering stubborn, hard-to-remember information after meaningful associations have been made. Returning to the Figure 5-15 material on symbiosis, you learned through meaningful associations how those types of symbiosis are alike (one organism always benefits) and different (a second organism is either unaffected, benefitted, or harmed) and how they might be exemplified (a crocodile and plover have a mutualistic relationship). However, you might not remember which type is which. Is commensalism the one where both organisms benefit, or is it the one where an organism is harmed, or is it something else altogether? Mnemonics can help:

- Commensalism sounds like comments. When a teacher comments on a student's work, the student is benefited and the teacher unaffected.

- Mutualism sounds like mutual. When a couple is in love with one another, their love is mutual and both people benefit.

- Parasitism sounds like parasite, and we all know that a parasite in our digestive system benefits and we get sick (harmed).

Returning to the start of the chapter, when you read about memory experts learning long strings of numbers, you learned that they did so largely through mnemonics. They artificially linked numbers to letters (1 was the letter d because d has one downstroke). They used those letters to create contrived words and images (such as rain and lid). And they placed those images inside locations (such as a bathroom) in a self-manufactured memory palace (such as a house).

Let's look at five well-established mnemonic techniques useful for making external associations: first-letter, narrative chaining, pegword, keyword, and mnemonomy.

First-Letter

Much of what must be learned is a list or a list in disguise. Consider: the process of photosynthesis, bones in the arm, points in a speech, or U.S. presidents. All lists. How can you remember list-like information such as the colors of the rainbow, the order of planets, the Great Lakes, the order of mathematical operations, or methods for learning effectively? The first-letter mnemonic is one way to remember. It involves using the first letter of the to-be-learned terms to create a memorable word or sentence, as shown below:

- **Roy G. Biv** is used to remember the colors of the rainbow in order: **r**ed, **o**range, **y**ellow, **g**reen, **b**lue, **i**ndigo, and **v**iolet.

- The sentence, "**M**y **v**ery **e**ducated **m**other **j**ust **s**erved **u**s **n**achos," helps you remember the order of planets from the sun: **M**ercury, **V**enus, **E**arth, **M**ars, **J**upiter, **S**aturn, **U**ranus, and **N**eptune.

- The word **HOMES** helps you remember the five Great Lakes: **H**uron, **O**ntario, **M**ichigan, **E**rie, and **S**uperior.

- "**P**lease **e**xcuse **m**y **d**ear **A**unt **S**ally" is a sentence used to remember the order of operations in math: **p**arentheses, **e**xponents, **m**ultiplication, **d**ivision, **a**ddition, and **s**ubtraction.

- **SOAR**, of course, is our first-letter mnemonic for remembering the learning process: **s**elect, **o**rganize, **a**ssociate, and **r**egulate.

When trying to remember Freud's five defense mechanisms presented in Figure 5-14, you might use first-letter mnemonics and think: "**S**ubmarines (sublimation) **d**eny (denial) **d**isplaced (displacement) **p**rojectiles (projection) **r**egularly (regression)."

Narrative Chaining

Narrative chaining is another list-learning technique. It involves associating to-be-learned ideas (chaining them) into a memorable story (a narrative). Narrative chaining helped my junior high science class remember a plant's reproductive parts. The teacher gave us this narrative chain: "*Stamen, stigma style*, or I'll shoot you with my *pistil*." And, "That's what Phil meant (*filament*) when he

---

Activity 5.6

Use first-letter mnemonics to remember these lists.

- **Six steps in the scientific method:** Question, Research, Hypothesis, Experiment, Analysis, Conclusion.

- **Four steps for treating a sprain:** Rest, Ice, Compression, Elevation.

went *ovary* his *anther*." This same teacher, who we coined Mr. Mnemonic, also gave us this story chain to help us learn about the circulatory system: "*Gene Cell* drove his little *red corpuscle* down *pulmonary vein* wondering if he *aorta* turn right to *Heart*land."

We can use narrative chaining to remember the Figure 5-5 forgetting terms:

> I *forgot* (forgetting) to mention that the *construction* of the sign behind a grove of trees made for a *distorted* (distortion) view. Thus, the sign had to be *reconstructed* (reconstruction) elsewhere. In *retro*spect (retroactive), allowing the trees to *interfere* (interference) with the sign's viewing was not a *pro*fessional (proactive) thing to do. Perhaps the old sign will *decay* among the trees.

And to remember the five evolutionary eras in Figure 5-8, we might spin this crazy story: To the stadium, *pre*dawn, he *came* with *Brie* (Precambrian) cheese in a *pail* (Paleozoic) to his seat in the *mezz*anine (Mesozoic). He did not spend a *cent* (Cenozoic) and screamed loudly to *psych* (Psychozoic) out the opposing team.

Pegword

The pegword method is especially useful for learning lists. To remember up to 10 items in a list (you can go much further, of course), first establish 10 visual pegs in memory, each associated with a number 1–10. These pegs are used to hang the list information you must learn, just as wall pegs are used to hang a hat, jacket, or book bag. These same pegs can be used over and over. My own peg for number one is a bun because it rhymes with one. Continuing the rhyming theme: two is a shoe, three is a tree, and four is a door. Five is golden rings, reflective of the number five in the carol "The Twelve Days of Christmas." Six is a six-pack. Seven is New York Yankee great Mickey Mantle, who wore number seven. Eight is a gate because eight and gate rhyme. Nine is a cat because a cat has nine lives. Ten is a tent because tent sounds like ten. When given a new list of items to learn, associate each with a peg, in turn, by creating a visual image.

Let's see how this might work for remembering the first 10 U.S. presidents:

1. Washington—Imagine washing a *bun*.

2. Adams—Imagine a *shoe* kicking you in the Adam's apple.

3. Jefferson—Imagine someone giving Jif peanut butter to his son sitting by a *tree*.

4. Madison—Imagine someone mad at his son because he won't open a *door*.

5. Monroe—Imagine a man rowing with a *gold ring* on each finger.

6. Quincy Adams—Quint means five, so imagine Adam Levine (from Maroon Five) carrying a *six-pack*.

7. Jackson—Imagine Reggie Jackson, another former Yankee slugger, swinging bats with *Mickey Mantle*.

8. Van Buren—Imagine a van burning outside a *gate*.

9. Harrison—Imagine a *cat* being warmed by a hairy sun.

10. Tyler—Imagine tying the flaps of a *tent*.

I find the visual associations I make to be rock solid when I am quizzed about the list. If someone asks me who the fifth president was, I find my golden rings, see them on a man's rowing hand, and remember Monroe. If someone asks me when the Harrison presidency occurred, I see the image of a hairy sun warming a cat, and report that Harrison was the ninth president. Although the pegword method might seem difficult, it is not. I've demonstrated it flawlessly many times, both in class and to liven up an occasional dying party. And I've taught it successfully to many, many students like you.

> **Activity 5.7**
>
> Create 10 pegs and use those pegs to remember the following list of school supplies: (1) ruler, (2) laptop, (3) backpack, (4) calculator, (5) stapler, (6) paper, (7) tape, (8) planner, (9) pen, (10) scissor.

Keyword

The keyword method is a most effective technique for learning new vocabulary, foreign words, science terms, states and capitals, and, really, any paired information, such as an artist and her work. Let's see.

Suppose you must learn the new vocabulary word "blain," which means an inflamed sore. Here's what to do:

1. Create a keyword that sounds like the target word blain—perhaps lane.

2. Create an image linking the keyword (lane) to the target word's meaning (inflamed sore). For example, imagine a fiery sore on a bowling alley lane.

That image—in your mind, or drawn on paper—helps you remember that blain means inflamed sore. Figure 5-16 shows a helpful illustration for that word pair and the set up for using the keyword method in general. I suggest that you set up all keyword learning in this helpful way.

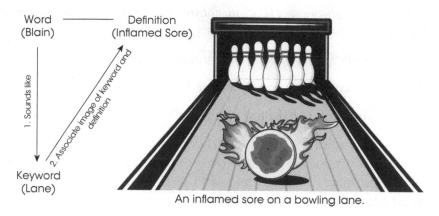

An inflamed sore on a bowling lane.

Figure 5-16 Keyword Method

Remember Freud's defense mechanisms in Figure 5-14? Here is how you might use the keyword method to remember that displacement means expressing feelings to a substitute target.

1. Create a keyword that sounds like displacement—placemat.

2. Create an image linking the keyword (placemat) to the target word's meaning (expressing feelings to a substitute target). For example, imagine a placemat yelling at a substitute player on the bench.

Or suppose you must learn that the German word Tannenbaum means fir tree. Here's what to do:

1. Create a keyword that sounds like the target word Tannenbaum—perhaps tied and bound.

2. Create an image linking the keyword (tied and bound) to the target word's meaning (fir tree). For example, imagine a fir tree tied and bound to a car's rooftop, as shown in Figure 5-17.

Figure 5-17 A Keyword Image Showing That Tannenbaum (Keyword: Tied and Bound) Means Fir Tree

Let's now use the keyword method to learn about the location of two different bones:

- Patella is the knee bone.

- Carpals are wrist bones.

Patella sounds like pat (keyword). Imagine patting someone's knee. Carpals sounds like car pals (keyword). Imagine pals in a car, handcuffed at the wrists.

Let's try a couple of states and capitals. Here, we'll create a keyword for both the state and capital and then create an image linking the two keywords.

- Topeka, Kansas: Topeka sounds like toe peeking. Kansas sounds like can. Imagine a toe peeking out of a can (see Figure 5-18).

Figure 5-18 Keyword Image for Remembering That Topeka (Keyword: Toe Peeking) Is the Capital of Kansas (Keyword: Can)

- Augusta, Maine: Augusta sounds like a gust. Maine sounds like mane. Imagine a gust of wind blowing a horse's mane.

Now, some artists and their works. Literary artist Willa Cather wrote *My Ántonia*. Willa Cather sounds like willow cashier. *Ántonia* sounds like ant on knee. Imagine a cashier in a willow tree with an ant on her knee. Artist Rosa Bonheur painted *Sheep by the Sea*. Rosa Bonheur sounds like rose and barn. *Sheep by the Sea* sounds like, well, sheep by the sea. (No reason to make this harder than need be.) Imagine a rose painted on a barn, surrounded by sheep near the sea.

Activity 5.8

Learn the following word pairs using the keyword method:

- Fennel—a carrot-like garden plant
- Jejune—dull
- Spondulicks—money
- Dover—Delaware
- Hemingway—*The Sun Also Rises*

Figure 5-19 Mnemonomy for Greek Goddess Aphrodite

The keyword method might seem pretty crazy or silly, but it works for remembering any word pairs.

Mnemonomy

A mnemonomy is an image or picture that helps learners associate and remember several related facts. For example, suppose you were learning about Greek gods and goddesses and needed to learn that (1) Aphrodite is the (2) daughter of Zeus and the goddess of (3) love and (4) beauty. To learn these four facts, create an interactive image, like that in Figure 5-19, containing all four facts: Aphrodite, who has an afro (to remember her name is Aphrodite), holds hands with a larger man (her father) who also holds a lightning bolt (the symbol for Zeus). She looks into a mirror (to behold her beauty) while hearts (for love) float about.

Let's try the Greek god (1) Apollo who is the (2) son of Zeus and god of the (3) sun, (4) archery, and (5) music. Perhaps imagine an Apollo space craft (to remember the god Apollo), being shot from a bow (to remember he is the god of archery) toward the sun (to remember he is the god of the sun). From the spacecraft come musical notes (to remember he is the god of music). A large figure looms over all of this, holding a lightning bolt (to remember he is the son of Zeus).

Suppose you needed to learn about painters and their works. For example, (1) Van Gogh painted (2) *The Starry Night*. The painting is (3) dreamlike and shows a (4) village and church beneath the stars. Van Gogh is also famous for (5) cutting off his ear. Imagine this: We see a van going (Van Gogh) to the stars at night (*The Starry Night*) as part of a man's dream (dreamlike). The man's bloody ear lies beside him. Beneath the stars we see a few simple houses (village) and a church steeple. Figure 5-20 shows this mnemonomy.

Figure 5-20 A Mnemonomy for Remembering Information About Van Gogh's Painting: *The Starry Night*

Next, check out the Figure 5-21 mnemonomy. This and similar mnemonomies proved highly successful at helping students learn biological classifications.

To remember that the subdivision <u>angiosperms</u> includes the class <u>dicotyledons</u>, which in turn includes the three orders <u>rubiales</u>, <u>sapindales</u>, and <u>rosales</u>, study the picture of the <u>angel</u> with the pet <u>dinosaur</u> that is walking up the <u>Rubik's cubes</u> so that he can lick the sweet <u>sap</u> that drips down from the <u>rose</u> tree,

Figure 5-21 Biological Classification Mnemonomy

Finally, Table 5-8 is a matrix comparing the five types of mnemonics.

Table 5-8 A COMPARISON OF MNEMONIC TECHNIQUES

	First-Letter	Narrative Chaining	Pegword	Keyword	Mnemonomy
Used for Learning	Lists	Lists	Lists	Vocabulary	Related facts
Method:	Use first letters to create word or phrase	Join (chain) ideas into story (narrative)	Visually associate new information with established number pegs	1. Create keyword that sounds like target word 2. Create image associating keyword to target word's meaning	Create interactive image relating several facts
Example	HOMES for remembering Great Lakes.	*"Stamen, stigma style* or I'll shoot you with my *pistil"* for remembering reproductive plant parts.	1=bun (peg). To learn the list's first item, Washington, imagine washing a bun.	1. Blain (target word) sounds like lane (keyword). 2. Imagine an inflamed sore (target word's meaning) on a bowling lane.	Aphrodite, who has an afro to remember her name is Aphrodite, holds hands with a larger man (her father) who also holds a lightning bolt (the symbol for Zeus). She looks into a mirror (to behold her beauty) while hearts (for love) float about.

Activity 5.9

Create a mnemonomy for the following information about Edgar Allan Poe (don't forget to include an image to remember his name):

- American writer
- Originator of detective fiction
- Wrote "The Raven"
- Wrote "The Tell-Tale Heart"

Answers to Focus Questions

1. Most memory experts are just average Joes using good memory techniques based on association. Memory researcher Anders Ericsson helped train two typical college students to eclipse 80 digits on the digit span task (Ericsson, 2007; Ericsson & Pool, 2016), and author Josh Foer (2011) trained his own memory well enough in one year to become a national memory champion. In these and other cases, the key to a strong memory is association—linking target information to other target information and to prior knowledge.

2. Internal associations are connections made among to-be-learned information; external associations are connections made between to-be-learned information and prior knowledge. When you are learning about moths and butterflies, recognizing that both proceed through four stages of development is an internal association. Surmising that a butterfly's colorful wings are likely that way to attract a mate is an example of an external association.

3. With hierarchical information, the question of what's above, below, and alongside is appropriate. With sequential information, the question of what's before and after is appropriate. With comparative information, the question of what categories cut across these topics is appropriate. The big internal association question is: What internal associations are within and across topics?

4. In a situation where multiple baseball teams are compared with respect to winning percentage (WP), batting average (BA), and earned run average (ERA), the following relationships might emerge. Within topic: The Yankees have a high team BA and low ERA. Across topic: The Dodgers have the best WP among the teams. Global: The lower a team's ERA, the higher their WP.

5. A chess master can remember a chess position better than a chess novice can because the master draws upon her prior chess knowledge to understand and remember the position. With just a glance, the master sees familiar chess patterns (e.g., a safely castled king or tension in the board's center) that a novice cannot see. The master is making and remembering meaningful external associations.

6. Examples aid understanding and memory of new terms and definitions. They also help you identify new examples when needed. For instance, when you are learning about capitalism, socialism, and communism, having examples of these terms helps you understand, remember, and later identify new examples of these terms.

7. First-letter, narrative chaining, and pegword are effective list-learning mnemonics.

8. Keyword is an effective mnemonic technique for learning word pairs such as a science term and its definition, a foreign language term and its meaning, a state and its capital, and an artist and his painting.

9. Creating a mnemonomy is helpful for learning a set of associated facts, such as various facts about a Greek god.

Figure Credits

Fig. 5.1a: Copyright © 2020 Depositphotos/Aleksei-veprev.

Fig. 5.1b: Copyright © 2011 Depositphotos/popcic.

Fig. 5.4a: Adapted from Copyright © 2015 Depositphotos/hobbit_art.

Fig. 5.9: Adapted from Kenneth A. Kiewra, *Teaching How to Learn: The Teacher's Guide to Student Success*, p. 78. Copyright © 2009 by Corwin Press.

Fig. 5.10a: Copyright © 2013 Depositphotos/graphixmania.

Fig. 5.12a: Copyright © 2017 Depositphotos/Marinka.

Fig. 5.12b: Copyright © 2010 Depositphotos/abrakadabra.

Fig. 5.12c: Copyright © 2017 Depositphotos/viktorijareut.

Fig. 5.17: Copyright © 2017 Depositphotos/KatBuslaeva.

Fig. 5.18a: Copyright © 2012 Depositphotos/KK-Inc.

Fig. 5.18b: Copyright © 2014 Depositphotos/Mr.Pack.

Fig. 5.20a: Copyright © 2017 Depositphotos/Tohey22.

Fig. 5.20b: Copyright © 2019 Depositphotos/satoof.mail.ru.

Fig. 5.20c: Copyright © 2018 Depositphotos/magicleaf.

Fig. 5.20d: Copyright © 2012 Depositphotos/agnieszka.

Fig. 5.20e: Copyright © 2018 Depositphotos/fandijki.

Fig. 5.21: Adapted from Mary E. Levin and Joel R. Levin, "Scientific Mnemonomies: Methods for Maximizing More than Memory," *American Educational Research Journal*, vol. 27, no. 2, pp. 301-321. Copyright © 1990 by American Educational Research Association.

Fig. 5.21a: Copyright © 2020 Depositphotos/Imaagio.

Fig. 5.21b: Copyright © 2012 Depositphotos/dvargg.

Fig. 5.21c: Copyright © 2015 Depositphotos/totallyjamie.

Fig. 5.21d: Copyright © 2015 Depositphotos/frostyara.

Fig. 5.21e: Copyright © 2014 Depositphotos/interactimages.

Fig. 5.21f: Copyright © 2016 Depositphotos/bioraven.

Fig. 5.21g: Copyright © 2014 Depositphotos/natis76.

CHAPTER 6

Regulation Strategies Let You Know What You Know

OVERVIEW

Objectives

1. Know how to regulate learning and understanding.

2. Recognize fact, concept, and skill test items.

3. Construct fact, concept, and skill test items.

4. Conduct error analysis.

Focus Questions

1. Match each regulation statement below to one of the SOAR learning components (select, organize, associate, regulate).

   a. Creating a mnemonic will help me learn this.

   b. My notes need more examples.

   c. A matrix seems useful here.

   d. I need to test myself to see if I can pick out instances of mutualism.

2. What evidence was presented to illustrate that self-testing works?

3. What are some ways you can obtain test information before the test?

4. Why is knowing that a test contains multiple choice items not so helpful?

5. What are the two types of fact items?

6. Why should concept items not ask test-takers to supply examples?

7. What are the two types of skill items?

8. Identify each question below on score dispersion as fact, concept, or skill.

   a. What is the formula for calculating variance?

   b. What is the standard deviation in this set of biology quiz scores: 7, 3, 7, 1, 3, 9, 6?

   c. To understand the dispersion of the biology quiz scores above, Mr. Campton did this: 9-1=8. What measure of dispersion did he derive?

9. Write a fact, concept, and skill question for the following information about contractions: A contraction is a word that shortens and combines two words. A contraction is formed when part of the second word is deleted and replaced with an apostrophe. For example: I am, I'm; we are, we're; they will, they'll.

10. List five test-taking strategies.

11. What are the three things learned through error analysis?

12. Create a hierarchy showing the three types of test questions and their subtypes.

13. Practice chapter regulation now by summarizing the main ideas learned in this chapter.

Read the passage below, and then rate it on a 1–10 scale for its comprehensibility, with 1 signifying low comprehensibility and 10 signifying high comprehensibility.

> *The man was worried. His car came to a halt and he was all alone. It was extremely dark and cold. The man took off his overcoat, rolled down the window, and got out of the car as quickly as possible. Then he used all of his strength to move as fast as he could. He was relieved when he finally saw the lights of the city, even though they were far away.* (Bransford, 1979, p. 196)

How did you rate it? Most students rate it as being fairly comprehensible, perhaps between 5–10. After all, there were no words too difficult to understand. Now, let me ask you a few questions about the passage:

1. Why was the man worried?

2. Why did he remove his overcoat if it was cold?

3. Why did he roll down the window if it was cold?

4. Why did he get out as quickly as possible?

5. Why was he relieved to see the city lights?

You probably could not answer these questions unless you knew this passage was about a submerged car in an icy lake, which you likely did not. Yet you likely rated the passage as comprehensible anyway, even though you did not really understand it. It was only when I raised these questions that you understood that you did not understand, knew that you did not know. It took my questions to reveal that the passage was largely incomprehensible and that your understanding was poor.

The message here is that you cannot assume that learning and understanding have occurred just because you read a passage or attended a lecture. And you cannot wait for someone else to assess your knowledge and reveal its gaps. Effective students don't wait for teachers to test them and assess their understanding. They test themselves so thoroughly beforehand that there is nothing the teacher can ask them that they haven't already asked themselves. Effective students regulate their own learning and know whether or not they know. And, if they find they don't know something, they do whatever's necessary to plug those gaps.

This chapter is about regulating learning. Regulation involves self-monitoring, or self-checking one's learning, regarding both the learning process (Am I listening carefully? Am I taking good notes?) and the learning outcome (Do I understand photosynthesis? Am I ready for the test?), often through the use of self-questioning. As youngsters, you depended on teachers to do this for you. Teachers prompted you to monitor learning when they asked questions like: Are you paying attention? Did you get that idea down in your notes? Did you read your text carefully? Did you study hard enough for the test? But more experienced and effective students don't depend on teachers to regulate their learning; they regulate their own learning from start to finish. This chapter shows you how.

Regulation in the Real World

Before you read about regulating your learning in college, it is important for you to understand that regulation is more than an academic skill; it transcends all domains and is a vital life skill. Regarding other domains, think about chess players, musicians, and golfers. All must regulate. The chess player regulates during a game: Why did she play that move? Is my king safe? Should I sacrifice that pawn, and what will she play if I do? A musician regulates when practicing: Should I hold that dotted quarter note longer? Am I rushing this passage? What mood is the composer trying to convey here, and how can I capture it? A golfer regulates when playing: Can I get there with a seven iron? Is hitting a flop shot here too risky? My tee shots are fading—is the problem in my grip or follow-through? Regarding life skills, regulation can keep you socially acceptable, employed, and safe. You need to regulate social encounters: Am I truly listening to what he is saying? How can I respond empathetically without validating his actions? You need to regulate job issues: Why might my supervisor want to meet with me today? What arguments might I make if I need to defend my handling of the Salzburg account? You need to regulate your and others' safety: Given the snowy forecast, should I postpone this road trip? Is it okay to ride my bike just a few miles without a helmet? Can the window blinds cord be a danger to my baby? Could that dresser be toppled by my toddler? Am I okay to drive? Should I call an Uber?

Successful people are regular regulators and are rarely surprised by what life throws at them. That's because they anticipate what might happen and are ready for what comes.

Activity 6.1

Suppose you were considering renting an apartment and were meeting the apartment manager later that day to see the apartment. List several regulation questions you might generate in advance of the meeting that might be answered by the manager or by your own observations.

Regulate Learning

In college, it's not enough to use learning strategies; you need to regulate their use by asking questions like: Am I using learning strategies? Am I using them effectively? But you can do far better than using only that general sort of regulation. Now that you know about SOAR strategies (and will soon know about motivation, mindset, and management strategies), you can ask more specific and effective regulation questions to guide learning. Here's how you might regulate SOAR strategies, including regulation strategies, which we have yet to address in depth.

Select:

- Am I recording main ideas, details, essential qualifiers, and examples in my notes?
- Am I on the lookout for note-taking cues, both importance and organizational cues?
- Am I "on the edge" as I listen to the lecture?

- Am I sitting in a good seat to avoid distractions?
- Am I using my laptop for class purposes only? Is it distracting me?
- Am I listening for and noting lecture topics and categories?
- Can I revise my notes and make them more complete?

Organize:

- Am I approaching this lesson with an organizational mindset?
- What type of organizer would best capture this information?
- What information is superordinate and subordinate to what I'm learning now?
- Should I add additional levels to my organizer?
- Is that an alert word, and what type of organizer does it imply using?
- Can I extend this organizer into a matrix?
- What categories cut across these topics?
- What labels and captions can I add to my illustration?
- Are multiple organizers needed?

Associate:

- What's above, below, and alongside this concept?
- What's before and after this concept?
- What categories cut across this topic?
- What internal associations can I make?
- How are these things alike and different?
- What do I know about this?
- What examples can I provide?
- What mnemonic technique works best here?
- Is my mnemonic strategy simple and memorable, and how might I improve it?

Regulate:

- What will the test be like?
- Will the test include fact, concept, and skill items?

- Do the fact, concept, and skill questions I've created follow item-writing guidelines?

- What type of errors am I making?

- What is the source of my errors?

- Am I ready to ace this test? If not, what more must I do?

As you learn, you must regulate learning to be sure you're learning maximally.

Regulate Understanding

Let's assume that you've selected and noted important lesson ideas, organized those ideas, and created internal and external associations; does that mean you're ready for a test? Not likely. You should do more. And doing more does not mean simply rereading your notes and rehearsing information over and over. Remember, from Chapter 2: *Re*dundant strategies are *Re*diculous! Instead, you should regulate understanding. You should test yourself in order to know if you know—before the instructor does.

In recent years, educational psychologists have uncovered the power of what's called the testing effect. They found that studying for a test should not be a passive process of simply rereading or reviewing one's notes or text. Instead, it is far better to self-test. Self-testing not only reveals what you know and do not know but also boosts and solidifies learning. It helps you encode information into long-term memory and later retrieve it from long-term memory, such as when you are tested by instructors. In one classic study (Roediger & Karpicke, 2006), students directed to learn from a text were assigned to a repeated-study condition (where they read the text multiple times) or a repeated-testing condition (where they self-tested multiple times). Those in the repeated testing group scored more than 20% higher, even though they read the text 11 fewer times than the repeated studiers. Self-testing works.

Perhaps Your Instructor Can Help ... or Not

So how should you self-test? If you were playing in a golf tournament next week, you'd want to know as much about the golf course as possible, including yardage, hazards, green conditions, and much more. Ideally, you'd like to play the course a few times before the tournament. Same with testing. You'd like to know as much as possible about the test and especially take some practice tests beforehand. One problem with anticipating testing, though, is that instructors often shroud the criteria in secrecy. They don't tell students much about the test, other than some rudimentary information such as, "It's multiple-choice." Why is that? In some cases, it's because instructors really don't know what the test is like, because they write the test just before springing it on students. Some instructors procrastinate too.

Or perhaps it's because they carry on the senseless tradition that befell them as students: "Nobody told me what was on the test, so I'm not telling my students."

Some instructors, fortunately, share vital test information with students. Perhaps they provide students with helpful test preparation aids, such as objectives that stress what should be learned, study guides that direct student learning, and even practice tests similar to the real thing. When such materials are made available, take full advantage of them. I'm shocked to see some students being unaware that these critical study aids are available, or being aware of them and ignoring them nonetheless. When instructors provide a testing roadmap, follow it!

What if instructors don't provide test preparation aids—what to do then? Be resourceful. Here are some possibilities. Contact students who took the course previously and ask what tests were like, or ask to see those tests if they were permitted to keep them. Look for practice tests in textbooks and online that pertain to course material. Form study groups, and as part of those groups, generate test questions and share them with group members. Ask! Ask your instructors to tell you about tests and to provide study aids, including practice questions. They can only say no. You can also ask specific questions, such as, "What must we know about theories of forgetting?" or "Are we going to need to calculate standard deviation?"

In the absence of test information, or even with it, you should prepare your own practice-test items to regulate your understanding of course material in order to know if you are test ready. To do so effectively, though, you must understand what types of test items there are and how to best construct them. The next section prepares you to do just that.

Preparing Practice-Test Items

Suppose you ask your instructor for test information and she says, "It's all multiple choice." Is that information really helpful? Take a look at the three multiple-choice questions below, pertaining to central tendency in statistics.

1. What score divides a set a of scores?

   a. Mean

   b. Median

   c. Mode

2. Looking at the test scores, Ms. Mallard said, "Looks like most of you scored 90%." What measure of central tendency did Ms. Mallard convey?

   a. Mean

   b. Median

   c. Mode

3. In five games, the team scored 2, 7, 9, 0, and 2 runs. What is the team's runs-scored mean?

   a. 2

   b. 3

   c. 4

   d. 5

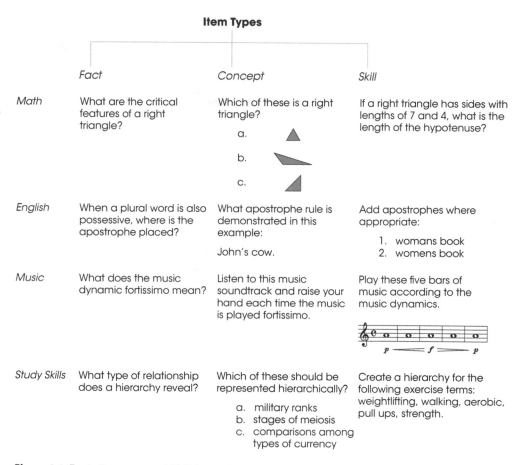

Figure 6-1 Fact, Concept, and Skill Items Across Subject Areas

Although all three items are indeed multiple choice, they are as different as boil and broil. Item 1 tests whether you *know* the definition of median. This item measures fact knowledge. Item 2 tests whether you can *recognize* a new example of the mode concept. This item measures concept knowledge. Item 3 tests whether you can *calculate* the mean, given a new set of numbers. This item measures skill knowledge. To give you a broader sense of these three item types, examine Figure 6-1, which shows item-type examples in various domains.

Rather than know a test's item forms, such as multiple choice, matching, or true-false, it's more helpful to know a test's item types: fact, concept, or skill. That way, you can regulate accordingly. For fact questions, you can practice recalling facts, such as the definition of "fortissimo." For concept questions, you can practice recognizing new examples, such as those for right triangles. And, for skill questions, you can practice solving new problems, such as adding apostrophes to words that are possessive singular or possessive plural. To regulate your readiness for different item types, you must be able to generate these different item types effectively when you study. Let's examine how to regulate for each item type in turn.

Activity 6.2

Classify each of the following test items as fact, concept, or skill.

1. Use the keyword method to learn that Salem is the capital of Oregon.

2. Describe the steps followed in using the keyword method.

3. To learn that "egalitarian" means all people deserve equal rights, the student created an image of an eagle flying over two people with an equal sign between them. What mnemonic strategy did the student use?

Regulate Fact Learning

Most test questions are fact questions that test your memory for previously presented information. Fact items are likely found on tests in all courses, from art (What are the characteristics of Cubism?) to zoology (Describe the process of natural selection). Fact items are most prevalent in information-based courses such as history, psychology, sociology, and philosophy. They are less prevalent in skill-based courses like math, chemistry, and statistics.

There are two main types of fact questions: single fact and relational fact. As the names imply, single-fact questions require you to know a single fact, such as *the Earth takes one year to revolve around the sun*, whereas relational fact questions require you to know the relationship among multiple facts, such as *all inner planets have rocky surfaces*.

If you already did a good job selecting, organizing, and associating information (the SOA in SOAR), then it's easy to create fact questions. Let's return to the apes graphic organizer introduced in Chapter 1 and now shown in Table 6-1. You can easily create single-fact questions by testing knowledge of a single fact, such as these:

- What do gibbons weigh?

- Where do gorillas live?

- How fast can orangutans move through trees?
- Which ape is called silverback?
- What do gorillas eat?

Table 6-1 GRAPHIC ORGANIZER FOR APES

	Gorillas	Orangutan	Gibbons
Weight (lbs.)	300	200	20
Height (ft.)	6	5	2
Tree speed (mph)	10	15	35
Diet	Herbivores	Omnivores	Omnivores
Defense	Gather in groups	Loud noises in groups	Brachiate away
Habitat	Ground	Ground	Trees
Unique facts	Least aggressive ape Males called silverbacks	Name means "man of the forest" Group cares for young	Cannot swim Dexterous movement in trees

Source: Tareq A. Daher and Kenneth A.Kiewra, "An Investigation of SOAR Study Strategies for Learning from Multiple Online Resources," *Contemporary Educational Psychology*, vol. 46, p. 12. Copyright © 2016 by Elsevier B.V. Reprinted with permission.

You can easily create relational-fact questions by asking for relationships between two or more facts, such as these:

- Which ape is the heaviest?
- What is the relationship between apes' weight and tree speed?
- What is the relationship between apes' height and tree speed?
- Which apes live on the ground?
- Which apes group together as a defense?

Note that you could create and answer single-fact questions by tapping what was in single-matrix cells and that you could create and answer relational-fact questions by tapping what was in multiple-matrix cells. That's another reason why graphic organizers are powerful learning tools: they can be used to generate questions. Also take note that answers to relational-fact questions should have been established earlier in the SOAR learning process, when internal associations were made.

Activity 6.3

Using this planets graphic organizer, create three single-fact questions and three relational-fact questions.

Planets

	Mercury	Venus	Earth	Mars	Jupiter	Saturn	Uranus	Neptune
	Inner				*Outer*			
Miles from the Sun	36 million	67 million	93 million	142 million	483 million	886 million	2 billion	3 billion
Revolution Time Around the Sun	3 months	8 months	1 year	2 years	12 years	30 years	84 years	165 years
Orbit Speed (Miles/Second)	30	22	19	15	8	6	4	3

Regulate Concept Learning

Concepts are things defined by their critical features and recognized in their wide range of examples. The concept of "bird" is defined by its critical features, which include beaks, wings, and feathers. There is a wide range of bird examples. There are big birds like condors and cranes and tiny ones like sparrows and hummingbirds. There are birds that fly, like robins and crows, and those that don't, like chickens and emus. Birds are found in a variety of colors: the red cardinal, the white dove, the black raven, and the multi-colored macaw. The concept of "triangle" is defined by its critical features, which include three connected sides and three angles. A wide range of examples reveals that triangles can be big or small, be thick or thin, come in all sorts of colors, include a variety of angle sizes, and be scalene, equilateral, right, or isosceles.

The world is filled with concepts that you've learned to recognize, such as shoe, sneaker, car, truck, sweater, hoodie, computer, tablet, hot, cold, area, perimeter, socialism, capitalism, and tens of thousands more. Of course, there are likely many concepts you've not yet learned, such as grivet (an African green monkey), grommet (a ring-shaped device to reinforce holes), and gravitas (a serious or solemn manner). Don't worry, you're learning new concepts all the time.

Let's look inside some school subjects. Here are a few chemistry concepts: anode, catalyst, density, enthalpy, molality, and reactant, to name a few. Psychology is ripe with concepts such as accommodation, agoraphobia, bipolar, classical conditioning, denial, and double blind. In art, sample concepts include impressionism, minimalism, abstraction, canvas, ceramic, and collage. Here are a few literature concepts: sonnet, haiku, alliteration, rising action, epilogue, fantasy, and metaphor. This book hopefully introduced you to several new concepts, such as memory palace, mindset, and SOAR.

There's really only one way to test concept learning, and that involves recognizing new, previously unencountered examples. Figure 6-2 contains well-constructed concept items from various domains. In each case, the learner must recognize a new example, often amid related nonexamples. This is often how things play out in the real world. A baseball announcer must report what kind of pitch was thrown, amid a variety of pitches such as fastball, slider, curve, and change. A botanist in the woods must recognize various plant species from one another. And a heating technician must identify furnace parts such as igniter, flame sensor, and air pressure switch when inspecting a furnace.

Concept Items Across Domains

Geometry   Which of these is a cone?

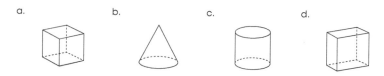

a.   b.   c.   d.

Psychology   Which is an example of satiation?

    a.   Matthew likes to light matches. His mother has Matthew light hundreds of matches until his fingers are tired and sore. Now Matthew never lights matches.
    b.   Ciera likes blowing bubbles in her soda to get her friend's attention. Her friend began to step away whenever Ciera did this and now Ciera no longer blows bubbles in her soda.
    c.   Stanley likes to cut the line. His teacher saw this and had him write "No cutting" on the board 100 times. Now Stanley does not cut the line.

English   When asked to wipe the counters, Randy replied, "This rancid rag reeks relentlessly."
Randy was using:

    a.   Onomatopoeia
    b.   Oxymoron
    c.   Metaphor
    d.   Alliteration

Biology   When bees sip nectar from a flower, they are fed. When they do, some of the flower's pollen attaches to the bees who then bring it to another flower, which results in flower pollination.

What kind of symbiotic relationship is this?

    a.   Commensalism
    b.   Mutualism
    c.   Parasitism

Study Skills   Tell what type of graphic organizer is best for each.

    1.   Adolescence follows childhood.
    2.   Expressive and adaptive creativity have several differences.
    3.   There are three main types of nerve cells.
    4.   The frontal and parietal lobes rest above the temporal lobe.

Figure 6-2 Examples of Concept Items

Concept items are somewhat difficult to create, and even seasoned test writers sometimes make mistakes that you'll want to avoid when regulating concept learning. Here are four concept item writing guidelines:

1. ***Do not test facts.*** You might think you're writing a concept question, but make sure you're not really testing facts.

   The following are fact questions testing reinforcement schedules:

   - What response pattern occurs in a variable interval schedule? (single fact)

   - Which two schedules are difficult to extinguish? (relational fact)

   Here is a concept question testing reinforcement schedules:
   - A car salesman earns a commission after every five sales. What schedule is this?

   Also, be careful that you don't develop fact questions disguised as concept questions. This occurs when the "example" to be recognized is actually nothing more than a restatement of the concept's definition or critical features. For instance:

   - A slot machine pays off after a varying number of pulls. What schedule of reinforcement is this?

   By including the words *varying* and *number*, we are restating the critical features of fixed ratio schedules. There is no true example to recognize. Someone need only know the critical features of fixed ratio schedules to answer this fact item. Here is a good concept question testing that same material:

   - A slot machine can pay off after just a few lever pulls or after dozens of lever pulls. No one knows when the next payoff is forthcoming. It dispenses reinforcement on a _____ schedule.

2. ***Do not ask for examples.*** Plain and simple, concept items require test-takers to recognize new examples, and providing examples is different than recognizing them. Here's why. Suppose, during instruction on literary elements, students are given this example of alliteration: "Sally sells seashells by the seashore." When later tested for concept learning, students are asked for an example of alliteration, and they repeat the instructional example: Sally sells seashells by the seashore. Would this be evidence of concept learning? Not at all. Students would simply be supplying a previously learned example. There would be no evidence that they could

recognize new examples. To assess concept learning, an item must require recognition of a new example, like this:

Which of the following is an example of alliteration?

a. The wind felt like a blowtorch.

b. The car putted up the hill.

c. The book's ending was bittersweet.

d. Condor came and Condor conquered.

3. ***Do not include previous or similar examples.*** Concept items must include new, previously unencountered examples. So don't include previously presented examples or examples similar to those previously presented. Suppose you were learning about schedules of reinforcement in your psychology class and the instructor presented this example for fixed ratio schedules: A factory worker is paid $10 for every five widgets assembled. It would be wrong to include this example on a practice test or actual test because it does not require recognition of a new example. Similarly, though, it would be wrong to include examples that are highly alike in their composition, such as:

- A factory worker is paid $10 for every five flanges made.

- A factory worker is paid $20 for every 10 couplets made.

These items are too similar to the original and do not guarantee that the test-taker can recognize a new example. A better item steers clear of previously presented examples, like this:

- Pitcher Roberto Pensato has a stipulation in his contract that he earns an additional $20,000 each time he amasses another eight saves.

- The car salesman is paid on commission: $5,000 for every 20 cars sold.

4. ***Test concepts amid related concepts.*** A concept is rarely learned or tested in isolation. When learning about the concept of alliteration, you are likely learning about related literary elements such as oxymoron, metaphor, and onomatope. When learning about the concept of commensalism, you are likely learning about related symbiotic concepts such as mutualism and parasitism. When learning about the concept of fixed ratio schedule, you are likely learning about related reinforcement schedules such as variable ratio, fixed interval, and variable interval. This idea of related concepts occurs everywhere. Types of clouds: cumulus, stratus, and cirrus. Types of brass instruments: tuba, trombone, French horn, and trumpet. Types of

research designs: case-study, causal, and descriptive. And types of graphic organizers: hierarchy, sequence, matrix, and illustration.

So, when you test concept knowledge, create items that require recognizing new examples against a backdrop of related and potentially confusing concepts. This is not only the strongest test for concept knowledge but also the most realistic. In the real world, you must distinguish robins from meadowlarks, Fords from Chevys, vegetable oil from olive oil, Macs from PCs, Phillips screwdrivers from flat-head screwdrivers, snow from sleet, friend from foe, and stop signs from yield signs. Here is a concept item requiring the recognition of three closely related operant concepts.

For each example below, determine if it represents positive punishment, negative punishment, or extinction:

- *When the offensive lineman held the defensive lineman, the offense was penalized 10 yards. This stopped the offensive lineman from holding again during that game. (Negative punishment.)*

- *When the puppy pulled on a walk, his owner pulled back on the leash, and the puppy stopped pulling. (Positive punishment.)*

- *Clarence's friend would use foul language to elicit an uncomfortable reaction from Clarence. Eventually, Clarence came to ignore the foul language, and it eventually stopped. (Extinction.)*

Activity 6.4

Here is a graphic organizer from Chapter 5, showing Freud's defense mechanisms. Create four concept questions pertaining to this material. Be sure your items follow concept-item writing rules.

Freud's Defense Mechanisms

	Regression	Displacement	Projection	Denial	Sublimation
Definition	Return to an earlier time when you were not so threatened.	Expressing feelings to a substitute target because you are unwilling or unable to express them to the real target.	Attributing to others your own negative thoughts or actions.	Blinding yourself to negative things you're too scared to deal with.	Diverting negative feelings into more socially acceptable activities.
Example (a parent with cancer)	Act in a child-like way when dealing with the situation.	Express remorse to a friend rather than the ill parent.	Believing that your sister is remorseful instead of you.	Believing that your parent is fine and will be okay.	Diverting anger by doing a lot of running.

Regulate Skill Learning

Skill learning abounds in college. In a research methods course, you might need to design a two-factor experiment, calculate standard deviation, and conduct a t-test to compare group performance. In an English course, you might need to punctuate sentences requiring quotation marks, replace passive verbs with active ones, and reduce prepositional phrase usage. In a physics course, you might need to calculate velocity, find the period of a pendulum, and determine the photon energy of a wavelength. In a learning strategies course, you might need to construct graphic organizers, create mnemonics, and regulate learning using fact, concept, and skill questions. All skills.

Most skills can be thought of as rules or procedures. Let's start with rules.

Rules

What is the solution to this problem: $13 - 4 \times 2 = ?$ Is the correct answer 18 or 5? The correct answer is 5, and we know that because there exists a rule for solving problems like this called order of operations. When multiple operations must be carried out, the rule states that they are carried out in a specified order: parentheses, exponents, multiplication, division, addition, and subtraction. In fact, you might have learned the first-letter mnemonic for remembering this rule: PEMDAS, or Please Excuse My Dear Aunt Sally. Following that rule, we first multiply ($4 \times 2 = 8$) and then subtract ($13 - 8 = 5$).

Rules are statements about how to generally do things, and they have widespread applicability. They govern behavior across settings. For instance, the order of operations rule just mentioned helps solve a variety of problems such as these:

- $44 - 3^2 \times 2 =$

- $6 \times (13-2) =$

- $4 - 4 + 4 \times 2 + 6 =$

You've acquired countless rules in your life that govern your behavior. Here is a small sample:

- If in doubt (about a food's freshness), throw it out.

- If you see a vehicle on the shoulder of a highway, move to the other lane and slow down.

- If someone is walking behind you as you approach a doorway, hold the door open for them.

- If your mouth is full, don't talk.

- If you're open near the basket, shoot.

- If you get an unwanted call, disconnect or block that caller.

- If you're playing chess, control the center of the board.

Although rules are statements about how to do things, it's imperative to test rule knowledge not by asking test-takers to state the rule but by asking them to apply the rule when they are given new material. Let's look at some grammar rules you might learn and how you might test them.

- Object of the preposition rule: Use whom, not who, as the object of a preposition.

Test item: Choose who or whom for each: (1) Carrie drove home with (who, whom). (2) (Who, Whom) was the winner? (3) For (who, whom) the curtain falls.

- Syllabication rule: When words have the letter configuration vowel-consonant-consonant-vowel, divide the word between the two consonants.

Test item: Divide each of following words into syllables: tennis, rather, commute, timber.

- Active voice rule: Write using the active voice instead of the passive voice.

Test item: Change the following sentences from the passive voice to the active voice: (1) At breakfast, four waffles were eaten by Marjorie. (2) The batteries in the smoke detector were changed by Callum. (3) The lunar eclipse was viewed by the class.

Of course, students might learn and be tested on several related rules, like those for forming plurals:

- Add s to form the plural of most words.

- Add es to words that end in a hissing sound.

- If the word ends in a consonant plus y, change the y to ie and add s.

- If the word ends in f or fe, change the ending to ves.

Activity 6.5

Here is a rule: When rounding numbers with decimals, round to the nearest tenth. Create four skill items to assess if this rule was learned.

Here is a test item to assess all those rules: *Change the following singular words to plural words: loaf, cemetery, wrench, carpet, pouch, army, knife, hat, mouth.*

Procedures

More complex skills, called procedures, involve the application of two or more steps. Figure 6-3 shows the procedure for dividing fractions. Figure 6-4 shows the procedure for conducting a one-sample t-test in statistics. Figure 6-5 shows the procedure for finalizing a tracked changes document. Notice that all procedures can be represented using a sequence organizer.

Of course, there are a wide variety of procedures to be learned in and out of school. Sample school-related procedures include: finding the hypotenuse of a triangle in geometry, adding mixed fractions in math, solving force problems in physics, balancing equations in chemistry, writing an essay in English, applying classical conditioning in psychology, and applying SOAR in any academic domain. Outside of school, you learn and apply procedures for driving a car, hitting a golf ball, making tuna noodle casserole, setting your DVR to record a series, and arranging a ride with a ride-sharing service.

Just as was true for rules, procedures are tested when test takers are asked to apply a procedure, not state it. Stating a procedure is fact learning; applying a procedure is skill learning. Here's a little mnemonic to help remember: Facts are for knowing; skills are for showing.

Don't ask: What is the procedure for adding mixed fractions?

Do ask: $6\frac{1}{4} + 9\frac{3}{4} = ?$

Don't ask: How do you calculate the mean of several scores?

Do ask: Calculate the mean of these scores: 2, 9, 4, 3, 3, 5.

Don't ask: How do you save a document without showing tracked changes?

Do ask: Save the document on your screen without showing tracked changes.

Finally, just as was true with concepts, skills—both rules and procedures—must be tested using new material. If the procedure for calculating the hypotenuse of a triangle with sides of 3 and 4 is shown in class, then that familiar problem should not be used for testing. Instead, create a calculate-the-hypotenuse problem with new numbers. Similarly, if shown how to apply forming-plural rules for the following singular words: bug, story, life, array, and bench, then those singular words should not be used for testing. Create new forming-plural problems using singular words not seen in instruction.

Activity 6.6

The formula for finding the hypotenuse of a triangle is $C^2 = A^2 + B^2$, where C = the hypotenuse and A and B = the other two sides. Generate three skill items to test that this procedure was learned.

Dividing Fractions

$$\frac{6}{11} \div \frac{3}{4}$$

Invert the divisor ➤ *Multiply dividend by inverted divisor* ➤ *Simplify if possible*

Example   Change $\frac{3}{4}$ to $\frac{4}{3}$ $\frac{6}{11} \times \frac{4}{3} = \frac{24}{33}$ $\frac{24}{33} = \frac{8}{11}$

Figure 6-3 Procedure for Dividing Fractions

Conducting a One Sample T-Test

Calculate the ➤ *Calculate standard* ➤ *Calculate the test* ➤ *Determine p-value*
sample mean   *deviation*   *statistic*

Calculation $\bar{y} = \frac{y_1 + y_2 + \ldots}{n}$ $sd = \sqrt{\frac{(y_1 - \bar{y})^2 + (y_2 - y)^2 \ldots}{n}}$ $t = \frac{\bar{y} - hv}{sd/\sqrt{n}}$ Find test statistic in probability table. Reject null hypothesis if p-value is < .05.

Index $y_{1, 2, \ldots}$ = the single observations sd = standard deviation t = test statistic

n = sample size hv = hypothesized value

Figure 6-4 Procedure for Conducting a One-Sample T-Test

Finalizing a Tracked Changes Document

Open Document ⟶ Click the Review tab ⟶ Click the dropdown arrow next to Accept ⟶ Select No Markup ⟶ Click the slider next to Tracked Changes ⟶ Click Accept All Changes

Figure 6.5 Procedure for Finalizing a Tracked Changes Document

Regulate Test-Taking

It's test day. You can tell. The classroom, usually half-empty, is filled with apparent strangers. Certainly you would have noticed those three offensive lineman sitting side by side, and the hiker gal with the Marmot top and Osprey backpack, had they been there before. And no one's on their phones. Instead, notebook pages are flipping like hotcakes. And what's that smell? Not hotcakes. More like a cornered animal. But you're not fearful as the instructor barks, "Fifty short answers, two essays, you've now got...42 minutes." You're prepared.

Test anxiety is for the unprepared. Most students who are anxious about tests should be anxious. They're not ready, and they know it. But because you attended all the classes, sat front and center on the edge of your seat, took copious notes, organized those notes, created associations, and generated and answered oodles of practice questions until you knew you knew, your regulation voice now confidently declares: "I'm ready. I'm prepared. Bring on the test! It's showtime."

Indeed. You are test ready. Still, here are some things you can regulate come test day to help you do your best.

1. **Eat properly.** When blood sugar drops, so does concentration. Eat a healthy snack or small meal about an hour before the test.

2. **Take a walk.** Before entering the classroom, take a brisk 10-minute walk to fire up your brain.

3. **Choose a good seat.** The best seat during lectures is front and center. Perhaps not so, come test day. In a testing room, every sound is amplified, every movement exaggerated. A sniffle sounds like a shop vac. A raised hand looks like a parade float. Choose a seat relatively free from distractions, perhaps along a side wall, away from flash points like doors and the instructor's desk. If possible, angle your seat toward the wall to further block distractions.

4. **Preview the test.** You wouldn't jump in a pool before checking depth and temperature. Don't jump into a test before checking the number of items and their point values. Then sketch out a quick time plan, allowing sufficient time for all parts.

5. **Read instructions carefully.** Don't assume you know what to do. Instructors have lots of latitude in how they construct tests. Directions might specify that multiple-choice questions can have more than one correct answer and all correct answers must be marked, that true-false items marked false must also be corrected, that alternatives in matching items might not be used at all or may be used more than once, or that only two of the three essay items need be answered.

6. **Answer easy items first.** Think of tests more as a buffet table than a seven-course meal. You need not start at the beginning of the test and work straight through. Go where you want, skip around—just be sure to answer all items eventually. I recommend starting with a section (perhaps multiple choice) or topic (perhaps photosynthesis) you're comfortable with and answering easy items first, to build confidence. Don't struggle too long with tough items during your first pass through the test. Come back to them later. Struggling with difficult items early on could dampen confidence, raise anxiety, and consume valuable time you could better spend accruing points answering easier items. Moreover, tests don't just request information; they provide information. As you work through the test, be on the lookout for information that helps you answer other items.

7. **Make notes on the test (if permitted).** That number two pencil can do more than mark answers—it can help you think, and reduce memory load. As you struggle with an item, for example, mark clearly incorrect choices with an X, unlikely choices with a dash, and likely choices with a check mark. Circle the item number, so you know to return to it later. Also, make test notes that help you interpret questions and formulate answers. Consider this item from a psychology test:

A student learns about the characteristics of short-term memory on Monday and about the characteristics of long-term memory on Wednesday. On Friday, he is tested on the topic of short-term memory. When tested, the student mistakenly lists several characteristics common to long-term memory. The student's error is best attributed to which type of interference?

In this case, first jot notes, like those you recorded in class and later studied, that represent the two types of interference: proactive and retroactive.

| Proactive: | Learn A | Learn B | Test B | A int with B |
| Retroactive: | Learn A | Learn B | Test A | B int with A |

Then jot notes germane to the test question.

Learn STM (A)   Learn LTM (B)   Test STM (A)   LTM (B) int with STM (A)

Writing such notes makes answering this question (retroactive interference) and other questions much easier.

8. **Ask questions.** Just as you should ask clarifying questions during class, do so during tests. Your instructors are trying to measure your knowledge, not trick you. They want the test to be clear, but sometimes things are not. Now's your chance. If you have a question—or a dozen questions— ask. Later is too late. Ask about directions you don't fully understand. Ask about vocabulary you don't know—so long as it's not vocabulary on which

you're being tested. If you're not sure how to interpret a question, ask: "The item says to describe the climate at the time she was elected. Does climate mean just political climate, or could it also mean social climate?"

9. **Retake the test.** After working through the entire test once, return to those items you couldn't answer or were unsure about. Having completed the rest of the exam, you can return to those items with greater confidence and perhaps enhanced knowledge from reading and answering other items. After that, "retake" as much of the exam as time permits. But, don't just check your work by rereading questions and answers. When you do, the tendency is to think everything is okay. Instead, cover your answers and try to answer each question anew, as if taking the exam for the first time. If you come up with a different answer, don't be afraid to change it if you can defend it. Don't believe those who say, "trust your first impression." That folktale probably originated with people selling white carpet. Don't trust your first inclination; trust your best inclination. As it turns out, the majority of changed answers are correct.

10. **Use all of the allotted time.** What's the rush to bolt the test room? Checking Facebook, texting your roommate, beating the coffee line? Relax and take your time. Revisiting items and retaking the test takes time. This is no time to misread instructions, leave items blank, or make careless erors. You've worked too hard in your test preparation to let that happen. And, if you need more time, ask. Maybe it will be provided.

11. **Sweep away anxiety.** Should you feel a bit anxious during the test, that's okay. Moderate anxiety actually raises performance. Should you become too anxious, take a few deep, cleansing breaths. Tense and relax your shoulder and neck muscles a few times. And maintain perspective. This test is not a life-or-death matter. Win, lose, or draw, there'll be other tests. You'll learn from this one and move on.

Regulate Test Errors

Learning does not end when you complete the test's last essay or pencil in the last bubble on the test's answer sheet. There is still much to learn from examining test errors. When you confront your mistakes, you can learn from them. The same holds true in other domains. Consider football. After the game, the team watches film of the game and coaches point out players' errors, such as lining up offside, missing tackles, and not holding blocks, so that players learn from those mistakes. Consider chess. Chess players notate their moves during games and later analyze those moves with opponents, coaches, or computer programs, so they can identify weak moves and rectify them in future games. Making mistakes and learning from them has produced life-changing products like the airplane and the lightbulb. The Wright brothers made numerous errors over many years trying to develop the world's first flying machine, but they analyzed their mistakes, made improvements, and got airborne. Thomas Edison did not invent the lightbulb on his first try either. He tested more than 3,000 lightbulb designs over several years before lighting the world.

Despite the importance of analyzing errors, most students shy away from their mistakes and forfeit opportunities to learn from them. After an exam, I post students' grades confidentially online. During the next class period, I reserve the last 10 minutes for students to view their marked exams to see what they got right and wrong, and I let students choose whether to stay or leave. In most cases, about 10% stay to examine their exams. Perhaps students leave to get a bit of free time. More likely, they leave because they don't realize how much can be learned from confronting errors and because they shun failure and criticism. They shouldn't. You shouldn't. Don't run from mistakes and shy away from corrective feedback. Confront mistakes. Invite and embrace feedback. Keep learning until you soar like the Wright brothers and shine like Edison.

When a graded test is returned, don't just look at the score; look at the errors and figure out what went wrong. This is called error analysis. Specifically, analyze error content, type, and source. Content refers to the topic of the question, such as Gothic architecture or proactive interference. Type refers to whether the test item was fact, concept, or skill. The item "Name the defining feature of Greek architecture" is a fact item. So is "Define proactive interference." The item "Which of the following illustrations depicts Greek architecture?" is a concept item. So is "Katy learned about Buddhism on Tuesday and about Zen Buddhism on Wednesday. When tested on Zen Buddhism on Thursday, Katy recalled little and instead recalled several facts about Buddhism. What theory of forgetting explains Katy's problem learning about Zen Buddhism?" Source refers to why an error occurred. Perhaps the student took incomplete notes or failed to create internal and external associations to aid learning and understanding. Once error content, type, and source are determined, isolated errors and error patterns can be corrected. Table 6-2 recaps the the three things you should determine through error analysis.

Table 6-2 THE THREE THINGS TO CONSIDER WHEN ANALYZING ERRORS

	Content	Type	Source
Description	The question topic	Fact, concept, or skill question	Why the error occurred
Example	• Gothic architecture • Proactive interference • Symbiosis	• Fact: Define proactive interference. • Concept: Which photo depicts Gothic architecture? • Skill: Calculate the mean of the following numbers ...	• Incomplete note-taking • Piecemeal learning • Failure to self-test

Let's see an example. Figure 6-6 shows a 10-item test on the topic of regulation. Begin the error analysis process by identifying the item content and item type for each item.

Regulation Test

1. What are the two types of fact items?

2. Name two rules for constructing effective concept items.

3. What are the two types of skill learning?

For items 4-7, identify the test item as (a) fact, (b) concept, or (c) skill.

4. Calculate the area of a rectangle with a base of 7 and height of 3.

5. What is the formula of calculating the area of a rectangle?

6. Which of the following figures is a rectangle?

7. What's the difference between area and perimeter?

For items 8-10, write a test item corresponding to the item type for the following material:

Students in an educational psychology class learned about the keyword method. The instructor said: "The keyword method is a great way to learn new vocabulary, such as hovel means a home made from dirt. To use the keyword method, the first step is to create a keyword (shovel) for the target word (hovel). The keyword should be a familiar word or phrase that sounds like the target word. The second step is to create an image linking the keyword (shovel) to the target word's meaning (a home made from dirt). You might imagine a shovel tossing dirt on a house."

8. Fact Item:

9. Concept Item:

10. Skill Item:

Figure 6.6 Regulation Test for Error Analysis

Table 6-3 shows an error analysis matrix for the regulation test shown in Figure 6-6. The Xs indicate incorrect responses. Examine the error analysis matrix and figure out what went wrong, especially trying to detect error patterns.

Table 6-3 ERROR ANALYSIS FOR REGULATION TEST

Item Number		Item Content	Item Type
1.		Fact Items	Fact
2.	X	Concept Items	Fact
3.		Skill Items	Fact
4.	X	Skill Items	Concept
5.	X	Fact Items	Concept
6.	X	Concept Items	Concept
7.	X	Fact Items	Concept
8.		Fact Items	Skill
9.	X	Concept Items	Skill
10.		Skill Items	Skill

Examining the Table 6-3 error analysis matrix, you should have detected the following error patterns: In terms of error content, the student missed all the items pertaining to the topic of concept items (Items 2, 6, and 9). In terms of item type, the student missed all the items assessing concept learning (Items 4, 5, 6, and 7). To sum up, this student does not get concept regulation—does not know about concept items (fact learning), cannot recognize concept items (concept learning), and cannot construct them (skill learning). What might be the source of these errors? Hard to know for sure, but perhaps the student was absent from class when the topic of concept regulation was presented. Perhaps the student was there but slept through that part of the lesson and recorded sketchy notes and no examples. Perhaps the student failed to create a matrix organizer for the three question types, associate them, use mnemonics to commit information to memory, practice recognizing new examples, and practice generating concept questions. Based on the students' errors, those are all logical error sources.

Activity 6.7

Conduct an item analysis for the following 6-item test. The student missed items 4–6.

For items 1–3, indicate what type of organizer (hierarchy, sequence, or matrix) the alert word suggests:

1. *After*
2. *Components*
3. *Different*

For items 4–6, create a preliminary organizer (hierarchy, sequence, or matrix):

4. *Four types of pliers*
5. *The three triangles differ with respect to angle equivalence*
6. *One thing led to another*

Answers to Focus Questions

1. These SOAR learning components match the given regulation statements:

    a. Associate
    b. Select
    c. Organize
    d. Regulate

2. Results from a study proved that self-testing works. Students in a repeated-testing group achieved 20% higher on a post-test than students in a repeated-studying group.

3. Before a test, try to obtain test information. Take advantage of test aids the teacher supplies, such as objectives, study guides, and practice tests. Ask students who've taken the course previously about their tests, and also confer with students in your class now about test expectancy. In addition, check for practice items in texts and online. And don't be afraid to ask your instructor about an impending test.

4. Knowing the form of a test (such as multiple choice, matching, or short answer) is not so helpful, because knowing item form tells you nothing about what you need to do with the content tested (know it, recognize it, or apply it). It is more valuable to know item type (fact, concept, or skill) than item form.

5. The two types of fact items are single-fact and relational-fact. Single-fact items require knowledge of a single fact, such as: The president of the U.S. administers the government's executive branch. Relational-fact items require knowledge of related facts, such as: Both the vice president and the cabinet support the president.

6. Concept learning can only be confirmed when students can recognize new, previously unencountered examples. Therefore, concept items should not ask test-takers to supply examples, because they might simply supply a previously learned example such as one presented during instruction.

7. The two types of skill items involve the application of rules and procedures. If a student can apply the rule, "Use a semicolon to join two main clauses," in a new setting, then that will show evidence of rule application. If a student can apply the procedure for adding mixed fractions when given previously unseen mixed fractions to add, then that will show evidence of procedure application.

8. Here is how each question should be classified:

   a. Fact

   b. Skill

   c. Concept

9. Here are sample questions about the topic of contractions:

   a. Fact: Define contraction.

   b. Fact: Describe how contractions are formed.

   c. Concept: Which of the following contain contractions?
      i. Let's go
      ii. Jon's bike
      iii. Horses' hooves
      iv. Couldn't decide

   d. Skill: Supply the contraction for the following word pairs:
      i. Have not
      ii. I will
      iii. Should have
      iv. You are

10. Several test-taking strategies were presented. Among them: choose a good seat, preview the test, answer easy items first, make notes on the test, and retake the test.

11. Error analysis reveals the content missed (such as simplifying fractions), the type of item missed (such as skill), and perhaps the source of the error (such as not practicing the skill).

12. Here is a hierarchy showing types of test items:

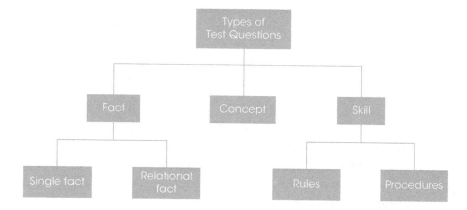

13. Students shouldn't let instructors be the first to test them. Students should test themselves so thoroughly in advance of tests that there is nothing instructors can ask them that they haven't already asked themselves. Students should try to find out or anticipate how they will be tested and test themselves accordingly, using appropriate question types: fact, concept, and skill. Also, students should regulate test-taking. There are several things students can do just prior to or during testing to maximize test performance. After the test, students should analyze test errors, by determining what went wrong in terms of item content, item type, and error source. Of course, students shouldn't wait to regulate learning until test time. They should regulate learning at all times as they select, organize, associate, and regulate.

Figure Credit

Fig. 6.5b: Microsoft Word is Copyright © by Microsoft.

CHAPTER 7

SOAR for Reading, Writing, Arithmetic, and Beyond

OVERVIEW

Objectives

1. Describe how SOAR was used to facilitate reading, writing, arithmetic, and real-world problem solving.

2. Apply SOAR strategies to facilitate reading, writing, arithmetic, and real-world problem solving.

Focus Questions

1. How is the application of SOAR strategies different for text than for lecture?

2. Is writing a natural—either you have it or you don't—ability?

3. What do most students do wrong when they write? What should you do?

4. How did the associations made prior to writing aid the writing process?

5. What sorts of things should a writer regulate?

6. What is the problem with how math skills are often presented in instruction, and how can SOAR help you overcome this problem?

7. How did SOAR impact the how-to-invest-money problem?

Y ou've learned how SOAR helps you *select* important lesson ideas and record complete notes, *organize* notes using graphic organizers where possible, *associate* lesson ideas with one another (internal associations) and with prior knowledge (external associations), and *regulate* learning and understanding. Let's now see examples of how SOAR can particularly help you with the 3Rs, reading, writing, and arithmetic, and with solving real-world problems.

SOAR for Reading

You saw in Chapter 3 how you might select text information using a text-marking system where you draw boxes around topics, draw circles around categories, underline details, and jot additional notes in the text margins. Here, those same text-marking selection strategies are demonstrated—along with other SOAR strategies for organizing, associating, and regulating—as you read the boxed text about tectonic plate movement. As you read a text, you can apply any and all SOAR strategies immediately in the text and its margins (assuming they're large enough) or on a separate page. In Figure 7-1, a combination approach was used where the text was marked (select), and numbers were inserted to designate other SOAR strategies (organize, associate, and regulate). Figure 7-2 shows a complete organizer for the tectonic plate material.

Tectonic Plate Movement Text

The movement of tectonic plates is classified by the type of boundary created between two plates as a result of their movement. There are three different types of tectonic plate boundaries: convergent, divergent, and transform.

Convergent Boundaries

Convergent boundaries are created when tectonic plates move toward each other. Plate convergence might involve two continental plates, two oceanic plates, or one of each. When two oceanic plates or an oceanic and a continental plate collide, the denser of the two plates dives underneath the other. This process is known as subduction. Because oceanic plates are denser than continental plates, they always subduct, go lower, upon convergence with a continental plate. When the subducting plate dives deep into the earth's interior, molten magma is created. Over time, this magma oozes up through the crust and the earth's surface and creates a chain of volcanoes.

However, when two continental plates collide with each other, subduction does not take place. Rather, in a process known as continental collision, the converging continental plates become welded together to form one, larger plate. When two continental plates collide, mountain ranges such as the

Himalayas are created as the smashing together of the plates causes them to rise up vertically. An analogy for convergent boundaries would be a head-on collision between two moving vehicles. Just as head-on collisions create substantial damage, convergent boundaries often result in the strongest of earthquakes. Earthquakes are measured on a magnitude of zero to ten, with ten being the greatest strength. Earthquakes created by a continental collision can reach a magnitude 9.

Divergent Boundaries

A second type of tectonic plate boundary is known as a divergent boundary. Divergent boundaries can occur when two plates move away from each other.

Divergent boundaries are formed through a process known as rifting. When rifting occurs, rising currents of pressure within the earth can pull plates apart. Molten magma rises into the fractures between the rifted plates, where it cools and solidifies, attaching itself to the edges of the rifted plates.

When rifting occurs in the ocean, the result is known as seafloor spreading. As oceanic plates move away from each other, openings occur on the ocean floor. These openings are filled with molten magma, which cools and hardens. This results in the extension of the ocean floor's surface.

Rifting can also occur beneath land, such as when two continental plates are moving away from each other. For example, the continental African and Arabian plates rifted and created a divergent boundary that filled with ocean water, which is now the Red Sea. If these two plates continue to move away from each other, the Red Sea may someday become the size of an ocean. Divergent boundaries can result in earthquakes as high as magnitude 8.

Transform Boundaries

A third type of tectonic plate boundary is known as a transform boundary. Transform boundaries are created when two tectonic plates grind alongside each other in opposite directions. As the giant slabs of rock slide alongside each other, the slabs are subjected to stress known as shearing. Because tectonic plates are rubbing alongside each other, their edges become ground up into smaller rocks that fall downward between the two plates, thus creating a valley. One example is the San Andreas Fault, where the North American and Pacific plates grind alongside each other. Along transform boundaries, powerful earthquakes up to 8.5 magnitude are experienced.

Tectonic Plate Movement

The movement of tectonic plates is classified by the type of boundary created between two plates as a result of their movement. There are three difference types of tectonic plate boundaries: convergent, divergent, and transform.[1]

Convergent Boundaries

Convergent boundaries are created when tectonic plates move toward each other.[2] Plate convergence might involve two continental plates, two oceanic plates, or one of each. When two oceanic plates or an oceanic and continental plate collide, the denser of the two plates dives underneath the other. This process is known as subduction.[3] Because oceanic plates are denser than continental plates, they always subduct, go lower, upon convergence with a continental plate. When the subducting plate dives deep into the earth's interior, [a]molten magma is created. Over time, this [b]magma oozes up through the crust and the earth's surface and [c]creates a chain of volcanoes.[4] However, when two continental plates collide with each other, subduction does not take place. Rather, in a process known as continental collision, the converging continental plates become welded together to form one, larger plate. When two continental plates collide, mountain ranges such as the Himalayas are created as the smashing together of the plates causes them to rise up vertically.[5] An analogy for convergent boundaries would be a head-on collision between two moving vehicles. Just as head-on collisions create substantial damage, convergent boundaries often result in the strongest of earthquakes.[6] Earthquakes are measured on a magnitude of zero to ten, with ten being the greatest strength. Earthquakes created by a continental collision can reach a magnitude 9.[R 1-7]

1. (O)

Tectonic Plate Boundaries

Convergent   Divergent   Transform

2. (EA)   When things converge, they come together– like spring breakers converging on Ft. Lauderdale.

3. (O)

Convergent Boundary

Continental Plate →   ← Oceanic Plate

Subduction: Denser plate dives below

4. (O)

Convergence

Magma created → Oozes through surface → Creates volcano chain

5. (O)

Continental Collision

Continental Plate →   ← Continental Plate

6. (EA)   Continental collision is like head-on collision. Also, both occur on land.

7. (O)

Divergent Boundary

← Plate   Plate →

8. (EA)   Diverge means separate. Recall the Robert Frost poem: "Two roads diverged in a yellow wood."

9. (O)

Rifting

Magma rises in fractures → Magma cools and solidifies → Magma attaches to rifted plates

10, 11. (IA) Rifting in ocean yields seafloor spreading, whereas rifting on land can create a body of water like the Red Sea.

12. (IA)   Continental collisions cause more powerful earthquakes (9) than rifting (8).

13. (O)

Transform Boundary

← Plate
Plate →

Regulation

1. _____ boundaries are created as two tectonic plates move toward each other.
   A) Divergent
   B) Convergent
   C) Transform

2. When two tectonic plates collide, the denser of the two plates will dive underneath the other and become consumed by the earth's interior. This is known as:
   A) Continental collision
   B) Rifting
   C) Shearing
   D) Subduction

3. The outcome of subduction is _____.
   A) Volcanoes
   B) Earthquakes
   C) Seafloor spreading
   D) Valleys

4. Which of the plate boundaries is associated with continental collision?
   A) Convergent
   B) Divergent
   C) Transform

5. Which plate movement can cause the strongest earthquake?
   A) Divergent
   B) Convergent
   C) Transform

6. Which 2 plates are involved in continental collision?
   A) Oceanic—Oceanic
   B) Oceanic—Continental
   C) Continental—Continental

7. What plate movement is shown in the image below?
   A) Subduction
   B) Continental collision
   C) Rifting
   D) Shearing

8. _____ boundaries are created as two tectonic plates move away from each other.
   A) Divergent
   B) Convergent
   C) Transform

9. Which tectonic plate process does the image below represent?
   A) Rifting
   B) Continental Collision
   C) Subduction
   D) Transformation

10. Seafloor spreading is a common result of _____ boundaries.
    A) Convergent
    B) Divergent
    C) Transform

11. Seafloor spreading is caused by _____.
    A) Subduction
    B) Rifting
    C) Shearing

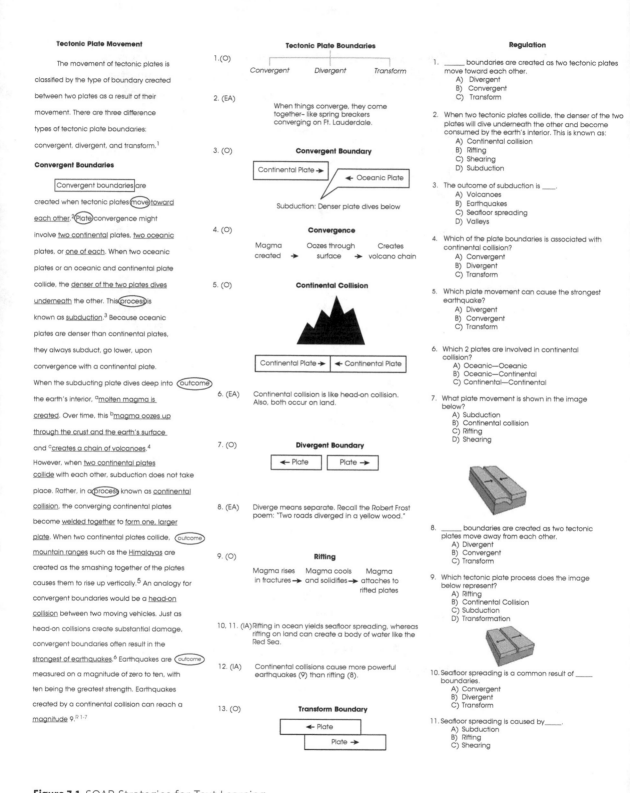

Figure 7-1 SOAR Strategies for Text Learning

Divergent Boundaries

A second type of tectonic plate boundary is known as a divergent boundary. Divergent boundaries can occur when two plates move away from each other.[7,8]

Divergent boundaries are formed through a process known as rifting. When rifting occurs, rising currents of pressure within the earth can pull plates apart and ᵃmolten magma rises into (outcome) the fractures between the rifted plates where it ᵇcools and solidifies,ᶜattaching itself to the edges of the rifted plates.[9]

When rifting occurs in the ocean, the result is known as seafloor spreading. As oceanic plates move away from each other, openings occur on the ocean floor. These openings are filled with molten magma, which cools and hardens. This results in the extension of the ocean floor's surface.[10]

Rifting can also occur beneath land, such as when two continental plates are moving away from each other. For example, the continental African and Arabian plates rifted and created a divergent boundary that filled with ocean water, which is now the Red Sea. If these two plates continue to move away from each other, the Red Sea may someday become the size of an ocean.[11] Divergent boundaries can result in earthquakes as high as magnitude 8.[12] R 8-13

Transform Boundaries

A third type of tectonic plate boundary is known as a transform boundary. Transform boundaries are created when two tectonic plates grind alongside of each other in opposite (movement) directions.[13] As the giant slabs of rockslide alongside each other, the slabs are subjected to stress known as shearing. Because tectonic plates are rubbing alongside each other, their ᵃedges become grinded up into smaller rocks that ᵇfall downward between the two plates, thus ᶜcreating (outcome) a valley.[14] One example is the San Andreas Fault, where the North American and Pacific plates grind alongside each other. Along transform boundaries, powerful earthquakes up to 8.5 magnitude are (outcome) experienced.[15,16] R 14-18

14. (O)

Shearing

Edges grinded into smaller rocks → Rock falls downward between plates → Create valley

15. (O, IA)

Earthquake Magnitude

Boundary:	Convergent	Divergent	Transform
Process:	Continental Collision	Rifting	Shearing
Magnitude:	9	8	8.5

All three boundaries can cause powerful earthquakes with Convergent>Transform>Divergent.

16. (O)   *See Figure 8-3.*

12. The Red Sea was caused by _____.
    A) Subduction
    B) Rifting
    C) Shearing

13. Many years ago, construction workers built a 5-mile long sidewalk. What these construction workers didn't know was that they built this sidewalk over a teotonic plate boundary. As time has gone by, a gap has appeared between two sections of the sidewalk as they have separated from each other. What type of a plate boundary did the construction workers build the sidewalk over?
    A) Convergent
    B) Divergent
    C) Transform

14. _____ boundaries are created as two tectonic plates slide alongside each other.
    A) Divergent
    B) Convergent
    C) Transform

15. Transform boundaries result in a type of stress called _____.
    A) Tensional
    B) Compressional
    C) Faulting
    D) Shearing

16. Transform boundaries produce _____.
    A) Volcanoes
    B) Seafloor spreading
    C) Valleys

17. Which type of boundary does the image below represent?
    A) Convergent
    B) Divergent
    C) Transform

18. What type of boundaries are shown in Images A, B, and C below?

Figure 7-1 SOAR Strategies for Text Learning (continued)

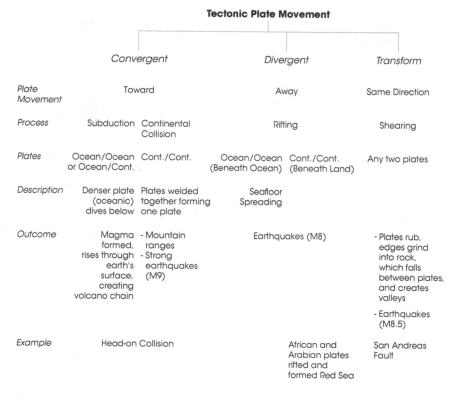

Tectonic Plate Movement

	Convergent		Divergent		Transform
Plate Movement	Toward		Away		Same Direction
Process	Subduction	Continental Collision	Rifting		Shearing
Plates	Ocean/Ocean or Ocean/Cont.	Cont./Cont.	Ocean/Ocean (Beneath Ocean)	Cont./Cont. (Beneath Land)	Any two plates
Description	Denser plate (oceanic) dives below	Plates welded together forming one plate	Seafloor Spreading		
Outcome	Magma formed, rises through earth's surface, creating volcano chain	- Mountain ranges - Strong earthquakes (M9)	Earthquakes (M8)		- Plates rub, edges grind into rock, which falls between plates, and creates valleys - Earthquakes (M8.5)
Example	Head-on Collision			African and Arabian plates rifted and formed Red Sea	San Andreas Fault

Figure 7-2 Complete Organizer for the Tectonic Plate Material

Activity 7.1

Apply SOAR strategies, in the manner used in this chapter section, as you read the following text passage about two body systems.

Digestive System

The digestive system is made up of organs that break down food into protein, vitamins, minerals, carbohydrates, and fats, all of which the body needs for energy, growth, and repair. After food is chewed and swallowed, it goes down the esophagus and enters the stomach, where it is further broken down by powerful stomach acids. From the stomach, the food travels into the small intestine. This is where food is broken down into nutrients that can enter the bloodstream through tiny, hair-like projections. The excess food that the body doesn't need or can't digest is turned into waste and is eliminated from the body.

Respiratory System

The respiratory system brings air into the body and removes carbon dioxide. It includes the nose, trachea, and lungs. When you breathe in, air enters your nose or mouth and goes down a long tube called the trachea. The trachea branches into two bronchial tubes, or primary bronchi, which go to the lungs. The primary bronchi branch off into even smaller bronchial tubes, or bronchioles. The bronchioles end in the alveoli, or air sacs. Oxygen follows this path, passes through the walls of the air sacs and blood vessels, and enters the blood stream. At the same time, carbon dioxide passes into the lungs and is exhaled.

SOAR for Writing

Writing is a learned skill, nothing natural about it. How do I know? Because before I published books and articles, I was a college student who three times failed the English Writing Exam needed to earn an English Education Teaching Certificate. I learned how to write in graduate school when my advisor picked apart my papers sentence by sentence, word by word, as we read them together in his office. He would say: "This sentence lacks parallel structure. Instead of writing, 'Short-term memory is limited in capacity and has a short duration,' you should write, 'Short-term memory is limited in capacity and duration.' Use the active voice here. Instead of writing 'The proposals were read by several reviewers,' write 'Several reviewers read the proposals.' Bad word choice here. You mean eager, not anxious. Anxious conveys nervousness; eager conveys anticipation. This section reads like a laundry list. Don't go at this topic by topic; discover and report similarities and differences across topics."

I also learned a valuable writing lesson when I once asked the editor of educational psychology's premier journal what made for a great article worthy of publication. His response: "Besides being scientifically sound, it must tell a story that all can understand and appreciate. I use the neighbor test: If my neighbor next door (who is not an educational psychologist) can read it, understand it, learn from it, enjoy it, and remember it days later, it is likely worth publishing."

Effective writing is one of the most important skills to master. If you cannot write effectively, you cannot share your ideas and discoveries. As a former journal editor myself, I saw many manuscripts presenting well-designed studies, addressing important research questions, and yielding important findings be rejected because the authors could not communicate effectively. Their wonderful ideas fell silent. They failed the neighbor test. Make it a priority to improve your writing now. SOAR can help.

Chapters 1 and 2 described research studies proving that SOAR boosted achievement. Research also proves that SOAR boosts writing. Before addressing how SOAR improves writing, let's start at the story's beginning: Most student writing is piecemeal and linear, like that laundry-list writing I did as a student that my advisor chastised. Student writers tend to address one topic at a time, one idea at a time, rather than synthesize information and report the important relationships and patterns hidden in the pieces. Students describe trees, not forests. But students are not alone in their topic-by-topic writing approach. Textbook authors do it too. As I thumb through a text on human development, I notice that Piaget's four stages of cognitive development are addressed one after the other and never synthesized. Ditto for Freud's psychosexual stages and for Erikson's psychosocial stages.

In two experiments Linlin Luo and I conducted, we found that students were inherently piecemeal writers (Luo & Kiewra, 2019a; Luo & Kiewra, 2019b). Left to their own devices, only 14% of students composed essays that synthesized information; the other 86% reported information in their essays piece by piece. When some students were later helped to use SOAR methods, those SOAR-aided writers wrote essays that were more complete, better organized—by categories cutting across topics rather than topic by topic—and more comparative—less piecemeal—than the essays written by their non-SOAR-aided counterparts.

Let's suppose that you're asked to write an essay about creativity after reading the creativity text in Table 7.1. Then, let's see how SOAR's four components (select, organize, associate, and regulate) can help.

Table 7-1 CREATIVITY TEXT

Expressive Creativity

Were you ever amazed by a musician playing progressive jazz? A comedian interacting wittily with the audience? These are examples of expressive creativity, which is the ability to generate a rapid and novel response in a spontaneous situation. Not only is expressive creativity demonstrated in performing arts, but it also shows up in other fields, such as when a football player skillfully feigns a would-be tackler in a game or when a college professor answers questions rapidly and succinctly in a classroom. Oftentimes, the expressively creative person displays creative responses within a few seconds or less.

The goal of the expressively creative person is to create a momentary flash of brilliance that fits the immediate situation yet stands apart from typical responses. That is, to create a response that is appropriate but seemingly novel. The means for achieving this goal is developing the ability to rapidly perceive patterns. This skill usually takes 8–12 years to develop. An important characteristic is timing. The person has to learn when to make the responses. For example, a funny response by a comedian might not be considered funny, but perhaps awkward and embarrassing, when spoken at the wrong time.

The myth associated with expressive creativity is that the creative response is spontaneous and that the person making the response is acting spontaneously. Upon more careful analysis, we discover that the person making the response has over-practiced the response. He or she has made a highly similar response, in highly similar situations, many times before. In a sense, the expressively creative person makes us believe that the response is spontaneous, much in the same manner that a magician makes us believe she's pulled a rabbit from a hat. In reality, the person has mastered a well-practiced style. The responses we observe are manifestations of that highly practiced style.

Adaptive Creativity

Adaptive creativity is the ability to solve everyday problems. The time needed to display adaptive creativity is usually within the span of a few hours to a few weeks. The characteristics of an adaptively creative person are the abilities to analyze day-to-day problems, plan effective solutions, and execute the plans successfully. For the adaptively creative person, the goal is to maintain the status quo or to slightly improve the status quo of daily life. To reach the goal, the adaptively creative person has mastered effective day-to-day problem-solving strategies.

Examples include any of the day-to-day problems that a homemaker or a skilled person in a profession or a vocation would have to solve. For example, a homemaker may have to use adaptive creativity to plan and execute a new house-cleaning and meal-preparation strategy after learning that unexpected guests will soon be arriving. A college professor may have to draw on past teaching experiences when planning a conference presentation for the first time.

The creativity stems from the characteristics of pattern recognition and flexibility. The adaptively creative person recognizes familiar patterns in new situations and then flexibly adapts past strategies to solve new problems.

The myth associated with adaptive creativity is the belief that the creative response is new. In actuality, adaptively creative people have overlearned effective problem-solving strategies that they simply adapt to new situations. They identify similarities between diverse situations and then use those familiar strategies to solve problems they perceive as similar to those they've solved before. Adaptive creativity, for these reasons, can only be mastered over a period of about 10 years.

Innovative Creativity

Innovative creativity refers to the person's ability to significantly change or alter a major process, product, or school of thought. Examples of innovatively creative people include inventors who significantly improve products or produce new products; writers, artists, and musicians who alter artistic styles; scientists who alter theories; or coaches who create a modification of the typical defensive strategies used in a match.

The goal of the innovator is to make significant change, to produce a better product or idea. That goal stems from dissatisfaction with the status quo. The innovatively creative dwell on their ideas for many years before producing their creative product or idea. Yet, in reality, they sometimes spend their total adult lives gaining the knowledge and experience that allows them to be creative. Thus, an important characteristic is a rich knowledge base.

The myth associated with innovative creativity is that innovative creativity stems from originality. In actuality, innovators reuse already-established ideas over and over again to guide their thought processes and actions. For example, most of Thomas Edison's inventions stem from his understanding of a few basic principles discovered early in his productive years. He was a master of analogical thinking—applying one idea to new situations.

Emergent Creativity

Throughout history, there are people who have given rise to intellectual, social, or political revolutions. For example, Einstein's groundbreaking theory of relativity laid the foundation of modern physics. Another example is Gandhi, the preeminent leader of the Indian independence movement. His non-cooperation movement not only led India to independence, but also inspired movements for civil rights and freedom across the world.

As these examples illustrate, emergent creativity refers to one's ability to profoundly change existing ideas, beliefs, or styles. The change is so profound that the whole direction of a discipline is reshaped. Obviously, such significant change involves a lifetime of experience in a particular field. And creative breakthroughs are usually displayed just once or twice in a lifetime.

The goal of the emergently creative is to set trends and redirect the future. They meet this goal by being great risk-takers. Another characteristic is their attack on basic assumptions. They have more faith in their own ideas than in the underlying assumptions of a discipline.

The myth associated with emergent creativity is the belief that the products or ideas of these great minds are uniquely novel and rise above the times. In actuality, it is the creators' deep and unparalleled mastery of the domain that positions them to see what others cannot envision. Their revolutionary changes are not giant leaps (to them) but the synthesis of available knowledge and the next calculated steps in a domain's direction and growth.

How SOAR Can Help

Select
Expressive Creativity

- Example: Musician playing progressive jazz, comedian interacting with audience

- Definition: Ability to generate a rapid and novel response in a spontaneous situation

- Example: Football player feigning a tackler, professor answering questions

- Time to display: Few seconds or less

- Goal: Create momentary flash of brilliance that fits situation yet is novel

- Means to goal: Rapidly perceiving patterns

- Time to develop: 8–12 years

- Characteristic: Timing—when to make response

- Example: Comedian responding at wrong time is not funny

- Myth: Person and response are spontaneous

- Myth dispelled: Person has mastered a well-practiced style, and similar responses were made before

Adaptive Creativity

- Definition: Ability to solve everyday problems

- Time to display: Hours to weeks

- Characteristics: Analyze day-to-day problems, plan solutions, execute plans

- Goal: Maintain/improve status quo of daily life

- Means to goal: Effective day-to-day problem-solving strategies

- Examples: Homemaker preparing for last-minute guests, college professor preparing conference presentation

- Characteristics: Pattern recognition, flexibility

- Myth: Creative response is new

- Myth dispelled: Person has overlearned problem-solving strategies; they adapt to new situations similar to past situations

- Time to develop: About 10 years

Innovative Creativity

- Definition: Ability to significantly change a major process, product, or school of thought

- Examples: Inventors who invent/improve products; writers, artists, musicians who alter styles; scientists altering theories; coaches creating new strategies

- Goal: Make significant change, produce better product or idea

- Means to goal: Dissatisfaction with status quo

- Time to display: Many years

- Time to develop: Adult life

- Characteristic: Rich knowledge base

- Myth: Creativity stems from originality

- Myth dispelled: Reuse already-established ideas

- Examples: Edison reused existing ideas

Emergent Creativity

- Examples: Einstein's theory of relativity, Gandhi's non-cooperation movement

- Definition: Ability to profoundly change existing ideas, beliefs, or styles and reshape discipline

- Time to develop: Lifetime

- Time to display: Once or twice in a lifetime

- Goal: Set trends and redirect future

- Means to goal: Risk-taking

- Characteristics: Attack basic assumptions, have more faith in own ideas

- Myth: Creativity is novel and rises above the times

- Myth dispelled: Creators have unparalleled mastery, and their revolutionary ideas are merely the next calculated step based on synthesis of that knowledge

Organize

	Expressive	Adaptive	Innovative	Emergent
Definition	Generate rapid and novel response	Solve everyday problems	Significantly change major process, product, school of thought	Novel and profound response that reshapes discipline
Examples	Musician— progressive jazz; comedian— interacting	Homemaker preparing for last-minute guests; professor preparing for conference presentation	Inventors; artists altering styles; scientists altering theories; coaches creating strategies; Edison	Einstein's theory of relativity; Gandhi's non-cooperation movement
Goal	Create quick, novel response	Maintain/ improve status quo of daily life	Make significant change; produce better product or idea	Set trends; redirect future
Means to Goal	Rapid pattern recognition	Day-to-day problem-solving strategies	Dissatisfaction with status quo	Risk-taking

Characteristics	Timing	Analyze problems, plan solutions, execute plans	Rich knowledge base	Attack basic assumptions; more faith in own ideas
Time to Display	Few seconds	Hours to weeks	Many years	1–2 times in lifetime
Time to Develop	8–12 years	About 10 years	Adult life	Lifetime
Myth	Person and response spontaneous	Response is new	Creativity stems from originality	Creativity is novel and rises above the times
Myth Dispelled	Response is similar to past responses and learned through practice	Response is reuse of overlearned problem-solving strategies adapted from past situations	Reuse already-established ideas	Creators' domain mastery and synthesis positions them to make next calculated (revolutionary) step

Associate

1. The creativity is progressively more sophisticated and profound, going from expressive (creating momentary brilliance) to adaptive (solving day-to-day problems) to innovative (creating/improving products) to emergent (reshaping disciplines).

2. As the types of creativity increase in sophistication, the time needed to both display and develop the creativity increase as well.

3. As the purposes become progressively more profound, the knowledge required by the creative person becomes broader, going from expressive (past responses) to adaptive (problem-solving strategies) to innovative (rich knowledge base) to emergent (unparalleled domain mastery and synthesized knowledge).

4. The goals for expressive and adaptive creativity seem personal (reacting to something in the moment or solving a day-to-day problem), whereas the goals for innovative and emergent creativity seem societal (striving to improve products, ideas, and disciplines).

5. All four types require pattern recognition—noticing similarities between past and present conditions.

6. In each case, there is really nothing new. All creative responses are based on past knowledge and experiences.

7. An example of expressive creativity is comedians doing improv.

8. An example of adaptive creativity is finding a better filing system for important papers.

9. An example of innovative creativity is Eli Whitney inventing the cotton gin. This example also dispels the myth because he actually adapted an already-existing gin.

10. An example of emergent creativity is Freud developing the theory of psychoanalysis.

Regulate

Checklist to monitor writing process and evaluate written product.

_____   Did I truly understand the creativity materials?

_____   Did I select their key ideas?

_____   Did I organize ideas in a way that aids comparison?

_____   Did I make meaningful associations among the topics?

_____   Am I including important information from all four texts in the essay?

_____   Am I organizing my points in meaningful ways?

_____   Am I using the associations I made as points of comparison?

_____   Did I write about how the topics are alike and how they are different?

_____   Did I tell a clear and convincing story my neighbor would understand, enjoy, and remember?

_____   Did I revise the essay several times to make it as perfect as possible?

Next is a sample essay that might evolve from using the SOAR method. Notice that the essay is not piecemeal (expressing one idea at a time) or linear (describing one type of creativity at a time) but instead synthesizes information across creativity topics. The end product is a meaningful essay that uncovers and expresses relationships across creativity types for all readers (or neighbors) to understand and enjoy.

Creativity Essay

There are four types of creativity: expressive, adaptive, innovative, and emergent. All four types involve a creative response, but those responses grow progressively more sophisticated and profound. Expressive creativity involves a rapid and novel response made spontaneously in a new setting, such as when a comedian reacts to a comment from the audience. Adaptive creativity involves a response made to solve an everyday problem, such as when a homemaker solves the problem of quickly preparing for an unexpected guest. Innovative creativity involves a response that significantly alters a process or product, such as when an inventor like Eli Whitney invents the cotton gin. Emergent creativity involves a response so novel and profound that it reshapes or even revolutionizes a discipline, such as when Einstein advanced his theory of relativity in physics.

The goals and characteristics of these creators fit with their creative outputs. Expressive creators seek to make quick, novel responses and do so by quickly recognizing familiar patterns and properly timing their response. Adaptive creators seek to maintain or improve the status quo in their lives and do so by analyzing problems, planning solutions, and executing them. Innovative creators are dissatisfied with the status quo and strive to create better products or ideas using their rich knowledge base. Emergent creators seek to set trends and redirect the future and do so by taking risks and attacking basic assumptions because they have complete faith in their own ideas.

As these types of creativity grow in sophistication, the time needed to display and develop them naturally grows. Expressive and adaptive creativity are quickly displayed. It takes just a few seconds for a comedian to react to a heckler (expressive) and just a few hours or weeks for a professor to adapt familiar teaching strategies to the planning of a first-time conference presentation (adaptive). Innovative and emergent creativity are displayed less quickly. An innovative creator requires many years, and an emergent creator a lifetime, to display a creative response. Similarly, acquiring the knowledge and experience to develop expressive or adaptive creativity takes about 10 years, whereas it takes a lifetime to develop innovative or emergent creativity.

Although these types of creativity yield impressive outcomes, there is a myth surrounding all of them. In each case, we think of the creativity as something extraordinary and beyond the capability of most people. In reality, though, these extraordinary outputs are easily explained by ordinary factors like long-term practice, reusing familiar ideas, and a deep knowledge base. For expressive creativity, the spontaneous response, such as reacting to a heckler, is actually a well-practiced response developed from having reacted to many hecklers before. For adaptive creativity, the seemingly new response, such as planning a conference presentation, is actually an adaptation of responses made in similar situations in the past, such as planning lessons for teaching. For innovative creativity, the seemingly original response, such as inventing a new product, is actually the outgrowth of reusing already-established ideas in somewhat new ways. Eli Whitney's invention of the cotton gin was actually a modification of a previous cotton gin. For emergent creativity, the seemingly revolutionary response, such as Einstein's theory of relativity, was actually the next calculated step for someone who had more knowledge of physics than any of his contemporaries.

SOAR for Arithmetic

Mathematics is a domain primarily comprised of skills. But open any math text, and you'll likely see math skills taught in a piecemeal fashion—one skill at a time, as if the skills were unrelated. Nonsense. Recall that Chapter 4 extolled the virtues of approaching material with an organizational mindset—striving to uncover how information is optimally organized and associated.

Consider what I saw when I examined a math book covering the area of polygons. There was a separate section about each polygon and no attempt to compare their area formulas. To make matters worse, the authors provided area formulas that made the polygons seem more disparate than they actually are. As you can see in the middle row of Figure 7-3, the authors indicated that the area formulas were Side x Side for square, Length x Width for rectangle, and Base x Height for parallelogram. Ludicrous. Assuming an organizational mindset, I realized that the formula is actually the same for all these polygons: Base x Height, as shown in Figure 7-3's bottom row. Yet countless math students were misled into believing these polygons were unrelated and into memorizing unnecessary formulas.

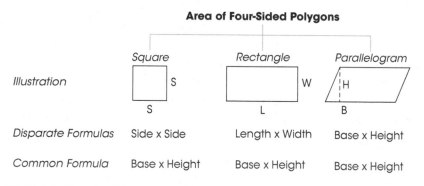

Area of Four-Sided Polygons

	Square	Rectangle	Parallelogram
Illustration			
Disparate Formulas	Side x Side	Length x Width	Base x Height
Common Formula	Base x Height	Base x Height	Base x Height

Figure 7-3 Matrix Showing Disparate and Common Area Formulas

When I perused another math book to learn the skills associated with adding, subtracting, and multiplying polynomials, I found much the same thing. There was a section on their addition, another on their subtraction, and another on their multiplication—as if these three skills had nothing in common. Crazy. To understand their relationship, I selected key information and created the matrix organizer found in Figure 7-4 (SOAR's select and organize components). Examining that organizer, it is easy to compare the rules for each operation along the top row (SOAR's associate). Of course, the organizer also contains a sample problem for each operation (which I intentionally kept uniform for comparison) and a worked solution directly below to easily see how rules are applied (SOAR's regulate). Moreover, all the worked examples are along the same row for easy comparison (SOAR's associate).

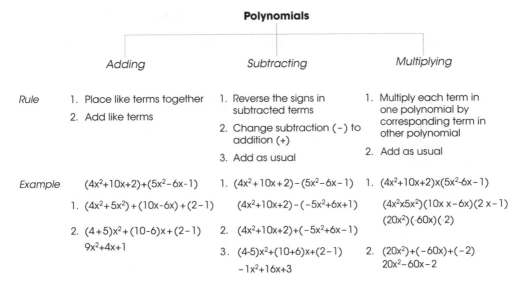

Polynomials

	Adding	Subtracting	Multiplying
Rule	1. Place like terms together 2. Add like terms	1. Reverse the signs in subtracted terms 2. Change subtraction (−) to addition (+) 3. Add as usual	1. Multiply each term in one polynomial by corresponding term in other polynomial 2. Add as usual
Example	$(4x^2+10x+2)+(5x^2-6x-1)$ 1. $(4x^2+5x^2)+(10x-6x)+(2-1)$ 2. $(4+5)x^2+(10-6)x+(2-1)$ $9x^2+4x+1$	1. $(4x^2+10x+2)-(5x^2-6x-1)$ $(4x^2+10x+2)-(-5x^2+6x+1)$ 2. $(4x^2+10x+2)+(-5x^2+6x-1)$ 3. $(4-5)x^2+(10+6)x+(2-1)$ $-1x^2+16x+3$	1. $(4x^2+10x+2)x(5x^2-6x-1)$ $(4x^2x5x^2)(10x\ x-6x)(2\ x-1)$ $(20x^2)(-60x)(-2)$ 2. $(20x^2)+(-60x)+(-2)$ $20x^2-60x-2$

Figure 7-4 Polynomials Matrix

What associations did I draw from this matrix?

- All three operations involve addition.

- All three operations involve placing like terms together, which is part of the addition process.

- Subtraction problems are transformed into addition problems by reversing the subtraction sign to addition and reversing each sign in the subtracted term. This makes sense because the inverse of subtraction is addition.

I can easily regulate understanding by solving an assortment of polynomial problems like the following:

- $(8x^2 + 9) + (6x^2 - 4)$

- $(x + 11) (4x + 3) (x - 1)$

- $(5x^2 + 2) - (7x^2 - 2)$

Activity 7-3

There are three statistical methods for understanding the spread of scores around the center of scores. Those three methods are interquartile range, variance, and standard deviation. Here is the formula for each:

- Interquartile Range (IQR): The first quartile is subtracted from the third quartile. To attain quartiles, divide the rank-ordered data set into four equal parts. The values that separate the parts are called the first, second, and third quartiles, respectively.

- Variance: Calculate deviation scores, square deviation scores, sum deviation scores, and divide sum by number of scores.

- Standard Deviation: Calculate deviation scores, square deviation scores, sum deviation scores, divide sum by number of scores, find square root of quotient.

Use the SOAR method to learn these three statistical methods.

SOAR for Solving Real-World Problems

You're shopping at the Dollar Store, cooking ramen noodles, and driving an old beater with a broken taillight. I get it—you're a poor college student. How would you like to someday be a millionaire? Interested in knowing how to make it happen? Well, here's comedian Steve Martin's two-step formula for becoming a millionaire and never paying taxes. "First, get a million dollars." Then, when the tax collector asks why you've never paid taxes, use these two simple words: "I forgot" (Martin, 1978).

Here's how to really become a millionaire in two easy steps: Invest early and invest regularly. Once you start earning money, start socking some away every month. Sure, you'll have other bills to pay, but always write that first monthly check or make that first monthly automated payment to you.

Here's why. I'm sure your parents told you that money doesn't grow on trees. True. But money does grow from money. Through the wonders of compounding interest and an ever-rising stock market, money accumulates. To better understand the value of investing early and regularly, examine the matrix organizer in Table 7-2. There, you'll see the monetary fates of two people: Early Erica and Late Larry. Erica began investing early, at age 20; Larry began investing later, at age 30. Each invested regularly: $100 per month. Erica, though, only invested this way for 10 years, until age 30. Larry invested this way for 30 years, until age 60. Erica invested a total of $12,000; Larry invested a total of $36,000. Naturally, you'd think Larry would have more money saved at age 60, right? Wrong. Even though Erica invested $24,000 less than Larry, Erica's age-60 nest egg was almost $20,000 more than Larry's (assuming 7% interest for both). It seems like magic, but it's simply the effect that early investing and long-term interest compounding have on money.

Although $140,000 is not chump change, it is not nearly a million dollars. To become a millionaire, you need only invest $400 a month from age 20 to 65. Like magic, that $216,000 investment becomes a million bucks. As for avoiding taxes, you can try Steve Martin's recommendation, or NOT!

Table 7-2 MATRIX SHOWING THE POWER OF INVESTING EARLY AND REGULARLY

	Early Erica	Late Larry
Age of First Investment	20	30
Monthly Investment	$100	$100
Years Investing	10	30
Total Invested	$12,000	$36,000
Age 60 Total	$141,304	$122, 709

Now that you're convinced that you should invest early and regularly, you'll need to figure out how to invest your hard-earned money. That's where SOAR comes in. When you browse money magazines or websites seeking investment advice, you'll want to select, organize, and associate that information and regulate the learning process. You'll also want to regulate the investments you eventually make. Here's an example of what you might encounter and how SOAR can help.

When you begin researching the investment world, you'll find out that there are three general types of investments: cash (savings accounts or CDs), bonds, and stocks. You can create a matrix like that in Table 7-3 to organize and compare those three investment types.

Table 7-3 MATRIX DISPLAYING GENERAL INVESTMENT TYPES

	Cash	Bonds	Stocks
Description	When you make cash investments, you are protecting (saving) your original investment.	When you buy a bond, you are lending money and collecting interest on the repayments.	When you buy stock, you are buying shares of ownership in a corporation.
Philosophy	Safety	Fixed income	Growth
Purpose	Short-term savings	Yearly income	Long-term growth
Short-Range Yield	Very low	Moderate	Variable (low to high)
Long-Range Yield	Very low	Moderate	High
Risk	None	Moderate	High

As with any graphic organizer, you want to examine it and make associations; see what it's telling you. Table 7-3 should be telling you that stock investments are the way to go for long-term savings, spanning your college graduation and retirement. Because time is on your side, you should be willing to absorb high risk and ride out market fluctuations to attain long-term growth, and only stock investments offer that.

Okay, assuming you've settled on stock investments, you read some more and learn that there are three stock investment options. You can purchase a single stock like Amazon, a few stocks like Facebook, Berkshire Hathaway, and Exxon-Mobil, or a mutual fund that pools money from investors and buys many stocks. You create Table 7-4 to organize and compare these three stock investments.

Table 7-4 MATRIX DISPLAYING STOCK INVESTMENT OPTIONS

	Mutual Fund	Few Stocks	Single Stock
Diversification	Most	Some	None
Risk	Least	Moderate	Most
Potential Gain	High	Higher	Highest
Potential Loss	Least	Moderate	Most
Investment Manager	Fund manager	Self or paid broker	Self or paid broker

You've likely heard the old adage: Don't put all your eggs in one basket (or both feet in the same pants leg). That's because if the basket breaks, you'll lose all your eggs. Same goes for investing, where the name of the game is diversification—spreading your money out over several companies. As you examine Table 7-4, in search of associations, it is evident that only the mutual fund option offers diversification. That option has other relative benefits too: It has the least risk, high potential gain, and a fund manager. You need not worry about moving your money around to other investments or timing the market. The fund manager does that.

You read some more about stock mutual funds, and wouldn't you know it—there are varying types of these as well: Balanced, Growth, or Sector, as shown in Table 7-5.

Table 7-5 MATRIX DISPLAYING TYPES OF MUTUAL FUNDS

	Balanced	Growth	Sector
Invests In	Diverse companies and bonds	Diverse companies	Companies in one area
Examples	Walt Disney, Coca-Cola, Treasury bonds	Berkshire Hathaway, JPMorgan Chase, Coca-Cola	Paper, electricity, or gold

Objective	Long-term growth and yearly income	Long-term growth	Short- or long-term growth
Diversification	Very high	High	Low
Long-Range Potential	Average gain	High gain	High or low gain

Time to make some more associations and some choices. Seems like the choice here might be growth funds. They have it all: long-term growth, high diversity, and high gain. What's not to like. Balanced funds, meanwhile, are actually a combination of stock and bond funds. That's nice for balancing things out as you grow closer to retirement age, but with so much time to invest, straight growth might be better. Meanwhile, sector funds invest in very narrow market sectors such as paper or electricity. Sector funds offer little diversification, just like single stocks did.

Almost there. Now you need only choose a growth mutual fund to park your money. That shouldn't be too hard. There are only about 10,000 mutual funds in the United States, with about 4,000 of these being growth funds. To narrow the search, you go to the website of a well-respected investment company and view their list of top-performing growth funds from last year. You choose five of their top-performing growth mutual funds and organize them as in Table 7-6. Take a look and make a pick.

Table 7-6 MATRIX DISPLAYING TOP-PERFORMING GROWTH MUTUAL FUNDS

	A	B	C	D	E
Average Total Return					
Last Year	19%	32%	17%	24%	22%
5 years	NA	NA	16%	21%	18%
10 Years	NA	NA	19%	14%	18%
Risk	Average	Above average	Average	Above average	Average
Bull Market Performance	*****	*****	***	*****	****
Bear Market Performance	NA	NA	***	**	***
Minimum Investment	$1,000	$2,500	$250	$1,000	$250
Load	3%	3%	None	None	None
Manager Stability	1 year	1 year	2 years	6 years	12 years

What fund did you chose? Examining the growth fund matrix and making associations, you might choose Fund E for several reasons. First, it has average risk. Selecting the overly risky Fund B or Fund D might make you uncomfortable. Second, the small minimum investment is appealing, especially if you prefer having investments drawn from your monthly paycheck. Investing a thousand dollars or more each month might be too steep, starting out. Third, Fund E has no load (investment fee). A 3% load like that for Funds A and B would reduce a yearly $2,000 investment by $60. No sense giving money away when there are high-performing, no-load options. Best of all might be Fund E's stability. It performs well in both a bull market (four of five stars when stock prices rise) and a bear market (three of five stars when stock prices dip), it has a great 10-year return, and its fund manager has handled the fund successfully for 12 years. Meanwhile, it is yet unknown how Funds A and B perform in bear markets, and it is evident that Fund D does not perform well when the market turns bearish. And, other than Fund D, all other funds are in relatively new hands.

As you journey through the investment choice process, you'll want to regulate along the way.

- "How much can I reasonably invest?"

- "What is my risk tolerance? Can I really handle market downturns?"

- "Should my investments be taxed now (Roth IRA) or when I eventually withdraw the money (traditional IRA)?"

- "What is the history and trend of bear versus bull markets?"

- "In what companies does this mutual fund invest? Am I socially comfortable with those companies?"

Activity 7-4

Suppose you want to purchase a new smartphone. Use the SOAR method to make an informed choice among three possible phones.

Of course, you'll need to regulate the investments you make, from time to time, to see how they are performing and to determine if they still meet your investment goals and risk tolerance. So get that taillight fixed, and stay the course to your first million. By the way, don't trust an educational psychologist for financial advice.

Answers to Focus Questions

1. Lectures are fleeting, so as they occur, there is really only time for you to select and note lecture information. The other SOAR strategies are more likely to occur later, as you work with your notes. When reading, though, you can apply any and all SOAR strategies as you go. For example, at any point, you can organize text ideas or generate regulation questions for self-testing. Another difference is that text can be marked. You can use boxes to denote topics, circles to denote categories, and underlining to denote details. You can also insert numbers in the text that reference

organization, association, or regulation strategies, shown in the text margins or on note pages.

2. Writing is not a natural—either you have it or you don't—ability. Like any ability, it is learned. Take, for example, my own writing experiences. As a college student, I couldn't pass the English Writing Exam given three tries. But I learned how to write as a graduate student, thanks to my advisor's tutelage and critical feedback.

3. Most students write in a piecemeal fashion—one idea or one topic at a time. A study I co-conducted showed 86% of college students writing in this way (Luo & Kiewra, 2019a; Luo & Kiewra, 2019b). When you write, look for patterns in the data, and report those patterns. Also, write for your neighbor next door. Writing should tell an interesting, understandable, and enjoyable story that an uninformed neighbor can read and retell days later.

4. The associations made prior to writing became the cornerstones of the written essay. The associations were a synthesis of the creativity topics and were reported in the essay.

5. Writers should regulate as they: select information for their essay (e.g., Did I select key ideas?); organize that information (e.g., Did I organize ideas in a way that aids comparison?); associate information prior to writing (e.g., Did I make meaningful associations among the topics?); write their essay (e.g., Am I writing about how the topics are alike and different?); and assess what they have written (e.g., Did I tell a clear and convincing story my neighbor would understand, enjoy, and remember?).

6. Math skills are often taught one skill at a time. For instance, instruction might cover the formulas for calculating the area of squares, rectangles, and parallelograms one after the other, as if there is no relationship among the formulas. SOAR can help because it imposes an organizational mindset that spurs you to seek and understand how seemingly disparate things might be related. When you construct matrices to compare area formulas for four-sided polygons or compare calculation formulas for adding, subtracting, and multiplying polynomials, you can see the vital associations among math skills that were originally addressed in a piecemeal fashion.

7. SOAR impacted the how-to-invest-money problem by helping potential investors select and organize potential investment options, understand their relative values through association, and regulate their investment choices now and in the future.

Figure Credits

CHAPTER 8

The Mighty Ms

Mindset and Motivation

OVERVIEW

Objectives
Focus Questions
Mindset
Motivation

Desire
Intention
Focus
Sustain

Answers to Focus Questions

Objectives

1. Describe characteristics of fixed and growth mindsets, recognize examples of those mindsets, and provide a growth-mindset response to new situations.

2. Describe the components and subcomponents of DIFS.

3. Apply DIFS to further your academic growth and self-growth.

Focus Questions

1. What evidence is there that abilities are not fixed but can grow?

2. How do fixed and growth mindsets differ?

3. What is the danger of a fixed mindset?

4. How can people turn fixed mindsets into growth mindsets?

5. What are the four DIFS components?

6. What four factors can shape desire?

7. What are the four characteristics of effective goals?

8. What are the three planning recommendations for intention?

9. What are the four focus recommendations?

10. How are lifestyle changes and rewards helpful for sustaining motivation?

Just because you know about SOAR strategies does not mean you'll use them. To take full advantage of them, you'll need a **mindset** that assures you that they work and are under your control, and you'll need the **motivation** to employ them. This chapter addresses mindset and motivation: the Mighty Ms.

Mindset

Indicate whether you believe each statement below is largely true or largely false:

1. Intelligence is something you are born with, and it cannot be changed substantially.

2. People who are creative started out with superior minds. They have a special something most people lack.

3. Rodeo stars are born with natural athletic ability.

4. People who are really smart in school don't have to work hard. Their high achievement comes naturally.

All of these statements are false, and it's okay if you didn't know that. What's not okay, what's downright dangerous, is holding the belief that one's ability is inborn and fixed. I'll offer some evidence to dispel each statement and then explain why an ability-is-fixed mindset is so dangerous.

Scores on intelligence tests can and do change. In one study (Wellcome Trust, 2011), researchers gave 33 adolescents IQ tests and scanned their brains, tracked them for 4 years, and then retested their IQs and rescanned their brains. Results showed some wide IQ changes, with scores rising or falling as much as 20 points for some adolescents. Twenty points is a lot, enough to move someone from the average intelligence category (90–110, where about 50% of the population resides) to the gifted intelligence category (121–130, where about 6% of the population resides). The researchers were confident that intelligence changes were real (and not due to testing effects such as people's effort) because IQ changes were accompanied by corresponding changes in the brain's structure, as measured by the brain scans. None of this should be surprising because numerous studies show that learning changes brain structure in the same way that physical training changes muscles or aerobic capacity. One of the best-known studies involved London cab drivers. London is a complex city with about 25,000 streets. To become a London cabbie, one practices navigating the London streets for years before taking a series of difficult navigational driving tests to obtain a cab license. Brain scans indicated that such training increased the size of the brain's hippocampus, where spatial navigation takes place (Jabr, 2011).

Creativity myths have been dispelled. It is now well established that creativity is made, not born. There is no gift from the gods, no flash of inspiration. Instead, creative people, like Mozart and Picasso, toil in a domain for 10 to 20 years before mastering the domain and taking the next calculated and incremental step that breaks a mold or reshapes a discipline. Creative people tend to have normal intelligence and use ordinary problem-solving strategies familiar to us all. It is their wealth of knowledge and experience earned along the way, high motivation, and willingness to take risks that separate them from the pack. Almost anyone could be creative if they followed this pack-separating blueprint.

Ever seen this cowpoke with the goat in her hands and the rope in her mouth (Figure 8-1)? Likely not. She's from a little town, not much bigger than a June Bug, called Broken Bow. But her talents and fame are bigger than summer thunder on the open prairie. This is Jayde Atkins, and she is a National High School Rodeo champion. How did Jayde find the winner's circle? Not through some rodeo gene.

Figure 8-1 Photograph of Rodeo Champion Jayde Atkins

Jayde was raised on a small ranch in rural Nebraska that was well equipped for rodeo training. There were acres of riding land; a rodeo pen; training apparatus such as saddles, mechanical calves, and rodeo barrels; a stately horse barn; and a horse trailer for traveling to rodeos. Jayde began riding there when she was 2, under the tutelage of her parents, who themselves were rodeo riders and horse trainers. Jayde's parents taught her by modeling good riding and rodeo techniques, stressing fundamentals, and helping her practice—something this horse-crazed cowgirl did 5 hours a day. Step in Jayde's boots and you could be a rodeo champion too.

What about school success? There is widespread belief that some fortunate students have natural gifts and don't really have to work hard at school. That's not what I found when I studied the cream of the crop: National Merit Scholars who also ranked near the tippy top of their high school graduating classes. One of the students I investigated worked strategically about 9 hours a day on schoolwork, and another spent 4–5 hours a day preparing for college entrance exams or advance placement tests when those tests were in season. And, because he was homeschooled, those work hours were all business, not time spent passing between classes or waiting for others to catch on or catch up. Being homeschooled allowed him to "work on challenging things and to focus on strengths and interests" (Kiewra & Rom, 2019).

Activity 8.1

Take a few minutes to Google someone you admire who is highly talented—perhaps an athlete, entertainer, or author. Read their biographical information, and uncover things that happened in this person's life to produce such talent. From this activity, you should see that talent was made, not born.

Now, I'll explain why believing that abilities like rodeo riding, music, art, or academics are inborn and fixed is so dangerous. According to psychologist Carol Dweck, author of *Mindset*, there exist two types of ability mindsets: fixed and growth. Those with fixed mindsets believe that abilities are innate and generally unchanging—kind of carved in stone. What you have is what you've got. Conversely, those with growth mindsets believe that abilities are modifiable through one's skill and will. Skill is the strategies one uses (like SOAR); will is motivation.

With appropriate skill and unrelenting will, high achievement is within reach for most every student. What you have today can be changed tomorrow. Table 8-1 summarizes Dweck's classic mindset study that was described earlier in Chapter 1, showing that mindset can be influenced by the type of praise you receive and that your mindset influences your choice of easy or difficult tasks, how failure is perceived, and future performance (Dweck, 2008).

Table 8-1 RESULTS FROM DWECK'S MINDSET EXPERIMENT

	Fixed	Growth
Performance on Easy Test	High	High
Praised For	Intelligence	Effort
Test Choice	Easy to look smart	Difficult to learn new things
Performance on Difficult Test	Failed	Failed
Effort	Low	High
Feeling	Miserable	Enjoyment
Attribution	Not being smart	Needing to learn more
Performance on Second Easy Test Compared to Original Score	20% lower	30% higher

This and other mindset experiments reveal several fixed- and growth-mindset characteristics that influence how one behaves in school and in life. These contrasting characteristics are shown in Table 8-2. Those with fixed mindsets believe that ability is innate and unchanging. They believe they are who they are. That's why their goal is simply to appear smart or competent. Meanwhile, those with growth mindsets believe their ability stems from learning and is modifiable. That's why their goal is to learn and improve. Fixed-mindset people avoid challenges that might expose their deficiencies. Moreover, they expend little effort and quit when faced with obstacles for two reasons: (1) they don't believe that effort is the pathway to success, and (2) trying and failing makes them feel even less competent. Meanwhile, growth-mindset people welcome challenges. They expend effort and topple obstacles to meet those challenges and reach their goals. Those with fixed mindsets are not receptive to learning about strategies or employing them. They do not believe that strategies can alter their innate

Table 8.2 FIXED- VERSUS GROWTH-MINDSET CHARACTERISTICS

	Fixed	Growth
Ability Belief	Innate and unchanging	Learned and modifiable
Goal	Appear competent	Learn, improve
Challenges	Avoid	Welcome
Effort	Useless	Path toward goal
Obstacles	Give up	Persist
Strategies	Useless	Path toward goal
Feedback and Criticism	Ignore	Embrace, learn from
Success of Others	Threatening	Find lessons and inspiration

abilities. Meanwhile, those with growth mindsets are eager to learn about and use strategies, seeing them as vital tools for success. When a task is completed, fixed-mindset people shun feedback. Hearing about their mistakes makes them feel threatened and inadequate. So too does the success of others. Meanwhile, those with growth mindsets embrace feedback as a means to learn and grow. And, when others succeed, they find lessons and inspiration for their own growth.

Activity 8.2

For each scenario below, tell what the student is likely to do if he/she has a fixed mindset or has a growth mindset.

1. Georgia was assigned a challenging piece for her violin recital in 6 weeks. She is not sure if she will be able to learn it in time. How will she proceed?

2. Gabe's drama teacher is trying a new activity in class today. Each student will act out a short scene, and classmates will provide feedback about their acting. How will Gabe react to student feedback?

3. Leona is required to submit weekly reflections for psychology class. On her first reflection, she received a score of 4 out of 10. Her friend Tyler earned a perfect 10. How will Leona react?

So what does all of this have to do with you? Many college students have fixed mindsets as a result of past experiences where teachers, coaches, and parents fed them a steady diet of negative, fixed-mindset comments like:

- Math just isn't your thing.
- You must have inherited my clumsiness and bad eye-hand coordination.
- You are not a singer.

Or, perhaps they fed them positive fixed-mindset comments like:

- You were born smart.
- Science is in your blood.
- Athletics just comes easy for you.

Either way, these abilities-are-born comments, even when meant to praise, are the recipe for a fixed mindset.

If you have a fixed mindset, believing that ability is largely inborn and fixed, then you're likely to ignore the two things most likely to improve learning and foster success: skill and will. You're likely to ignore the SOAR strategies presented thus far that can boost your skill, and also likely to ignore the upcoming motivation lesson that can boost your will. If you have a fixed mindset, you're like the anorexic hermit crab mentioned in Chapter 1 that was afraid to grow, shed his confining protective shell, and step into a challenging new world where much can be experienced and learned (J. Waitzkin, 2007).

Fortunately, it's not too late to change, not too late to turn that fixed mindset into a growth mindset. Here are three easy steps:

1. *Believe that ability is made, not born.* At the start of this chapter, you were given evidence that intelligence, creativity, rodeo riding, and school success rest in the palm of your hand. All abilities do. As mentioned in Chapter 1, psychologist Benjamin Bloom (1985) studied 120 of the most talented people in six domains (piano, sculpture, swimming, tennis, mathematics, and neurology). His final conclusion was this: What any person in the world can learn, almost all persons can learn if provided with the appropriate conditions of learning. Ralph Waldo Emerson said, "Every artist was first an amateur" (Emerson, 1904). Believe it.

2. *Recognize and change mindsets.* Recognize when you are operating with a fixed mindset and change your approach to a growth mindset, as shown in Table 8-3.

Table 8-3 RECOGNIZING AND CHANGING FIXED MINDSETS

Fixed Mindset	Growth Mindset
I can't learn chemistry. I don't have a scientific mind.	If I use effective strategies, work hard, and seek help when needed, I can learn chemistry. I'm up for the challenge.
Oh shoot, I got a 63 on the first chemistry quiz. I'm dumb. I can't do this.	This is a wake-up call. I can do much better. I need to figure out what went wrong on the chemistry quiz and correct it.
If I try to learn to play the piano and fail, that will be embarrassing.	Learning to play the piano will be challenging but enjoyable. Every day I'll learn something new and improve a bit.
It makes me sick to see how much better Josh plays piano than me after 6 weeks.	Josh is doing great. Good for him. I need to find out how he's practicing and try some of his methods. I'm happy I've improved as much as I have in just 6 weeks. I'm in this for the long haul.
It stinks that I broke my finger. That's it, I'm done with piano.	It stinks that I broke my finger, but I can still practice and improve. I can really work on my left hand while my right one heals, and I can listen to piano pieces and practice mentally.

3. *Cultivate a growth mindset.* Take stock each day of your growth-mindset perspective. Ask and answer questions like these each day:

- What did I learn?

- What mistakes did I make that taught me something?

- What did I try hard at?

- What obstacles were in my way? How did I overcome them?

- Who can I go to for help?

- What challenges should I confront tomorrow?

In the end, develop a childlike appetite for personal growth and a thirst for learning and knowledge. Josh Waitzkin was a champion chess player as a child. He was so good that Hollywood made a movie about him called *Searching for Bobby Fischer*, based on a book written by his father (F. Waitzkin, 1988). As a young adult, Josh took up a totally new interest: martial arts. Josh approached martial arts with a childlike yearning to learn and develop, a growth mindset. He wasn't a famous champion anymore but just another guy in the room searching for martial arts wisdom. While other students checked out their appearance in the mirror or checked their watches, Josh was one with teacher, relishing every opportunity, consuming every subtle pointer. When it came time to train, Josh chose to fight those far beyond his skill level. He even asked these powerful opponents to target his weaknesses so he could strengthen his frailties. Time after time, he was knocked down, tossed from the ring, or thrown into plaster-shedding walls. But if Josh fell down seven times, he stood up eight. He was losing to win. Even when Josh broke his dominant hand, he trained his weaker hand until it became dominant. Throughout Josh's martial arts journey, he abandoned the safety of the shell and welcomed and embraced all challenges. His growth mindset drove him to do his best and to eventually claim a world title in a domain where he was once just another guy in the room (J. Waitzkin, 2007).

Activity 8.13

Describe an upcoming challenge you will face, and detail how you will take on that challenge with a growth mindset.

Motivation

What did you accomplish in the past 46 days, 8 hours, and 36 minutes? Perhaps you passed a couple college tests, did Pilates a few times at the rec center, got a haircut, and had the oil changed in your car. Not a bad month-and-a-half. Now let me tell you what Pete Kostelnick did in that time: He ran across America. The 29-year-old financial analyst from Lincoln, Nebraska ran 3,067 miles from San Francisco to New York and smashed a 36-year-old record for running across

America (yes, there are records for that too). To complete this odyssey, Pete averaged—hold on—over 72 miles a day, nearly three marathons a day. Each day he began his run at 3:00 a.m., ran 40 miles in about 7 hours, ate lunch (wouldn't you?), and then ran another 30 or so miles into the night. In total, he ran about 14 hours a day for 6 weeks. How are you feeling now about that 4-mile bike ride through the park last month?

How was Pete's accomplishment possible? Was he born with the running gene, with incredible running ability? You know that's not true from our mind-set discussion. Abilities are made, not born. In fact, Pete's a good runner but hardly elite. His best marathon time, for example, is 2:41, while the world record hovers just above 2 hours. An elite runner could claim his marathon prize and then run another 8+ miles before Pete finished the 26-mile race. Moreover, Pete is like the rest of us, not superhuman. He once thought it inconceivable that he would ever run a half-marathon (about 13 miles), thinking that distance was ridiculously far. And when he became ill and parked his running shoes for a while, he had to almost begin anew and slowly work his way back to his former fitness level.

The two keys to Pete's accomplishments are, of course, skill and will. Pete built his endurance skill one step at a time, as he trained as much as 200 miles a week and 10,000 miles a year while maintaining a full-time job. Pete's will, his motivation to do all this, arose from several sources. Primarily, Pete loved running. He enjoyed the movement, the comradery of other runners, and the wonderful destinations running led him. Pete also loved setting challenging goals, which were largely improvements in his own training and racing records, and he loved charting his daily progress toward goal attainment. He found these marked improvements in distance or time rewarding. As to why Pete set out to run across America faster than anyone before him, he was inspired by other runners who made that attempt or made other ultra-running attempts that pushed human endurance to its limits. Another motivator Pete had for completing the run was his wife. During his 6-week run, Pete never saw his wife until she hugged him at the finish on the steps of New York City Hall. Pete said, "My wife and I decided my biggest motivator would be to wait and see her at the very end" (Fox, 2017).

Pete's story speaks to the power of motivation. Motivation is the wind that turns the mill, the steam that drives the engine. Without it, things don't run—not Pete, not you. You need motivation to grow and succeed, academically and beyond. But know that motivation is not a disposition: "I really want to run a marathon," or "I really want to get an A in psychology." Talk is cheap. Instead, motivation is ultimately an action. It is taking the steps necessary to run a marathon or to earn an A in psychology.

The remainder of this chapter introduces you to a motivation method called DIFS, so that you can take action in any situation—from earning an A in psychology to completing your first marathon. DIFS is a first-letter mnemonic for remembering the method's four steps: **D**esire, **I**ntention, **F**ocus, and **S**ustain. And here are two more mnemonic hints for remembering DIFS: (1) "DIFS makes the difference." It is the difference between mediocrity and success. (2) Remember the sentence: "Do It For Success." Motivation's four factors, DIFS, help you Do It For Success.

Desire

You've met them: people with little or no desire. They go where the wind blows them. They bob up and down in life's waters. They are pawns—mere foot soldiers—in the chess game of life. They are cruisers, slackers, and laggards who don't expect much, do much, or get much. Then there are those with great desire who know what they want and want it badly. People like ultra-distance runner Pete Kostelnick. People like inventor Thomas Edison. One of Edison's many scientific desires was to create a better storage battery. During his quest, Edison went to his lab every morning by 7:00, ate a short lunch at noon (What's with these talented people and lunch?), and ate dinner at 6:00. By 7:30, he returned to the lab and often toiled until 2:00 or 3:00 in the morning. This schedule was followed for 5 months, 7 days a week. During this time, Edison conducted more than 9,000 experiments but never produced a suitable solution. When asked, "Isn't it a shame that with the tremendous amount of work you have done you haven't been able to get any results?" Edison responded, "Results! Why, man, I have gotten lots of results! I know several thousand things that won't work!" (Dyer and Martin, 2013). Real desire cannot be quashed.

Where does desire come from? Some psychologists believe that some people are naturally inclined toward challenge seeking and hard work. Some are born with a rage to master, in the same way border collies are born with a rage to herd. Perhaps. But psychologists know too that desire can be manufactured when one is exposed to (a) information, (b) emotional arousal, (c) models, and (d) rewards. Let's take a look.

Information can increase desire:

- Information about the accelerated rate of global warming might boost your desire to reduce your carbon footprint.

- Information about skin cancer might boost your desire to wear sunscreen and protective clothing when outdoors.

- Information about growth mindset might boost your desire to approach challenging tasks with an "I can do this" attitude.

- Information about the Battle of Marathon might boost your desire to learn about other events in the Persian Wars.

Emotional arousal can increase desire:

- Seeing a haunting news story about local families in need might boost your desire to sponsor a family during the holidays.

- Seeing a heartbreaking video about wildlife being tangled in plastics might boost your desire to reduce and recycle plastics.

- Hearing the powerful story of how Dick Hoyt, a once sedentary man, pushed or carried his disabled son Rick through hundreds of endurance events because it made Rick feel whole and exhilarated might boost your desire to one day give fully to your children.

- Reading the surprising story about Abraham Lincoln's many failures before being elected president might boost your desire to persevere in the face of failure or defeat.

Models can increase desire:

- Watching astronomer Carl Sagan in an episode of the historic television documentary *Cosmos* might boost your desire to become an astronomer or learn more about science.

- Listening to the music of Johnny Cash, Willie Nelson, and Kris Kristofferson might boost your desire to become a country singer or at least download some traditional country tunes.

- Experiencing your parents' devotion to their aging parents might boost your desire to show similar devotion to your parents as they age.

- Observing your English professor's love of writing might boost your desire to write.

Rewards can increase desire:

- Receiving high grades can boost your desire to study.

- A paycheck can boost your desire to show up for work.

- A compliment on your appearance can boost your desire to keep rocking Aviator glasses and a 3-day growth.

- A low utility bill can boost your desire to keep setting the thermostat a few degrees higher in summer and a few degrees lower in winter.

Activity 8.4

Provide actual examples where your desire to accomplish something was raised by (a) information, (b) emotional arousal, (c) models, and (d) rewards.

Once you recognize your desire, it is important to express it as a **goal statement**, a statement that says what you'll accomplish. Goal statements direct effort. They are the bull's-eye you aim at, the North Star you follow. Without goals, you're likely to drift like a balloon riding changing currents. Political strategist Scott Reed (n.d.) aptly said, "This one step—choosing a goal and sticking to it—changes everything."

Here are four tips for writing effective goal statements: Make them challenging, behavioral, long- and short-range, and public.

Challenging Goals

Architect Daniel Burnham said, "Make no little plans; they have no magic... Make big plans, aim high in hope and work" (Moore, 1921). Michelangelo said, "The greater danger for most of us isn't that our aim is too high and we miss it, but that it is too low and we reach it" (Robinson, 2009). Don't aim to pass a college course; aim to consume it, master it, and ace it. Don't aim to graduate; aim to graduate with distinction. Don't aim to get a job; aim to land a job that challenges and nourishes you. Don't aim to cut down on fatty foods; aim to be physically, mentally, and emotionally healthy. Don't aim to get married; aim to marry a life partner you love and cherish. Don't aim to save a few bucks for retirement; aim to pocket a million or more. You get the idea. To jump high, you must aim high. Motivational speaker Les Brown (n.d.-a) said, "No one rises to low expectations...If you go through life being casual, you will end up a casualty."

Behavioral Goals

Behavioral goals state the actual behaviors necessary to meet the goal. They are specific and measurable. They tell you exactly what to aim for and exactly what must be accomplished. For example, don't say, "I want to be healthy." This is too vague. It fails to specify the behaviors you'll demonstrate when the goal is met. A more behavioral goal might be, "I will lower my weight by 10 pounds and lower my resting heart rate to 68 beats per minute." Don't say, "I want to study psychology for an hour." That's also too vague. Specify the behavioral outcome: "I will study the four schedules of reinforcement. I will create a matrix to compare them, generate associations specifying how they are alike and different, and commit the information to memory using mnemonics." Now that's specific and measurable.

Activity 8.5

Write a goal statement for each of the following situations. Each goal statement should be challenging and behavioral.

1. Improving your diet.

2. Improving your time management.

3. Improving assignment completion.

Short- and Long-Range Goals

Because some goals you set will be long-range and take a while to accomplish, it would be helpful to also set some short-range goals that help you reach those longer-range goals. For example, you might set the long-range goal of becoming an attorney. Short-range goals you'll need to set and accomplish along the way might include minoring in political science, completing law-related internships, preparing for and scoring high on the LSAT, applying to law schools, and talking out of both sides of your mouth. You might set the long-range goal of hiking the 2,650-mile Pacific Crest Trail. Short-range goals might include reading extensively about the trail, gathering all the necessary equipment, completing a series of shorter backpacking excursions, saving the money needed to make the attempt, and subletting your apartment. Short-range goals are the stepping stones to meeting long-range goals.

Public Goals

When you make your goals public—sharing them with family and friends—two positive things can happen. First, others can support you on your journey. As you prepare for a marathon, they can offer training advice, buy you a subscription to *Runner's' World*, accompany you on training runs, or massage your sore calves. As you tackle semester courses, they can loan you books, send you care packages, meet you for a movie, or listen to your gripes about tyrannical professors. Second, they can remind you of your goals and encourage you should you veer off track. In *The Lion King*, Rafiki kept Simba on track in his quest to be king by striking him in the head and saying, "Oh yes, the past can hurt. But you can either run from it, or learn from it." My college English professor told me he had doubts about chasing his dream of earning a doctoral degree because he was already 36 years old. He shared his doubts with his father, saying, "It'll take 4 years; I'd be 40 when I graduate." His father offered this sage and convincing advice: "The way I figure it, you'll be 40 in 4 years anyway, with or without your doctorate."

Even posting goals, for your eyes only, can help remind you what you're trying to achieve. When I began running, my first big goal was to run a sub-3-hour marathon. I wrote that goal on index cards. I posted one on my nightstand to pull me out of bed to train on cold, dark mornings. I posted another on the refrigerator to discourage overeating. Many athletic teams post signs in locker rooms or in the walkways onto the field, offering one last reminder of what they seek to accomplish. Post your goals where you can't miss them: on calendars, inside notebooks, on your computer homepage and phone screen, and on shower walls (laminated). Paul H. Nitze (1991, p. 177), former secretary of the Navy, said, "One of the most dangerous forms of human error is forgetting what one is trying to achieve."

Intention

A goal without a plan is just a wish.

—Antoine de Saint-Exupéry (n.d.)

Intention is the planning that is done to meet the goal. Just as coaches need plans to win a game or architects need plans to build a house, you'll need plans to achieve your goals. As you draft your plans, consider three planning guides: (a) plan for success, (b) plan a foundation, and (c) plan time.

Plan for Success

I sometimes ask students anonymously what score they plan to achieve on a test. Many say 80, some say 70, and a few say 60. Say what? Why plan to scrape by or even fail? Why not plan for success?

Don't be a pessimist; they rarely succeed. Helen Keller said, "Believe. No pessimist ever discovered the secrets of the stars or sailed to an uncharted land or opened a new heaven to the human spirit" (Keller, 1903). Be an optimist; believe you can succeed. Philosopher Ernest Holmes (n.d.) said, "Believe as though you are, and you will be." An Arabic proverb advises: "Throw your heart out in front of you and run and ahead to catch it" (Arab Proverbs, n.d.).

The world record for the mile is 3:43. There was a time, though, that people thought it impossible to break the 4-minute barrier. Then, one day in the 1950s, Roger Bannister finally broke the barrier. After that, many runners eclipsed 4 minutes, including grandmothers and pastry chefs. Why? Because they now believed it possible and planned for success. Plan to succeed, not to scrape by or fail.

As you plan to reach your goal, list reasons you'll succeed. Students facing a test in a few weeks might offer these reasons for success:

- I plan to study 2–3 hours each day for the test.

- I plan to use SOAR strategies as I study.

- I have aced tests before, and I will do it again.

Plan a Foundation

Pete Kostelnick didn't run across America without support. He had a support team with him every mile of the way. They drove the support van across America, kept Pete on course, cooked his meals, washed his clothes, treated his wounds, massaged his sore feet, and offered encouragement. Pete was also joined by a cadre of local runners along the way, who helped the miles pass by more quickly and enjoyably. All these people were Pete's foundation, his rock. Pete had other foundational supports, such as satellite watches to show his amassed time and route for official record keeping, numerous pairs of running shoes, running garb for all sorts of weather, medical supplies, and food (Fox, 2017).

When Nebraska swimmer Olivia Calegan broke a slew of state records, she didn't do it alone. Olivia had a strong foundation. She had two older brothers who were champion swimmers, a father who quit his job to help train her, an Olympic-level coach, and elite teammates who pushed her to excel. She also had access to pools and gyms for training and high-tech competition suits that shed water like a duck.

As you plan to reach your goals, plan foundations that support you. As you strive to achieve an A in psychology, plan to find a study buddy or assemble a study group, locate distraction-free places to study, and collect additional study materials. As you strive to complete a marathon, plan to build a foundation for success. Seek running clubs, exercise partners, health food stores, running literature, comfortable running shoes, and seasonal running gear. Whatever your goals, align yourself with positive and helpful people who can guide and help you. As Les Brown said, "If you run around with losers, you'll become a loser," and "You can run faster with 100 people that want to go than with one hanging around your neck" (Reelblack, 2019).

Plan Time

Do you like classic rock? If so, you know that some classic bands weighed in on the topic of time. The Rolling Stones (1964) said, "Time is on my side, oh yes it is." But Crosby, Stills, and Nash (1982) said, "And there's so much time to make up everywhere you turn, time we have wasted on the way." Both ideas are in tune. When it comes to planning, time is a great ally—it's on your side. Time affords you opportunity to meet your goals. But it is also true that we waste time, running off course or never getting out of the starting block. To meet your goals, you need plans that allocate sufficient time, begin today, and involve regular investment.

Allocate sufficient time. Author Beryl Markham (1942) said, "If a man has any greatness in him, it comes to light—not in one flamboyant hour, but in the ledger of his daily work." Edison's inventions took years to develop. Calegan's state swimming records punctuated years of training. Great works, even those of luminaries like Mozart or Picasso, only come to fruition after years of preparation. Want to become a chess grandmaster? Figure on spending at least 10–20 years doing intensive study. Remember that experts are not born, they're made through hard work over many years. Whatever your goals, realize that achieving them will take time, so plan accordingly.

Begin today. Supreme Court Justice Sandra Day O'Connor said, "Slaying the dragon of delay is no sport for the short-winded" (Day O'Connor, n.d.). Don't delay in achieving your goals; plan to get started now. Mark Twain said, "The secret of getting ahead is getting started" (Twain, n.d.). Remember from Chapter 7 how starting now can make you a millionaire later. Spending 10–20 years becoming a chess grandmaster is a long time, but the sooner you begin, the sooner you get there. Too many students procrastinate. One interviewer asked students if they procrastinate. Twelve percent immediately said no, 46% thought they did, and 42% said they'd tell the interviewer later. Don't wait for approaching deadlines to get started. If you need to read 10 psychology chapters before midterm exams, read two this week and two each week following. Reverend Cardinal Cushing (n.d.) cleverly reminds us to "Always plan ahead. It wasn't raining when Noah built the ark." Christopher Parker said, "Procrastination is like a credit card: It's a lot of fun until you get the bill" (Pinola, 2011).

Invest time regularly. Regular investments—even small ones—pay off. Do you like to read? Are you amazed that some people read dozens of books a year? Don't be. Most do so by doing a bit of reading each evening after supper or before bed. Small investments become big ones over time. Want to run 1,000 miles this year? Just 3 miles a day. Find little pockets of time each day to get things accomplished, perhaps when waiting for a bus or medical appointment or when passing time between classes or before dinner. Use those precious few minutes to chip away at your goals. Also, don't lose sight of where you're going. Say no to requests that pull you off track. When someone tries to pull you downtown when you plan to exercise or study, say no. Warren Buffet said, "The difference between successful people and very successful people is that very successful people say 'no' to almost everything" (Blaschka, 2019).

Activity 8.6

Create a goal statement for a goal that you have. Then, detail your (a) plan for success, (b) plan for building a foundation, and (c) plan for allocating time.

Focus

> *Dreams don't work unless you do.*
>
> —John C. Maxwell

> *A knowledge of the path cannot be substituted for putting one foot in front of the other.*
>
> —M. C. Richards

Focus is getting down to work. Moving toward your goal. Following your plan— one step at a time—despite obstacles in your path. Here are four focus guidelines: (a) set a launch date, (b) work hard, (c) record progress, and (d) overcome barriers.

Set a Launch Date

Why wait to turn your intentions into actions? Get started soon; get started today. But getting started today is never easy while tomorrow beckons. Untold dreams have withered and died on tomorrow's doorstep while opportunity knocks today. If you're like most people, you pledge to begin next year, or this summer, or after things settle down at work, or a week from Tuesday, but that starting day never arrives. You become paralyzed in the starting block, locked in the launch pad. Don't be. Set a launch date to begin working toward your goal—the sooner the better—and stick to it. Pete Kostelnick's run across America began with a single step. Take that first step, and the others will follow. Author Wolfgang Von Goethe said, "Whatever you can do, or dream you can, begin it ... Seize this very minute ... Only engage and then the mind grows heated. Begin, and then the work will be completed" (Winokur, 1999). The philosopher Hillel simply said, "If not you, who? If not now, when?" (Taylor, 1897). Quoting an unknown source: "One day or day one? You decide" (Mirchevski, 2020).

Work Hard

Getting out of the starting block is vital, but so are the many strides that follow. Much work is needed to complete the journey. You've seen in this chapter that success does not come in a flash of inspiration, a dash of good fortune, or a dip in a potent gene pool, but through hard work. Recall the nose-to-grindstone stories of Olivia Calegan, Pete Kostelnick, Josh Waitzkin, Thomas Edison, the Merit Scholars, the London cabbies, and Jayde Atkins. All walked the walk. Author Jeffery Archer trumpeted that hard work trumps inborn talent: "Never be frightened of those you assume have more talent than you do, because in the end energy will prevail. My formula is this: Energy plus talent and you are king; energy and no talent and you are still a prince; talent and no energy and you are a pauper" (Archer, n.d.). Author Sarah Brown (n.d.) clucked, "The only thing that ever sat its way to success was a hen."

Record Progress

One key to Pete Kostelnick's ultra-distance success is charting progress toward his goals. Pete is a habitual recorder who meticulously tracks his workouts, mileage, and race results. He loves the recording process and loves seeing the progress he's made. You should do the same. It is reinforcing to record progress on a phone app, to place a tic mark alongside a completed goal, or to make a notation on a calendar proclaiming the day's accomplishment. These tiny marks of triumph feel good and are indelible footprints on the road to success.

Overcome Barriers

Pete Kostelnick's trek across America was not without obstacles. Pete battled snowstorms in Utah, fierce winds across the plains, a severely swollen ankle just 7 days from the start, and an accident that totaled his support van. Of course, fatigue and doubt were also unwelcomed companions nipping at his heels for 42 days.

As you sail life's seas following your North Star, there will be troubled waters—maybe blistering heat, fierce storms, and choppy surf. Faced with such barriers, you can abandon ship or sail on. On the sea, in school, and in life, barriers abound. The key is overcoming them, one way or another, come heat or high water. Maybe you go over, go through, or go around. But you go. No turning back. Publilius Syrus said, "Anyone can hold the helm when the sea is calm" (Lyman, 1856). President Woodrow Wilson said, "You should nurse your dreams and protect them through the bad times and tough times to the sunshine and light that always comes" (Williams, 2002).

Remember Isabelle from Chapter 3: late for class, back-row seat, sketchy notes, cyber-slacker? Surprise! She didn't have a good start to her college career. First semester GPA: 2.13. But it wasn't her fault—so she says. All kinds of barriers got in her way, such as these:

- "History class was too early; I'm not a morning person."
- "My sociology professor was boooooring!"
- "My biology class was too large. It was like 200 people."
- "I had little time to study, working 30 hours a week."
- "I caught a couple colds and couldn't go to class."
- "In math, the midterm test was unfair."
- "My boyfriend broke up with me, and I couldn't concentrate."

These all seem like barriers and legitimate explanations for Isabelle's low achievement. But let's look more closely and see if these barriers are outside Isabelle's control or if she is making excuses for situations she can overcome. Of course, we're not just talking about Isabelle; we're talking about you.

Don't be like Isabelle and try that "**I'm not a morning person**" excuse on your boss or drill sergeant. Arrive late or uninspired for work or roll call, and you'll likely be fired or dropping down for 100 push-ups. If you don't like getting up early, choose classes later in the day. Can't do that? Choose to go to bed earlier. Moreover, choose to get up well before class, exercise to get that blood flowing, take an invigorating shower, and eat a nourishing breakfast—all before class. You won't be tired then.

Let's assume Isabelle is right that her **professor is boring**. He speaks in a low monotone voice and barely has a pulse. Some statues move more. Ugh! No one wants that. But, if that's what you got, choose to deal with it. Boredom is a choice. As mentioned in Chapter 3, be on the edge of your seat, lean into the lesson, and take copious notes. Also, search the lesson for golden nuggets you'll want to save and re-examine. Remember that some people devote their lives to sociology. What do they find so interesting? Challenge yourself to learn despite the instructor's boring style.

When you go to a concert, there might be 10,000 other screaming fans; maybe 80,000 rabid spectators surround you at a football game. Large crowds don't detract at concerts or football games, and they need not dampen Isabelle's or your educational experience either. **Large classes** can seem intimidating or impersonal, but they needn't. As advised in Chapter 3, choose to move to the front of the classroom. This way, the class does not seem so big, and there are few distractions between you and the instructor. Also, choose to ask questions and offer comments; this makes the class seem smaller and more personal. Most instructors welcome student participation—even when a class is large. They too like when a class feels smaller and more intimate.

College is a **full-time job**, and Isabelle and you should treat it as such. If you're taking 15 hours, figure you should be studying another 30 hours on top of that. That's a full-time job. So choose not to work if you don't have to. If you believe you must work, ideally, choose to work about 10 hours a week at a job related to your major. But ask yourself if you really need to work. If you're choosing to work in order to keep your car insured and on the road, ask yourself if you really need a car while in college. Chances are, you don't. If you're choosing to work because all costs fall to you, ask yourself if a loan is a better option. Sure, it stinks paying back loans, but now is the time to reap the full college experience. If at all possible, choose to delay working. Throw yourself fully into college and seize all of its opportunities and benefits.

Getting sick is a drag. When you are sick, it is important to take good care of yourself and get better as soon as possible. But a few sniffles and a runny nose should not send Isabelle or you to the sidelines. Ask yourself if you are well enough to make it to class. But perhaps ask the question this way: "If today I had tickets to a concert, was competing in the conference volleyball finals, or was getting married...could I make it?" Because if you could, you could also make it to class. Don't be like poet Shel Silverstein's (2003) Peggy Ann McKay, who is only sick if it's a school day:

"I cannot go to school today,"

Said little Peggy Ann McKay.

"I have the measles and the mumps,

A gash, a rash and purple bumps.

My mouth is wet, my throat is dry,

I'm going blind in my right eye...

My brain is shrunk, I cannot hear,

There is a hole inside my ear.

I have a hangnail, and my heart is—what?

What's that? What's that you say?

You say today is...Saturday?

G'bye, I'm going out to play!"

If you must miss class due to illness, let your instructor know you are sick and not just skipping class. This tells your instructor you are not a slacker and paves the way for possible allowances, such as extra time to complete an assignment. Also, arrange for a friend to record the class (with the instructor's permission) so you don't miss a word.

Maybe Isabelle's **test was unfair**. Sometimes tests are unfair. Questions might be poorly constructed and not match objectives. And grading might not always be accurate or reliable. After all, most college instructors were never trained in evaluation. If you believe there was a problem with a test, you should politely and privately voice your concerns to the instructor, and on up the line to chairs and deans if you must. That said, you should primarily figure out what *you* did wrong by conducting error analysis, as described in Chapter 6. What content was missed? What type of items (fact, concept, or skill) were missed? Why were these errors made: Did you miss class, take sketchy notes, mindlessly read the text, or spend little time studying? Blaming the test for your poor performance is a dead end because it produces no positive changes on your part. You keep doing what you're doing and getting what you're getting—more low grades. Assigning blame to an unfair test even causes some students to become oppositional and give up. I've seen it; you've seen it. When the class goes over the test, the oppositional student challenges every test answer marked wrong. The student repeatedly whines, "Why wasn't my answer right?" The student isn't interested in understanding why an answer is wrong, only in challenging the instructor. Then the quitting starts. Instead of moving past a low test grade, the brooding student retreats to the rear of the classroom, sits sideways with folded arms and a look of defiance, and eschews note taking. Occasionally, steam pours from the student's ears. Of course, all of this counterproductive behavior can only lead to more low test scores, poor course performance, and misplaced blaming. When the student eventually fails the course, the instructor is again blamed for giving a failing grade. What students must realize, of course, is that instructors don't choose grades; students do. Students can choose to earn an A or F.

Isabelle's breakup was perhaps devastating. She and you are likely to experience occasional **personal problems**—from physical ailments to lost jobs to deteriorating relationships—in college and beyond. That's life. Personal problems hurt, but they need not disable. When a personal problem arises, it can consume your thoughts as you attend European history or study American literature, if you choose to let it. Instead, choose to isolate the problem. Set aside time to deal with the problem directly. For example, set aside time, outside of class or study time, to talk with a counselor or friend, record feelings in a journal, or simply be alone with your thoughts. Make dealing with personal problems a priority—but on your schedule, not theirs. Know too that history is filled with people who endured personal problems but achieved great success. Consider Mozart. In his later years, Mozart struggled with a lack of work, financial debt, poor health, and depression, yet he continued to compose outstanding works. Consider President Franklin D. Roosevelt. Roosevelt was crippled by polio and confined to a wheelchair, yet he became one of the greatest U.S. presidents. Don't let personal problems deter you from your goals.

Here are three other common barriers students experience and how you might overcome them.

"I'm bad at math. I stink at sports. I'm not musical."
This "I-lack-ability" barrier and its many flavors is distasteful now that you've consumed a growth mindset. The natural-ability belief is poisonous, because it dismisses the two things that really matter when it comes to attaining success: skill and will. If you believe that the blueprint for success is inborn rather than drawn by your own hand, then you won't bother applying proven strategies (skill) or trying hard (will). Your growth mindset reminds you that *you* draft all plans and outcomes. You can always improve your skill or bolster your will to attain your goal.

"I'm the product of a bad situation."
There is no shortage of bad situations: people encumbered by unemployment, a sour relationship, a devastating weather event, or just plain bad luck. And there is no shortage of people blaming bad situations for their failures. Talk shows and courtrooms are overrun with people blaming others for their misfortunes. With blame comes the abandonment of responsibility, the loss of hope, and yet another somebody-did-me-wrong country song. Cut it out. The blame game has no winners. Employment guru Robert Half (n.d.) said, "The search for someone to blame is always successful." What follows is a true story reported by *60 Minutes* showing that bad situations are reversible.

Franklin County, Mississippi is a rural place in the buckle of the Bible Belt. "Half the county is covered by national forest, the other half it seems by churches" (Alfonsi, 2017). Seven thousand people populate the county, which has only two stop lights and one elementary school. The pace is slow, the economy slower, and most people hold modest hopes for advancement given their isolated and near-poverty situation. That changed when a wealthy benefactor funded a school and community chess program. The benefactor found that chess positively

influenced kids in inner-city Memphis and wondered if similar results were possible in the country "where a chessboard was as out of place in the county as a
skyscraper." Dr. B, a charismatic and knowledgeable chess instructor, was hired
to make the best moves for the Franklin community. Chess was taught as part
of the school curriculum, just like math and science, and offered as a voluntary
after-school activity. In a short time, chess took hold in the classroom and after
school, with a couple hundred kids joining in for the extra lessons. And, after
that, most went home and played some more. Within 2 years, the magic of chess
instruction was revealed. The kids of Franklin County dominated the Mississippi
state chess championship, leaving one proud parent to explain: "What happened
is a bunch of hillbillies beat the snot out of a bunch of really educated, sophisticated people." That's not all. The players later traveled to the national chess
championship, where they competed against 1,500 scholastic players from 644
schools. Results were staggering. The fifth-grade team finished eighth in the
country, and the sixth-grade team placed 10th. But the most magical thing was
how minds were transformed, despite bad situations, from losers to winners.
One chess parent runs a café in town but believes that her son will [now] do
more than flip burgers for a living, saying it's fun to "see your kids dream a little
bigger than the county line." Another parent said, "You always want to see your
kids go further. And I think chess can be a vehicle to take 'em there...This gives
them a window at a young age, that, 'Hey, there's a whole world out there. I
don't need to set my goals at making eight dollars an hour, I need to set my
goals at whatever I want 'em to be.'" When four players were asked if the world
champion might someday emerge from Franklin county, they optimistically
responded, "Maybe. Absolutely. Absolutely. It's super possible." Dr. B taught
the community that chess pieces don't care about your rural roots or income;
success comes from learning and practicing good moves. When asked if chess
has made the community more hopeful, Dr. B optimistically said, "It's starting
to ... This flower hasn't blossomed yet ... There's a lot to come" (Alfonsi, 2017).

"I failed."

Of course you did! Everyone fails, everyone loses, even the great ones. Thomas
Edison and his team tested more than 3,000 bulb designs for 3 years before
inventing the light bulb. American fiction writer F. Scott Fitzgerald, author of
the *Great Gatsby* and many other great works of fiction, once had 122 rejection
slips pinned to his walls. How about contemporary horror writer Stephen King?
His first novel, *Carrie*, was rejected 30 times before it was published. Ditto for
author J. K. Rowling. Twelve major publishers thumbed their noses at her *Harry
Potter* script before a minor publisher accepted it. Know what happened to Walt
Disney before his Mickey Mouse fame? The editor of the *Kansas City Star* fired
him because he "lacked imagination and had no good ideas" (Mahalingam, 2015).
By now, you've likely heard that Michael Jordan, perhaps the greatest basketball

player ever, was cut from his high school basketball team. Did you know that Abraham Lincoln was defeated in seven elections before being elected the 16th President of the United States or that the Wright Brothers failed dozens of times over a 5-year period in their attempts to invent the first airplane? Harvard psychologist Howard Gardner (1997) studied extraordinary people and found that all shared a common virtue called framing. All framed their defeats and failures in positive ways. They saw failure not as an end but as an opportunity to learn what to try next. They saw failure as the price of improvement. General Colin Powell (n.d.) said, "There are no secrets to success. It is the result of preparation, hard work, and learning from failure."

In **summary**, choose toppling barriers over blaming and excuse-making. Cartoonists Don Wilder and Bill Rechin said, "Excuses are nails used to build a house of failure" (More, 2014). Elaine Maxwell (n.d.), an educational consultant, sums up focus and the importance of overcoming barriers best:

> My will shall shape my future. Whether I fail or succeed shall be no one's doing but my own. I am the force; I can clear any obstacle before me or be lost in the maze. My choice; my responsibility; win or lose, only I hold the key to my destiny.

Activity 8.7

Here are four barriers your friend says keep him from succeeding. In each case, convince him that these barriers can be overcome.

1. "My wrist injury will prevent me from practicing basketball."
2. "The best grade I can hope for in anatomy is a C. There are just too many things to memorize. I have a lousy memory."
3. "Schoolwork is going to suffer this semester as I pledge a fraternity."
4. "I can't get homework done because my roommate is always blasting music, having friends over, or telling me about his personal problems."

Sustain

Getting going on the road to success is great, but you must keep going. Motivation must be sustained, and that's not easy. Think about all the resolutions swept away like fallen confetti on New Year's Eve. One third are broken before the calendar turns to February, and 80% are never fulfilled. People tend to return to familiar paths and slip back into old habits. That's why people quit smoking ... umpteen times, or go on a diet ... again and again. But sustaining motivation produces remarkable results. Remember that the plodding tortoise kept going and won the race while the speedy hare slept. Understand that a small trickle of water for a million years reshapes landscapes more than an upstart earth-quake or volcano. Similarly, a student who plugs away throughout the semester and throughout college is likely to accomplish a great deal. My graduate school advisor dispensed a lot of valuable advice, but perhaps none more valuable than his parting advice following each meeting: "Stay with it now." What great advice. No matter how difficult or impossible things seem, no matter how many times you've failed, just stay with it, keep plugging away, keep moving toward your goals. Here are some ideas to help you sustain motivation, to help you stay with it.

First, understand that people are habitual characters. Forty-three percent of our daily actions stem from habits we developed. And habits, once established, are hard to break. Consider what happened in a research study that recruited two types of people: those who typically eat a lot of popcorn when they go to the movies and those who don't. Both groups were given popcorn to eat as they watched movie trailers. Half the people in each group were given fresh, tasty popcorn; the others were given old, stale popcorn. Among those who rarely ate popcorn in movies, they consumed a lot of the fresh popcorn but ate little of the stale popcorn, as you might expect. Among those who regularly ate popcorn, they consumed both types. Moreover, regular popcorn eaters eating the old, stale popcorn reported that it tasted awful. Why then did they eat old, stale popcorn they knew was bad-tasting? Habit. Eating popcorn is what they habitually do in movie theatres, so they ate the crummy popcorn even though they found it distasteful (Vendantam, 2019).

Second, understand that habits hold up even when people know they're not right, even when people want to make a change for the better. When health experts championed the benefits of eating five fruits or vegetables a day, people did not increase their fruit and vegetable intake, even though they knew they should and wanted to do so, because it was not their habit. When the Surgeon General made clear that smoking was a lethal habit linked to lung cancer and emphysema, smoking did not decline among habitual smokers, even though they knew that smoking was dangerous and that they should quit. Habits are stronger than information, stronger than willpower. How, then, can bad habits be broken and good habits be established?

Make Lifestyle Changes

Lifestyle changes can build and sustain positive habits. Smokers did not quit when they knew smoking was dangerous, but they did when their lifestyle changed because of government policies that choked out smoking. The price of ciga-rettes skyrocketed. Alluring cigarette ads were replaced with deadly warnings. Cigarettes were no longer easy pickings in store aisles and vending machines. They were forbidden fruit, tucked behind a protective counter. Smoking was outlawed on planes and busses, in restaurants and bars, and in offices and parks.

Of course, you don't need the federal government in order to build and sustain positive habits. You can choose to make your own lifestyle changes. If you want to stop eating sweets, don't rely on willpower. Remove sweets from your home and replace them on your grocery list with fruits and vegetables. If you want to exercise regularly, build a lifestyle compatible with regular exercise. Kick fitness-draining habits like partying, overeating, and late nights to the curb. Build a lifestyle compatible with exercise: plenty of sleep, healthy foods, and water. Make exercise convenient by doing it close to home. One study found that people living 3.5 miles from the gym went there five times a month, while those living 5 miles from the gym went there just once a month. To make sure she stuck to her morning exercise routine, Wendy Wood (2019), author of *Good Habits, Bad Habits: The Science of Making Positive Changes That Stick*, wore her exercise clothes to bed.

Dispense Rewards
Rewards are also vital to habit development. Many of our bad habits, like eating sweets, smoking, and drinking alcohol, bring on an immediate dopamine rush in the brain that rewards and sustains those nasty habits. Healthy habits like eating vegetables, drinking water, and running do not produce the same dopamine rush and reward and have little chance for survival—unless you make such activities more immediately rewarding. So find the immediate rewards in what you do. Mix vegetables into a delicious stir-fry casserole. That's rewarding. Add a slice of refreshing lemon to enliven your drinking water. That's rewarding. Run in wondrous places along the shore, through the woods, or at sunrise. That's rewarding. Although we know that healthy behaviors will eventually yield long-range health benefits that are in themselves rewarding, it helps to receive temporary rewards that keep us on course along the way.

Activity 8.8

Suppose your goal is to read more. What lifestyle changes might you make to sustain your efforts toward this goal? Indicate too how you might use rewards to sustain your reading efforts.

Reinvent
Another idea to consider in establishing and sustaining new habits is **reinvention**. When our lifestyle goes topsy-turvy because of life disruptions such as moving, a new job, or marriage, this tumultuous time is actually ripe for reinvention— trying new things. And if you are just getting started in college, then you are a prime candidate for reinvention. Things are new and fresh, and nobody knows the old, high-school you when you acted above it all, like you didn't care about school. Reinvent. Try new things in college, like you are trying on new clothes. Be like George on *Seinfeld*. Try the opposite. If your everyday instincts have come up short, try the opposite. Come prepared to class. Sit in the front of the room. Speak up. Meet with your professor outside of class. Smile and show your

excitement for learning. Study hard. Join academic clubs. Play intramural field hockey or bass guitar. Grow a mustache. Wear a fedora. Reinvent yourself. Create a lifestyle that can carry you where you really want to go … minus the fedora.

Table 8-4 summarizes the DIFS motivation method. The subsequent box presents a DIFS motivation method example.

Table 8-4 SUMMARY OF DIFS MOTIVATION METHOD.

	Desire	Intention	Focus	Sustain
Definition	Goal you want to reach	Plan for reaching goal	Hard work for reaching goal	Sustained effort and habits for reaching or maintaining goal state
What to Do	Develop challenging, behavioral, public, and long-and short-range goals	Plan for success, plan a foundation, and plan time	Set a launch date, work hard, record progress, and overcome barriers	Make lifestyle changes, dispense rewards, and reinvent

Example of DIFS Motivation Method

Sasha is struggling with bad grades and a downcast disposition early in her first college semester. She is not engaged in classes, in college activities, or with other people. She thinks the root of her problem might be an overuse and misuse of her smartphone. She seems to be forever on her phone. So she naturally fires up her phone to collect some **information** and finds a site describing the ramifications of digital distractions. She learns:

- Technology can become negatively addictive.
- Smartphones drain brains and distract. Your ability to think is hindered when phones are within reach, even if they are silenced or powered down. The urge to check your phone can be overpowering.
- The more you are on social media, the worse you feel about yourself.
- Excessive screen time is associated with less sleep and poor sleep quality.
- An app on Sasha's phone indicates that she is using her phone 8–10 hours a day.

Sasha also experienced **emotional arousal** recently, while home for a weekend. Both her family and friends noticed her phone dependency and lack of human socialization. They made comments like, "Can't you put that phone away and talk to us?" and "Maybe we should text or FaceTime you?"

Sasha has also noticed that her roommate is breezing through her studies, is involved in several activities, has a lot of friends, seems happy, and is rarely tied

continues

down by technology. Sasha thinks her roommate is a **model** for how she would like to be.

Sasha wants to change; she wants to cut down on unhealthy phone use. To do so, she is guided by DIFS.

Desire

Challenging and behavioral long-range goal: Cut phone use to 1 hour per day maximum and restrict its use to necessary communication and website browsing by January 15.

Short-range goals: Cut daily phone use to 6 hours by October 15, to 4 hours by November 15, and to 2 hours by December 15.

Goal posting: Post goals on my phone and computer screen (I certainly look there a lot), on my bathroom mirror, and on the center console of my car. Share my goals with my family and roommate, all of whom have agreed to support me.

Intention

Plan for success: I plan to be successful because I have successfully committed to things before, such as rehearsing every day for show choir in high school. I also have no choice but to succeed. I see my grades suffering and my college future on the line. My long-held goals of graduating from college and becoming an engineer are in jeopardy. Moreover, I don't like the sullen person I've become, and there are people willing to help me.

Plan a foundation: People-wise, my family and roommate will watch over me, making sure that I am not checking and using my phone too much. I gave them free reign to comment when they see excessive use. From an environmental standpoint, I plan to leave my phone in the residence hall when I go to classes and to turn it off and place it in my purse when I study. I also plan to replace some of my previously spent phone time with more healthy and social activities. I plan to play intramural tennis, join a study group for my engineering class, and take a 30-minute walk each day with my roommate (sans phone). I plan to regulate phone time to certain times of the day.

Plan time: I've restructured my days to look like this for the first month, as I set out to meet my goal:

- 7:00-8:00, phone time
- 8:00-9:00, walk and dress
- 9:00-10:00, breakfast with friends in dining hall
- 10:00-12:00, classes
- 12:00-1:00, phone time and lunch on own
- 1:00-5:00, classes and study time
- 5:00-6:00, phone time
- 6:00-7:00, dinner with friends in dining hall

continues

- 7:00-8:00, tennis
- 8:00-9:00, phone time
- 9:00-11:00, study time
- 11:00, bedtime

Focus

Set a launch date: With goals and plans in place, I begin tomorrow morning.

Work hard: It will be work to make these drastic life changes. I'm committed to change and will do my best every day to follow the plan.

Record progress: I will use the "plan time" schedule above to keep track of my progress. In addition, I will check my phone-use app each night and record my total phone time. I will also chart my course grades and intend to see those rising throughout the semester.

Overcome barriers: The biggest barrier will be the ongoing temptation to grab my phone. I'm so used to that. And once it's in my hand, I go through a whole routine of texting, checking Facebook, and browsing my go-to apps and websites. My plan to leave the phone in my room while in classes and turned off in my purse while studying should help, as should my involvement in healthier and more socially appropriate activities. Another barrier will arise as I seek to further curtail phone use throughout the semester, because more unstructured time will come available. I plan to fill that additional time by studying more and by joining the university STEM club. Both activities should also help me meet my college success and engineering occupation goals. Another barrier is simply feeling out of touch if people are trying to contact me and my phone is off or not with me. To overcome this barrier, I simply must realize that most contacts are not so important and can wait a few hours for a response, if one is even necessary. Hey, for centuries people lived without instant communication, and so can I.

Sustain

Make lifestyle changes and reinvent: I already described several lifestyle changes that will help me sustain curtailed phone use, such as a restructured day, incorporating healthy social and physical activities throughout the day, placing my phone off-limits where it cannot be reached at most times, and designating specific phone-use times. In addition, I will reinvent myself and better play the role of an engaged college student. I will attend all classes, sit toward the front, take copious notes (in a notebook, not on a laptop), speak up in class, and visit with my professors.

Dispense rewards: Charting and seeing my progress will be rewarding. So too will the physical enjoyment of walking and playing tennis. It will also be rewarding to socialize in person with others in study groups, clubs, sports, classes, and meals. Seeing my grades rise will be rewarding. Although less quantifiable, simply feeling happier and more fulfilled might be the greatest reward.

Answers to Focus Questions

1. There are many lines of evidence that abilities are not fixed and can grow. IQ scores can rise as many as 20 points over a few years. Creativity does not come via high intelligence or in a flash of inspiration but from toiling in a domain for 10–20 years, having high motivation, and taking risks. Rodeo champion Jayde Atkins succeeded because of early opportunities and training, parental instruction and support, and a lot of practice. School success is no different. National Merit Scholars were highly motivated, were hard workers, and had superior educational opportunities.

2. Table 8-2 is a good summary of how fixed and growth mindsets differ. Most importantly, those with fixed mindsets believe that abilities are fixed and unchanging, whereas those with growth mindsets believe that abilities are learned and modifiable. The goal of fixed-mindset people is to appear competent, so they avoid challenges. They don't expend much effort or use strategies because they believe both are useless. They give up when confronted by obstacles, ignore feedback, and are threatened by others' success. The goal of growth-mindset people is to learn and improve, so they welcome challenges. They try hard and are strategic because they believe both will lead them to their goals. They persist in the face of obstacles, embrace feedback, and find lessons and inspiration in others' success.

3. A fixed mindset is dangerous because it leads one to dismiss the two things most likely to yield success: skill and will. Those with fixed mindsets are not likely to try hard (will) or use strategies (skill) because they believe abilities are innate, not made.

4. Fixed mindsets can be turned into growth mindsets by (a) believing that abilities are made, not born as described in Focus Question 1, (b) recognizing fixed mindset reactions and consciously changing them to growth mindset reactions (e.g., "I can't play tennis; I'm not athletic" becomes "If I get some coaching and practice hard, I can learn to play"), and (c) cultivating a growth mindset by taking stock each day of growth mindset perspectives (e.g., "Look what I learned today by analyzing my test errors").

5. The four DIFS components are Desire, Intention, Focus, and Sustain. Desire represents the goals you desire to attain. Intention represents your plan for attaining your goals. Focus represents the hard work you do to attain goals. Sustain represents your sustained effort to attain goals and maintain your new status.

6. The four factors that can shape desire are information, emotional arousal, models, and rewards. Why might someone desire to wear seatbelts? Perhaps he reads information like the following: Seatbelts reduce the risk of

death by 45% and critical injury by 50%. Perhaps he reads an emotional story about five adolescents dying in a car crash when none were wearing seatbelts. Perhaps his parents and close friends are role models for regular seatbelt usage. Perhaps he is praised (rewarded) by others for seatbelt wearing and once came through a minor accident without injuries because he wore a seatbelt.

7. The four characteristics of effective goals are: (a) challenging, (b) behavioral, (c) long- and short-range, and (d) public. Goals should be challenging. To quote Les Brown (n.d.-b), "No one rises to low expectations." Goals should be stated behaviorally. They should be specific and measurable so that it's clear when you've achieved them. Don't say, "I want to be a good student." That's vague. Perhaps say, "I want to earn an A in history and in English literature and attain at least a 3.5 GPA this semester." If you set a long-range goal such as earning teacher certification, then you should also set short-range goals that help get you there, such as completing required courses and completing student teaching. Making goals public, such as telling family and friends or posting them on Facebook, is helpful because others can support you and remind you of your goals should you veer off track.

8. Intention is planning to meet your goals. When you plan, you should plan for success, plan a foundation, and plan time. Plan to succeed, not fail. Draw on past experiences and future actions that ensure success. For example, "I know I'll nail my piano recital because I have done it before, and I'm going to spend 3 hours a day perfecting it." Plan a foundation that can support you on your quest. If your goal is to earn an A in history, then support that effort by lining up a study group and scheduling weekly meetings, meeting occasionally with your instructor to ask questions, acquiring online resources, setting aside ample time to study each day, and securing a quiet place to do your work. When you plan how you'll spend time meeting your goal, be sure to invest ample time each day, beginning today.

9. The four focus recommendations are (a) set a launch date, (b) work hard, (c) record progress, and (d) overcome barriers. Goals and plans are nice, but you've got to get down to work to realize your dreams. Don't wait for the optimal time to begin. It might never come. Set a launch date—as soon as possible—and simply begin. Remember that one's accomplishments are largely a function of hard work. Anything worth achieving is likely to involve some heavy lifting. Record your progress as you go, to be sure you're making progress toward your goals. Recording progress is also rewarding as you check off or list accomplishments. No matter how hard you work, barriers will arise. Most, though, are self-imposed (such as work obligations

or fatigue) or seem more imposing than they really are (such as a large class or personal problems). Whatever the barrier, remember that you have the freedom to find ways around it, over it, or through it. Don't be denied.

10. It is difficult to sustain motivation. To do so, it's best if you can adjust your lifestyle to your goals and behaviors. That way, your actions and lifestyle are compatible and not at odds. If you want to achieve running goals, then leading a lifestyle that involves smoking, partying, fatty foods, and late nights is incompatible with reaching or maintaining that goal. So adapt your lifestyle to one compatible with the running goal: no smoking, ample sleep, a healthy diet, and positive and supportive friends. Rewards also help you build habits of success. Achieving the end goal is certainly rewarding in itself but could be a long way off. So create reward opportunities along the way. While you're striving to break 36 minutes for a 10K run, find and enjoy rewards along the way, like running 10K in 40 minutes, the company of other runners, beautiful running paths, and your increasingly healthy body. Finally, when opportunity for a fresh start beckons: reinvent. Try on a new lifestyle.

Figure Credit

Life and Time Management

OVERVIEW

Objectives

1. Describe the characteristics of effective life management and explain how you can apply each characteristic to achieve academic success.

2. Describe the time-management investment principles and explain how you can apply each to improve your use of time.

3. Generate block, semester, and weekly time schedules for the current semester.

Focus Questions

1. "Every artist was first an amateur." What does that mean?

2. What does *follow your bliss* mean?

3. What is focused integration?

4. What is a center of excellence, and what roles do such centers play in attaining domain expertise?

5. What is deliberate practice, and how does it differ from how most people practice?

6. Summarize the daily routines of productive scholars and creative people.

7. Why are study groups useful, and how should they be formed?

8. What are the components of a block schedule?

9. How can the principles of investing early and investing daily be applied when you are assigned a term paper?

10. What goes in a semester planner and in a weekly planner?

Life Management

Take a look at Table 9-1. There you'll see the staggering publication numbers of three highly productive educational researchers at the times I interviewed them. As you can see, the three scholars produced an average of 6–11 publications per year over 20–35 years. And, just so you can see that the scholars did more than publish, here is a listing of some of Michael Pressley's accomplishments from just one year:

- Published articles—18
- Published books—3
- Edited books—2
- Journal editor—2 journals
- Journal editorial boards—9
- Major awards—2
- Department chair

Table 9-1 PUBLICATION TOTALS FOR PRODUCTIVE EDUCATIONAL RESEARCHERS

	Michael Pressley	Patricia Alexander	Richard Mayer
Published Books	8	8	27
Published Articles	203	173	329
Years in Service	20	30	35
Average Publications/Year	11	6	10

You already know from reading this book that the talent displayed by these educational scholars wasn't born, but made—as are all abilities, from archery to zoology. The key question now is: How were their talents made? What allowed them and the other educational researchers I studied to be so productive? The answers to this question have important implications for anyone who seeks to be successful, in school and beyond, in any area. Like you.

Take the Leap

You look at these amazing scholarly publication numbers, or those of top fiction authors like Danielle Steele and Michael Connelly, and think, "I can't do that; the gap between them and me is too far." When I interviewed Michael Pressley, he told this story about the gap:

> A child comes before a tribal leader for his initiation into adulthood. The boy must jump from a cliff. The leader nudges the boy toward the edge; the child recoils in fear. The sage leader calmly says, "Go ahead and jump. It's not as far as it looks."

Pressley faced and bridged the gap. He said:

> If anybody had really told me when I was in graduate school that I'd be sitting where I am right now, I probably wouldn't have believed it, but in retrospect it isn't as far from there to here as I would have thought at the time (Kiewra & Creswell, 2000).

Don't be intimidated by those farther along the path; be energized. Know that they started at the same place as you. Remember what Ralph Waldo Emerson (1904) said: "Every artist was first an amateur." Scan the horizon, take a deep breath, and take the leap. It's not as far as you think.

Follow Your Bliss

When I asked productive educational researchers what advice they would dispense to budding scholars, all said the same thing in one way or another: Don't play it safe. Don't be content following someone else's path. Follow your bliss! Want to become a veterinarian? Pursue that. Want to become a circus clown? Pursue that. Be like Alexander Hamilton in the musical *Hamilton* and don't throw away your shot.

Motivational speaker Les Brown warned, "There is no safe position in life. You can't get out alive. You can die on the field or in the bleachers. You might as well come out on the field and have a good time" (Reelblack, 2019). Don't throw away your shot. Come out on the field. Follow your bliss. Here's how.

Don't follow the crowd. Carve your own path. Richard Anderson, another productive scholar I interviewed, urged budding scholars to conduct pioneering science. He said: "I feel that too many people are contributing footnotes to other people's history rather than making some substantial and unique—at least distinctive—contribution on their own" (Kiewra & Creswell, 2000). Anderson warned against being a normal scientist who nudges the field along by simply making slight modifications to other people's work.

They say when you're about to die, your life flashes before your eyes. New York Comedian Woody Allen offers this humorous life-flashing take:

> And suddenly my whole life passed before my eyes. I saw myself as a kid again. Kansas. Going to school. Swimming at the swimming hole. Fishing. Frying up a mess-o-catfish. Going down to the General Store. Getting a piece of gingham for Emmy-Lou. And, I realized it's not my life. They're going to hang me in two minutes [and] the wrong life is passing before my eyes. (Allen, 1999)

Make sure that doesn't happen to you. Apple founder Steve Jobs (2005) said, "Your time is limited, so don't waste it living someone else's life." Live the life you dream. Follow your bliss.

Stay Focused

In the Shakespeare play *Hamlet,* Polonius said, "To thine own self be true." Stay true to yourself, to your bliss. It's certainly right to help others, but it is imperative that you help yourself. Sometimes, you must say "no" to others in order to stay focused on your dreams and tasks. When psychologist Mihaly Csikszentmihalyi (1996) studied creative people, he found that they focused on their work and commonly ignored things that got in the way of completing their work. Here is how one creator responded when invited to participate in the study:

> I hope you will not think me presumptuous or rude if I say that one of the secrets of productivity is to have a VERY BIG waste paper basket to take care of ALL invitations such as yours. Productivity in my experience consists of NOT doing anything that helps the work of other people but to spend one's time on the work the good Lord has fitted one to do, and do it well. (Csikszentmihalyi, 1996)

I would add that when you do say "yes" to something, no matter how big or small, say it with all your heart and soul. Be mindful, fully in the moment, and exert your best effort.

Staying focused does not mean you need be one-dimensional. Michael Pressley credited his widespread productivity to what he called focused integration. Many professors teach classes, conduct research, and serve their profession as if those were three distinct and separate jobs, with little connection among the three. They're pulled in three or more directions. Not Pressley. He integrated teaching, research, and service. For example, when his research interest turned to strategy instruction, he taught a class on this topic and wrote a strategy instruction book with students in the class that served educators everywhere. Rather than be pulled in multiple directions, Pressley focused his efforts on integrated goals (Kiewra & Creswell, 2000). This way, Pressley was able to feed two (or more) birds with one scone. You can employ focused integration too. If you're studying zoology in college, find volunteer work related to animals and join clubs related to science or animals.

Hone Your Knowledge and Skills

Whatever domain you pursue, each has unique information and skills to be acquired and mastered. In chess, for example, you must obtain knowledge and skill about hundreds of openings such as French Defense and Ruy Lopez, numerous tactics such as fork and skewer, and numerous principles such as controlling the center and trading pieces when ahead. In astronomy, you must acquire knowledge about, well, the universe—galaxies, stars, planets, black holes, and deep space. And you must acquire technical skills for observation, calculation, and statistics. The main sources of knowledge and skills are instruction and practice.

Not all instruction is equally effective. The productive educational researchers I studied knew that and gravitated to centers of excellence—the best colleges and graduate schools in their field. There, they were mentored by top scholars and worked with other students on the discipline's cutting edge. Richard Anderson, who was mentioned earlier, received his doctorate from Harvard University, where he was mentored by a famous psychologist linked to a long line of other famous psychologists rolling back to the dawn of psychology. Michael Pressley left his own graduate school for a time and gravitated to another university where top researchers were studying his intended topic—memory strategies (Kiewra & Creswell, 2000). I also investigated four highly productive scholars tied to a single center of excellence: Ludwig-Maximilian University in Munich, Germany. Three graduate students gravitated there to work with and be mentored by Professor Hans Mandl. In about a decade, the quartet produced over 200 collaborative works. Wow. One of Mandl's students, Alexander Renkl, said, "I grew up in a rich academic environment where it was clear you had to be productive ... It's important for young students to go to a productive group because you adapt to what others do. If you're in the Mandl group and all others are publishing, then you want to do the same. If you're in a group with people who are only publishing once a year, then you do the same" (Flanigan et al., 2018).

Centers of excellence, talent hotbeds, exist in every domain. Mozart, Freud, and others during the classical period gravitated to Vienna, Europe's intellectual hub. Movie stars have long basked in the bright lights of Hollywood, theater actors in the stage lights of Broadway. Musicians gravitate to The Juilliard School, engineers to MIT, and tech-savvy folks to Silicon Valley.

Mentors not only guide you through teaching and collaboration, they also open doors that might otherwise be closed to you. They can help you publish, get grants, get jobs, and establish a professional network with other influential scholars. Hans Gruber, another Mandl protégé, credits his mentor for involving him in research, escorting him to conferences, and helping him build a professional network, particularly with two prominent scholars who shaped Gruber's career (Flanigan et al., 2018). Patricia Alexander, one of the three productive scholars mentioned at the outset, said, "[My mentor] set my life on a trajectory that I still pursue. She was a superb role model for what it means to be a scholar, and I took those lessons to heart … No one [becomes successful] without others supporting, guiding, and mentoring. Everyone who is successful had a successful mentor somewhere in his/her life" (Patterson-Hazley & Kiewra, 2013). You get the idea. Sniff out the best places and people and gravitate there, or connect with them through visits, professional conferences, or electronic correspondence. Throughout my career I've helped dozens of faculty, students, or parents who did nothing more than send me a request for assistance. People like to use their talents to help and nurture others. Simply ask.

You've heard the old joke. A stranger in New York City asks a local passerby, "How do I get to Carnegie Hall?" The response: "Practice, practice, practice." Training in a center of excellence is an important stop on the way to Carnegie Hall, but the passerby was right. Only practice, practice, and more practice can deliver you.

Practice, though, is different than logging a lot of playing time. I know this firsthand. For years, I played a lot of golf but never improved much. Just knocking balls around the course or spraying a bucketful around the range never transformed me from duffer to Tiger. To do that, I'd have to practice like Tiger—spending hour after hour perfecting my putting stroke, shaping golf shots on the range, repeating shots from various lies, and lifting weights. I'd have to practice the right way, doing what psychologist Anders Ericsson calls deliberate practice. Deliberate practice is focused on subtle skill improvement. It is arduous and intense. It requires full concentration, is often carried out alone, and is not necessarily enjoyable. In one study, Ericsson investigated the practice routines of musicians over a 15-year period. Although all the musicians spent similar time engaged in music activities, those who spent the most time engaged in deliberate practice were the most accomplished (Ericsson & Pool, 2016). This is not surprising because others have found that experience alone—years on the job—does not lead to improvement and can actually lead to worse performance over time. Why? The person is not practicing deliberately, not challenging himself, not learning new things. His skills erode. He gets worse. Psychologist Benjamin Bloom also touts the importance of deliberate practice. Bloom was the psychologist who studied the 120 most talented Americans in six domains. Although siblings in those families shared similar genetic stuff and were raised in the same environment, only a few ever came close to the level of accomplishment of their talented sibling. The sibling who made it was the one who practiced most and best (Bloom, 1985).

So what does deliberate practice look like? I studied two record-setting high school swimmers in Lincoln, Nebraska. Practice was deliberate and exhausting. Although the swimmers were nearly Olympic caliber, practice focused on minor technical improvements. Over and over, the swimmers practiced proper elbow position, arm reach, and hand pitch. And they practiced to exhaustion. Here's Caroline Thiel:

> Some days in practice you're just so exhausted. You're sore and your entire body aches, and it's hard to find motivation. But you remember your goals and you find motivation. You push through each 100-, 50-, or 25-yard sprint. Your brain shuts down but your body keeps going through the muscle aches and heavy breathing and throwing up. People don't realize how hard swimming is and how hard we practice. People think you just get in the pool and swim a few laps. (Kiewra, 2019)

Deliberate practice in academic circles is much the same, minus the throwing up. Take writing. To improve writing skill, set a challenging goal like improving sentence structure. Consult writing books that show what polished sentence structure looks like. Read widely and find examples and non-examples of polished sentence structure. Practice improving the tarnished sentence structure of others. Write something new every day, always striving for flawless sentence structure. Have a writing expert read your writing and offer sentence structure feedback. Once sentence structure is mastered, practice another writing skill like transitions.

Activity 9.1

What is your bliss? How can you follow your bliss now while in college? How can you stay focused and hone your knowledge and skills?

Get Into a Routine

Among the productive scholars I interviewed, most work about 50 hours a week, a rather modest workload given their high productivity. All agreed that productivity is a function of how those hours were spent. Most adopt a daily routine. In most cases, this involves preserving and protecting the morning hours for writing because writing is their most important activity and because they are fresher in the morning. Ideas and words flow more easily. Most put off more perfunctory tasks like meetings, answering correspondence, administrative tasks, and teaching (sorry students) until afternoon whenever possible. Most take work home and spend a portion of evenings and weekends writing or completing other professional tasks. All value personal health and carve out ample time for family, socializing, exercising, and leisure activities.

My own rhythm is much the same as I write this book. I claim the morning hours. I'm up early, and I write in my home office from 6:00 until noon. I turn off email and other notifications in order to work undistracted. Then I exercise. Later in the afternoon, depending on the day, I attend meetings, handle professional obligations, and teach. I schedule classes in the afternoons or early evenings and schedule them so that they meet just once per week, which cuts preparation and contact time. If I need not go to the university, I don't. That's a huge time saver in terms of dressing for the office and traveling. Evenings are spent with family and usually involve outdoor activities like walking or tennis.

Psychologist Mihaly Csikszentmihalyi (1996), who interviewed dozens of creative people across multiple occupations, offered this advice to all for building effective life rhythms:

- *Protect creative energy.* "Erect barriers against distractions, dig channels so that energy can flow more freely, find ways to escape outside temptations and interruptions." His study took place before smartphones, but today he might specifically recommend their limited and controlled use.

- *Develop habits of discipline that save time.* For instance, address electronic correspondence just twice a day rather than as emails arrive. Shop when stores are less crowded. Make enough food for multiple meals when you cook. Exercise early in the day, so you need just one shower. The habits can be trivial, like Albert Einstein always wearing the same old sweater and baggy pants. Doing so cut down on shopping and dressing time. Suppose it takes just 2 minutes a day to choose what to wear. That's 730 minutes, or 12 hours a year, that Einstein could contribute to physics. Now think of all the repetitive things you do most days such as grooming, shopping, cleaning, traveling, and corresponding. Don't dare eliminate that daily shower, but eliminating or routinizing some things frees up time and creative energy. Every hour saved from drudgery can be spent more productively.

- *Shape your space.* To the degree possible, create functional and harmonious work spaces. Whatever you need should be at hand, such as books, your computer, a spacious but uncluttered work surface, and good lighting. Things that distract should be absent or tucked away, such as phones, unpaid bills, unfolded laundry, and gaming consoles. Be ready to work on the go, too. Be portable. Pack your laptop with all needed documents, contacts, and websites, so you can work anywhere when opportunity knocks, such as when waiting for class to begin or waiting for a medical appointment. As a college student, I often sought out-of-the-way study havens that were deserted and distraction-free. I'd study in empty classrooms at night, in the deserted bleachers along the college soccer field at the far end of campus on warm sunny days, and in the third-floor hallway of our under-construction library, well beyond the barriers and yellow tape.

- *Make time for reflection and relaxation.* The productive scholars I studied and the creative giants Csikszentmihalyi studied all saw reflection and relaxation as vital to a healthy mind and body and made those things a priority. And they didn't just wait for such opportunities to happen; they scheduled them. They also claimed that the best relaxation is not doing nothing, but doing something physical. Educational researcher Richard Mayer especially enjoyed walking his dog, hiking, and mountain biking. Educational researcher Richard Anderson liked to cook, enjoyed outdoor photography, and camped and canoed in the wilderness (Kiewra & Creswell, 2000). When Csikszentmihalyi contacted ordinary people throughout the day at random times and asked them to rate how creative they felt, they reported higher levels of creativity when involved in physical activities like walking or swimming (Csikszentmihalyi, 1996). Those claims were confirmed in recent research out of Stanford University showing that walking improves creative thinking. For me, I've probably had more good ideas bubble to the surface when out walking or running than in other facets of my day.

Activity 9.2

Describe a routine you can follow, based on chapter ideas, to be a more productive college student.

Tailor your days for success, because how you spend your days is how you spend your life. Arrange your days to follow your bliss.

Collaborate

The productive scholars I studied were big-time collaborators and owed much of their productivity to collaboration. For instance, Michael Pressley collaborated with others on 85% of his publications, Patricia Alexander on 76%, and Richard Anderson on 74% (Kiewra & Creswell, 2000; Patterson-Hazley & Kiewra, 2013). Staggeringly high numbers. The scholars agreed that collaboration permitted them to work on more projects, share the workload, and do better work. Because of collaboration, the scholars often worked on as many as 10 different research projects at a time. And each project was completed efficiently and effectively, because many hands make light work and because scholars contributed most in their strength area, be it research design, data analysis, or writing. Scholars could play to their strengths rather than be jacks-of-all-trades. Here is what Michael Pressley said about collaboration:

> When I went through graduate school there was a tremendous sort of egocentricism about the whole thing, a sort of "you've got to become famous by standing on your own." I think that maybe you can still become famous on your own, but that the breadth and depth of your thoughts and certainly your personal fulfillment is going to be a lot greater if you spend your life doing important things with other people ... We need to train young people ... to be lifetime collaborators. (Kiewra & Creswell, 2000)

Collaboration can play a big role in your college studies. When you imagine college studying, you likely conjure up an image of a solitary figure hunched over a stack of books and papers, in a darkened room lit by a small lamp. Although much study should be done alone as you read, record notes, construct organizers, build associations, and regulate learning and understanding, there is much value in group (collaborative) study too. Group study, when done properly, is highly effective. It provides a forum for sharing study materials and ideas and offers opportunities for feedback. Others might recognize your weaknesses and errors better than you might recognize them. Group study can increase your course understanding and mastery. Here are some group-study guidelines:

1. *Form a study group for each class.* If you are taking European history, psychology, and calculus, then form a separate group for each subject that includes members from that class.

2. *Include 3–5 serious members.* Don't create a group too big or too small. Too big, and accountability gets lost as members assume someone else will do the work. Too small, and the benefit of sharing work and ideas is limited. Include only serious members who pledge to attend all sessions and pull their load. No freeloaders allowed.

3. *Hold weekly meetings.* Begin in week one and meet every week throughout the semester. Cramming is as ineffective for groups as it is for individuals.

4. *Make written assignments.* At the end of each session, assign each group member to create written study materials for next time, such as organizers, associations, or practice tests. Completed materials are shared with group members before or during subsequent sessions.

5. *Stay on task.* Your job is to study, not socialize or gripe about the class. Don't tolerate chatterboxes or complainers. This is a study group, not a support group.

6. *Be cooperative.* Follow the Golden Rule: Treat others as you would want them to treat you. Help others succeed, and they will help you. Don't shy away from dispensing and accepting constructive criticism, though. If someone's work is substandard or their ideas misguided, correct them for their betterment and that of the group. The fate of the group and its members depends on the sharing of knowledge, not ignorance.

7. *Dismiss noncontributors.* Those who skip meetings, fail to complete and share assignments, or are uncooperative should be asked to leave the group. Group study is optional and is only for those seriously committed to it. Agree at the start to provide one warning before dismissing a non-contributing member. One rusty cog can grind the entire group to a halt.

Frame Failure

You've read about failure framing in other parts of this book, but it is vital here too, in a section on life management. To recap: You will fail, but failure is the pathway to success. In life, there will be wins and losses, hits and flops, acceptances and rejections—even for the productive scholars I studied. When failure strikes, you must get up off the mat and learn from it. Michael Pressley said, "[When a manuscript is rejected], I always spend time with the reviews and try to figure out what they are telling me. Every one of those points is always telling me something [that I must] react to" (Kiewra & Creswell, 2000). Early in Richard Mayer's graduate school tenure, he submitted a paper to his mentor, Jim Greeno, who responded, "I don't understand what you're saying." Following this deflating response, Mayer revised the work to improve clarity and resubmitted. This time Greeno responded, "Now that it is written clearly, I don't think you have a very good idea" (Patterson-Hazley & Kiewra, 2013). Even the great ones, like Mayer, must embrace failure and learn from it. Speaking of failure and mentors, my graduate school mentored counseled, "Learn to live with failure; just don't live with it too long."

Time Management

Isabelle is back from the lunch she planned during history class back in Chapter 2, when she should have been paying attention and taking complete notes. This time she's talking time management with classmate Satie.

Isabelle: Satie, can you believe someone in our class pulled a 100 on the physics test? That nerd must be president of the Albert Einstein fan club.

Satie: No, just treasurer. I got the 100.

Isabelle: Wow! I got a lousy 67 and I studied 2 whole hours last night. How much did you study last night?

Satie:	None. I went to my son's band concert. He had a trombone solo.
Isabelle:	When did you study?
Satie:	I studied over the past 5 weeks, about 10 hours a week.
Isabelle:	My goodness! That's more than I'm likely to study over 4 years of college. How do you study so much, work part-time, and take care of your family? Is your family going to file charges against you for neglect?
Satie:	Not at all. I miss very few chances to spend time with family. I begin studying about 5:00 each morning when they're all still asleep and the house is peaceful and my mind is clear.
Isabelle:	Five o'clock? My mind is still mostly cloudy when I wake up around 9:30. I'm not a morning person.
Satie:	After we all eat breakfast together, I drive my kids to school and head right over to campus. On my way, I replay lectures I recorded on my phone.
Isabelle:	Ugh, talk about moldy oldies. Hearing lectures once is more than enough.
Satie:	I get to campus around 8:00, and parking is no problem then.
Isabelle:	For me, it's usually about 20 laps around campus before I land a spot. That's why I'm often late for physics or don't make it at all.
Satie:	Once I arrive, I usually head straight to the library, where I read assignments until my first class.
Isabelle:	If I have time, I usually hit the coffee shop for a bagel and cream cheese. Have you had the asiago bagel? It's heavenly.
Satie:	Nope, missed out there. When I get to class, I spend time reviewing notes from the previous class before the instructor begins.
Isabelle:	If I'm early—fat chance—I check Facebook.
Satie:	After my psychology class, I grab a quick bite from a sack lunch I bring. That saves me time and money. Ka-ching! I lunch with all the psychology bigwigs—B. F. Skinner, Howard Gardner, Carol Dweck...
Isabelle:	Ugh, you study while you eat? I heard that's bad for digestion. I usually cruise across town to Hot Diggity Dog. Love their deep-fried hotdog on a stick. It's really murder finding another parking space when I return though. Students circle the lots like buzzards.
Satie:	After lunch, I go to my research assistant job in the psychology department. It's just two hours a day. It's fun and I'm learning tons. I'm considering graduate school in educational psychology.
Isabelle:	After my 2:30 class, it's back across town to my job at the Holiday Hotel. My title is resort steward, which is a fancy way of saying I make beds and clean toilets. It's gross.
Satie:	Gross is watching my son blow spit through the spit valve on his trombone. Anyway, after wrapping up at the psych department, I

	pick up my kids from school at 3:30, and we go play tennis, ride our bikes, or walk the dog.
Isabelle:	I'm too busy to exercise.
Satie:	My husband gets home around five. He and the kids make dinner while I study for another hour. After dinner, it's family time. We usually read stories, play games, and talk about our days.
Isabelle:	More Facebook for me and computer games. Sometimes I go to the study lounge in the residence hall to talk to people.
Satie:	Once the kids are tucked in, I study for another hour or two before turning in.
Isabelle:	I'm too beat to get work done then.
Satie:	On weekends, we all do chores Saturday morning. It's more fun when everybody pitches in.
Isabelle:	I can't face cleaning my room after cleaning up after slobs all week.
Satie:	The rest of Saturday, we play. Saturday night, my husband and I have a late supper together after the kids are in bed and watch a movie. Sunday morning I'm up before dawn and banking some study hours before church. Sunday afternoon, I can usually find another 3–4 hours to study and plan for the upcoming week, while the kids are out playing and my husband's out with his friends doing whatever they do.
Isabelle:	I avoid studying on Sundays. I want to be sure I'm fresh for the new week. And I never plan. I like to study when the mood strikes.
Satie:	Hmmm, you might want to consider taking our college's study skills course, Isabelle. It really helped me nail down some great time- and life-management strategies and improve my study strategies.
Isabelle:	Perhaps ... if I can find the time.

Based on that admittedly contrived conversation between Isabelle and Satie, answer the following questions:

1. Which student is likely to earn a higher college GPA?

2. Which student would you invite to join your study group?

3. Which student seems to lead a more fulfilling life?

You probably answered Satie for each question, because Satie seems on top of things and is flourishing; Isabelle seems buried beneath things and is floundering. Satie is a time master; Isabelle a time waster. It need not be this way for Isabelle—or for you. Following a few time-management principles, based on investment principles, can lead you to success in school and beyond.

"Time is money." You've heard that expression. Is it true? Seems so. First, both are valued. You value time and money because each can be redeemed for things you enjoy. When you have money, you can purchase golf clubs or a Hawaiian vacation. When you have time, you can spend it playing golf or vacationing in Hawaii. Second, both are earned. You spend time earning money at your job, and you spend money earning time, such as when you pay someone to fix your car rather than doing it yourself. Last, both are wasted. You waste money on frivolous investments like swampland in Florida or buying a $12 hamburger. You waste time spending hours on social media or watching Adam Sandler movies. Because time and money are intertwined, many of the principles governing the investment of money can be applied to the investment of time. Below are seven time-management principles culled from the world of financial investment, each with a fingernail description. Following that, is a complete description of each.

> ### Activity 9.3
>
> After reading through the rest of the chapter, address each of Isabelle's statements in the dialogue above and give her time-management advice along the way.

1. Invest time—Success takes time. The time you put in determines what you take out.

2. Invest in time—Time can be purchased or manufactured. Do so to get more time.

3. Invest early—The earlier you begin, the sooner you'll arrive.

4. Invest daily—Regular investments add up and pay big dividends over time.

5. Invest wisely—Preserve time and put it where your priorites are.

6. Monitor investment—Check to be sure your time investments are paying off.

7. Enjoy investment—Reward yourself for time well spent.

Invest Time

If you had a bank that credited your account each morning with 86,400...
That carried over no balance from day to day...
Allowed you to keep no cash in your accounts...
And every evening canceled whatever part of the amount you had
*   failed to use during the day...*
What would you do?
Draw out every cent, of course, and use it to your advantage!
Well, you have such a bank...and its name is "TIME."
Every morning, it credits you with 86,400 seconds.

Every night, it writes off as lost whatever of this you have failed to
   invest to good purpose.
It carries over no balances.
It allows no overdrafts.
Each day, it opens a new account with you.
Each night, it burns the records of the day.
If you fail to use the day's deposits, the loss is yours.
There is no going back.
There is no "Tomorrow."
It is up to each of us to invest this precious fund of hours, minutes, and sec-
   onds in order to get from it the utmost in health, happiness, and success!
                                                                    —Levy, 2005

If you want to be rich, you'll need to invest money. If you want to be successful, you'll need to invest time. Rome wasn't built in a day. The world's great structures, like the Roman Coliseum or the Egyptian pyramids, took decades to build. The world's great people, like Amadeus Mozart and Marie Curie, took decades to hone their talents.

To be a successful student, you must invest time. How much time, you wonder? Whatever time it takes to master course material. Use your regulation skills to monitor course mastery, and don't stop until you get there. At a minimum, you should follow the long-held rule of thumb and spend about 2 hours studying outside of class for every hour in class. That means that if you are taking a 15-hour course load, you should be studying about 30 hours per week outside of class. Add that all up, and your total academic time investment is about 40–50 hours weekly. Your college education is indeed a full-time job.

If possible, spend time now earning a good education that pays dividends the rest of your life. In this time of escalating college costs, some college students work full-time jobs to pay for their education and treat their education like a part-time job, thereby shortchanging the very thing they're working for. Instead, work full-time, even overtime, in summers and during school breaks to help pay for school. During the academic year, strive to reduce work hours to 10 hours weekly, 20 hours max, and try to get a job on campus related to your academic and professional goals. Students who work on campus tend to outperform those who work off campus. They are also more involved in their college community and enjoy college more.

Whatever time you have, make the most of it by completing a block schedule framework like that in Table 9-2. A block schedule is your general guide for how you'll spend your time each week throughout a semester. Don't worry; the schedule is not carved in stone. It's modifiable. You might have to deviate from the schedule from time to time, or create a whole new one, if things change or the schedule is not working. That's okay. But having a general time management plan can really help you stay on track for school success. The completed block

Table 9-2 BLOCK SCHEDULE FRAMEWORK

	Sunday	Monday	Tuesday	Wednesday	Thursday	Friday	Saturday
6:00-7:30							
7:30-8:30							
8:30-9:30							
9:30-10:30							
10:30-11:30							
11:30-12:30							
12:30-1:30							
1:30-2:30							
2:30-3:30							
3:30-4:30							
4:30-5:30							
5:30-6:30							
6:30-7:30							
7:30-8:30							
8:30-9:30							
9:30-10:30							
10:30-11:30							

Source: Kenneth A. Kiewra and Nelson F. DuBois, *Learning to Learn: Making the Transition from Student to Lifelong Learner,* p. 82. Copyright © 1998 by Pearson Education, Inc.

schedule in Table 9-3 shows the four things you should include in your block schedule: (a) classes and commitments, (b) life tasks, (c) study times, and (d) leisure activities.

Record Classes and Commitments

First, fill in all class times. These are the most important thing on your schedule. The Table 9-3 schedule shows classes in history, French, algebra, psychology, and chemistry. Next, include other regular time commitments. The Table 9-3 schedule shows these commitments: religious service and meeting, tennis practice, work, and teacher aid volunteering. Notice how most non-class commitments are scheduled later in the day or on weekends, outside the school day, when possible. This allows you to use the main part of the day for classes and studying.

Table 9-3 COMPLETED BLOCK SCHEDULE

	Sunday	Monday	Tuesday	Wednesday	Thursday	Friday	Saturday
6:00-7:30		Exercise Breakfast	Exercise Breakfast	Exercise Breakfast	Exercise Breakfast	Exercise Breakfast	
7:30-8:30		Study	Study	Study	Study	Study	
8:30-9:30	Breakfast	History	Study	History	Study	History	Exercise
9:30-10:30	Religious Service	Study	Psych	Campus Errands	Psych	Psych	Breakfast
10:30-11:30	Religious Service	French	Study	French	Study	French	Chores
11:30-12:30	Chores	Lunch	Lunch	Lunch	Lunch	Lunch	Chores
12:30-1:30	Chores	Study	Chem	Study	Chem	Teacher Aid	Chores
1:30-2:30	Lunch	Study	Chem	Study	Chem	Teacher Aid	Lunch
2:30-3:30	Leisure	Study	Study	Study	Study	Study	Study
3:30-4:30	Leisure	Tennis	Tennis	Tennis	Tennis	Tennis	Study
4:30-5:30	Leisure	Tennis	Tennis	Tennis	Tennis	Tennis	Work
5:30-6:30	Supper	Supper	Supper	Supper	Supper	Supper	Work
6:30-7:30	Study	Algebra	Work	Study	Work	Study	Work
7:30-8:30	Study	Algebra	Work	Study	Work	Study	Work
8:30-9:30	Study	Algebra	Work	Religious Meeting	Work	Leisure	Supper
9:30-10:30	Study	Leisure	Work	Leisure	Work	Leisure	Leisure
10:30-11:30	Bed	Bed	Bed	Bed	Bed	Leisure	Leisure

Source: Kenneth A. Kiewra and Nelson F. DuBois, *Learning to Learn: Making the Transition from Student to Lifelong Learner,* p. 83. Copyright © 1998 by Pearson Education, Inc.

Record Life Tasks

Perhaps you were shielded from many life tasks such as laundry, cleaning, shopping, food preparation, and car maintenance before shoving off to college. Now, on your own, many such tasks fall to you. That's life. And, life takes time, so invest time accordingly. As shown in Table 9-3, block out time to get essential life tasks done such as morning exercise, meals, campus errands, and weekend chores. Try to minimize the time needed for life tasks. Exercising first thing in the morning rather than later saves showering time and preserves water. Folding laundry while watching your favorite show allows you to complete a chore and enjoy some leisure time simultaneously. When dropping your car off for service, you can do some homework while you wait. Reducing your lunch hour to twenty minutes is a time-saver too. Finally, try to handle chores in the evening or on weekends, rather than during your school day and prime study times.

Record Study Times

Next, fill in a sufficient number of study hours. Do not indicate the subject you'll study, though, since this could change from week to week. Remember to budget about 2 hours of study time for each hour you spend in class. The Table 9-3 schedule shows 28 scheduled study hours for 15 class hours. Of course, more study time can be found if needed, for example, while waiting for classes to begin or by shortening lunch hours.

When you plan study times, ideally make them 1–4 hours in length. If you try to study much longer in one sitting, you might get tired and lose your sharpness. Of course, take short breaks as needed to rejuvenate. A brisk walk outdoors should be the ideal refresher. Shorter study episodes are fine too. Every bit helps. When you study, try to get right down to business. Some students, like my friend Tom in college, suffer from *prolonged study warm-up*. Tom would announce nightly on the residence hall floor all the studying he planned to do ... right after he showered, made some phone calls, fixed a snack, folded his laundry, and organized his desk ... Don't procrastinate. Get busy.

Record Leisure Time

A college student on semester break was at a restaurant near the college when she saw her favorite professor there. The professor asked her how break was going. The student commented on the school work she was accomplishing. The professor nodded approvingly, but then asked, "What are you doing for fun?" The student reported that she had twice been skiing, had attended a concert, was playing a lot of ping pong, and was reading her third novel. With that, the professor smiled and said, "Good, good, good, that's what college should be all about." From that point on, the student and her roommate wryly echoed those words whenever one or both of them was headed out to hike a mountain trail, attend a party, or curl up with a good book: "Good, good, good, that's what college should be all about."

And, in many ways, it should. It should be among the best 4 years of your life—8 years, if you're like Bluto in *Animal House*. College provides a balance of intellectual and social opportunities. Although excelling in the classroom is your primary college objective, take advantage of the smorgasbord of stimulating and enjoyable opportunities college offers. Attend concerts, films, plays, and talks. Join groups and clubs. Hang out with friends and have fun. If you don't find time for leisure and fun, you'll surely find time for drudgery and illness. Therefore, make leisure a priority and incorporate leisure time in your schedule.

And don't be a servant to your block schedule. If a leisure opportunity arises, such as a bluegrass afternoon in the college square or an impromptu Groundhog Day party, go with it if time permits. Remember, though: Don't steal time, borrow it. If an unscheduled leisure activity cuts into a scheduled study session, return the favor later by using a scheduled leisure period to study.

<table>
<tr><td>

Activity 9.4
_____

Use the blank block schedule in Table 9-2 to record how you actually spend time over the next week. How effective was your time management, based on the chapter's investment principles? Next complete a block schedule in line with the chapter's investment principles.

</td></tr>
</table>

Invest in Time

We can invest in our financial wealth by doing things to make extra money, such as working second jobs or working overtime. We spend time to make money. Conversely, we can invest in our academic wealth by doing things to make extra time, such as paying someone to fix our car so we don't have to do it. We spend money to make time. Investing in time—buying time—is particularly valuable for college students who need a lot of time to handle all the things in their block schedules.

Here are some ways you can invest in time:

- Pay others to do the things you can't do, can't do efficiently, or simply don't want to do. Perhaps things like servicing your car, preparing meals, or doing your taxes.

- Live on campus. This saves time commuting, parking, shopping, preparing food, and cleaning up. It brings social and leisure activities to your doorstep.

- Form study groups. Workload is reduced, as each member prepares detailed study notes for one another.

Remember: Time is valuable and worth most any price.

Invest Early

You saw in Chapter 7 the benefit of investing early into your retirement account. Early Erica banked more retirement savings in 10 years than Late Larry did in 30 years, just because Erica began saving 10 years earlier. Ditto for financing a college education. When your kids are ready to attend college, costs might range from $50,000–$100,000 a year. If you want to pay for your children's education, this leaves two options: Powerball winnings or investing early. Good luck with the former. You'll want to start socking away college money early, around the time of the first sonogram. Not ready to think about kids? What about a new car? If you want to keep that shiny new car in great shape for many years, you'll need to invest early by waxing it and servicing it early on, not waiting 3 or 4 years. Should you miss your opportunity to invest early, then invest now. The best time to plant a tree was 20 years ago; the second best time is today.

In terms of college, jump on assignments early. If you have a term paper due in 6 weeks, start this week. If you have twelve chapters to read for the midterm, read two chapters this week and every week hence. Why wait? Studying works best when done in a distributed manner—a bit at a time—over the semester rather than cramming as deadlines approach. If you have too much schoolwork to do in December, you weren't doing enough in September.

Investing early also means that you should shoot from the starting blocks when a semester starting gun sounds. As mentioned in Chapter 3, some students believe they can ease into classes when a semester begins. After all, not much happens that first day other than some syllabus perusal. Wrong! Let me remind you what could happen, and does happen, in my study skills class. Students who miss the first day lose 2 points for being absent, another 2 points for missing a graded class activity, another 3 points for not turning in assigned homework the next class period, and 3 points on a quiz Day 2 that covers Day 1 material. Add it up. That's 10 points from 100 possible points for the course. Missing the first day can cost students a full letter grade.

Invest Daily

> *Each day that we awake is a new start, another chance. Why waste it on self-pity, sloth, and selfishness? Roll that day around on your tongue, relish the taste of its freedom. Breathe deeply of the morning air, savor the fragrance of opportunity. Run your hands along the spine of those precious 24 hours and feel the strength in that sinew and bone. Life is raw material. We are artisans. We can sculpt our existence into something beautiful, or debase it into ugliness. It's in our hands.*
>
> —Cathy Better

Seize the day! Regular investments can pay large dividends. Let's talk money. If you invest $400 a month for 40 years at 10% interest, you'll have saved a cool 2.2 million. Wow!

Do you like to read? How would you like to read 15–20 novels a year in addition to your textbooks? To do so, invest daily. Read for about 15 minutes before bed each night, and "presto," you've read 15–20 books in a year. Wow!

For academic learning, investing daily not only produces more learning but also produces *better* learning. Consider the cases of Jack and Jill, students in Psych 100. Jack studies his lecture notes for 20 minutes after each psychology class. Each week, he spends an additional hour integrating and studying class notes for that week. The week before his psychology midterm, Jack studies an additional hour each day. In total, Jack studies about 20 hours for the midterm exam. Jill does not study until 2 days before the midterm exam. She studies

10 hours each day. Which study plan is likely to be more effective? Before you answer, let's shift to running. Jack and Jill pledge to run 90 miles in a month. Jack invests early and daily—running 3 miles a day right from the start and throughout the month. Jill puts off running until the last 3 days of the month. By then, it's too late. She'd have to run 30 miles a day to meet her goal—and she's no Pete Kostelnick, yet. She's likely to pull a hammy 5 miles in, if she even gets that far.

It's obvious that Jack's daily investments are more likely to pay off on the track and in the classroom than Jill's last-minute scrambling. By investing daily, Jack actually improves his aerobic fitness throughout the month. Midway through the month, 3 miles a day is a snap, and Jack starts upping his mileage. By studying psychology daily, Jack "stays up" with the instructor and understands newly presented material better than Jill. As he masters material, it is easier to learn more. Moreover, Jack brings energy to his daily study sessions and does not feel overwhelmed or anxious as the test approaches.

To help you invest time early and daily, consider using a semester and weekly planner in addition to your block schedule.

Develop a Semester Planner

A semester planner highlights the dates of all tests and assignments in all subjects throughout the semester. These are written in the spaces of a monthly calendar, as shown in Figure 9-1 (although this one just includes psychology). For example, this semester planner shows the psychology midterm on October 22nd and the psychology term paper due on November 15th. In addition, divide long-term assignments and test preparation plans into segments, and record these self-imposed due dates on the semester planner too. For example, this semester planner shows the chapters to be mastered each Thursday on the way to the psychology midterm and final. It also shows the due dates for completing portions of the psychology term paper, such as choosing a topic (September 10th), reviewing the literature (September 25th), and writing a first draft (October

Activity 9.5

Develop a semester planner.

25th). Breaking tasks down in this way and setting self-imposed deadlines pushes you to invest early and daily. But don't be like those students who say, "I love deadlines. I love the whooshing noise they make as they go by."

Develop a Weekly Planner

The weekly planner illustrates the week's tests, assignments, and activities. The activities might apply to tests and assignments occurring this week or in future weeks. Examine the weekly planner in Table 9-4. It schedules study time for three history chapters on Monday, Tuesday, and Wednesday in preparation for a future test. French study is scheduled for Sunday, Monday, and Tuesday for a test on Friday. A final review for an algebra test on Tuesday is scheduled for

Semester Planner

September

Sun	Mon	Tues	Wed	Thurs	Fri	Sat
1	2	3	4	Ch. 1 5	6	7
8	9	Choose Topic 10	11	Ch. 2 12	13	14
15	16	17	18	Ch.3 19	20	21
22	23	24	Review Lit 25	Ch. 4 26	27	28
29	30					

November

Sun	Mon	Tues	Wed	Thurs	Fri	Sat
					1	2
3	4	5	6	Ch. 10 7	Write Polished Draft 8	9
10	11	12	13	Ch. 11 14	Term Paper Due 15	16
17	18	19	20	Ch. 12 21	22	23
24	25	26	27	Ch. 13 28	29	30

October

Sun	Mon	Tues	Wed	Thurs	Fri	Sat
		Create Structure 1	2	Ch. 5 3	4	5
6	7	8	9	Ch. 6 10	11	12
13	14	15	16	Ch. 7 17	18	19
20	21	Mid Term 22	23	Ch. 8 24	Write 1st Draft 25	26
27	28	29	Write 2nd Draft 30	Ch. 9 31		

December

Sun	Mon	Tues	Wed	Thurs	Fri	Sat
1	2	3	4	Ch. 14 5	6	7
8	9	10	11	Ch. 15 12	13	14
15	16	17	18	Final Test 19	20	21
22	23	24	25	26	27	28
29	30	31				

Figure 9-1 Semester Planner for Psychology.

Table 9-4 WEEKLY PLANNER

	Sun	Mon	Tues	Wed	Thurs	Fri	Sat
History		Study Ch. 4	Study Ch. 5	Study Ch. 6			
French	Study French	Study French	Study French			French Test	
Algebra	Test Review		Test			Complete Assign 3	
Chem		Write Lab Report	Write Lab Report		Lab Report		
Psych				Study Ch. 3	Study Ch. 3		

Source: Kenneth A. Kiewra and Nelson F. DuBois, *Learning to Learn: Making the Transition from Student to Lifelong Learner*, p. 92. Copyright © 1998 by Pearson Education, Inc.

completion on Sunday. Algebra assignment 3 is to be completed on Friday. In chemistry, a lab report due Thursday is completed Monday and Tuesday. And Chapter 3 in psychology is scheduled for study on Wednesday and Thursday in preparation for a future test.

The weekly planner's matrix structure is powerful because it helps you clearly see the week's activities by day (with just a quick vertical glance) or by subject (with just a quick horizontal glance). You should create a weekly planner each Saturday for the upcoming week. Table 9-5 is a summary of the three time-management schedules.

Activity 9.6

Develop a weekly planner.

Table 9-5 SUMMARY OF THE THREE TIME-MANAGEMENT SCHEDULES

	Block	**Semester**	**Weekly**
Structure	Days of week by times of day	Monthly calendars for each month during a semester	Course subjects by days of the week
Purpose	Show general schedule for each hour of each day	Show all important semester tasks by day for each month	Show a week's testing, assignment, and study activities by subject and day
Includes	1. Classes and commitments 2. Life tasks 3. Study times 4. Leisure times	1. Test dates 2. Assignment due dates 3. Self-imposed due dates for test preparation and assignment completion	1. Test days by subject 2. Assignment due days by subject 3. Study activities by day and subject

Invest Wisely

People waste time complaining, watching TV, checking Facebook, updating social media, playing email ping pong, piling instead of filing, traveling and shopping during peak hours, and attending pointless meetings. If that's you … Stop it! Your time is valuable. Invest it wisely.

Put your time where your priorities are—things like school, health, family, friends, and leisure. Remember that it's okay to say no to things that don't take you where you want to go. Spend your spare time smartly. Use the few minutes before classes to review notes. When driving, replay lectures you've recorded. Waiting for a bus: Read a text assignment. Waiting for a medical appointment: Read *War and Peace*. Also, accomplish chores more efficiently. Beat the crowds by shopping for groceries in the morning or at night, not at 5 p.m. or on weekends. Better yet, shop online and have them delivered. Travel off-peak if you can, after morning traffic dies down and before evening traffic picks up. Avoid banks and post offices. Have money direct-deposited. Set up bill pay on your computer. Send e-cards. Remember what Benjamin Franklin said: "Lost time is never found again."

Monitor Investment

Imagine investing your hard-earned money in the stock market and then not monitoring the performance of those investments. Crazy. The same is true for time. You should monitor whether your time is well spent.

Begin by monitoring (regulating) your current time practices. Complete Activity 9-4 by filling in a blank block schedule, like that in Table 9-2, with your actual time expenditures. For one week, simply record how you spend your hours and days. You might be disappointed to learn how much time you waste but encouraged to learn how much more time is actually available for studying or other activities.

After constructing block, semester, and weekly schedules, monitor how well you stick to those schedules and monitor the schedules themselves. Don't hesitate to make schedule changes that result in better outcomes, including your own mental and physical health. No sense trying to stick to schedules making you sick. Remember that these schedules are simply guides to help you achieve your goals. They are yours and yours alone. Make them work for you.

Apply the ultimate acid test. Set your phone alarm for 10:30 each night. When it sounds, ask yourself this one simple question: Was your day productive and enjoyable? If not, adjust accordingly tomorrow.

Enjoy Investment

Just as you should enjoy the fruits of your financial investments—luxuries like a lakeside cottage, a golf membership, and movie theater popcorn—you should also enjoy the benefits of time well spent. Reward yourself for getting your school work done in an effective and timely manner. Once work is completed, shoot some hoops, play a video game, or socialize with friends. Two precautions. First, the reward should follow the prescribed academic activity, never precede it. Work before play. Second, keep rewards in line with task accomplishments. Study for a couple hours, then perhaps enjoy a 30-minute reward activity. Put in a good day accomplishing things, and perhaps enjoy a couple hours of leisure or rest at day's end.

Speaking of rest ... Two woodcutters chop wood. The first chops straight through the day without a break and assembles an impressive pile of logs. The second chops throughout the day as well but stops every hour for a 10-minute break. Much to the first woodcutter's surprise, the second woodcutter assembles an even larger pile of logs. "How did you do that?" asks the first. "I never stopped chopping." The second woodcutter replies, "Each time I stopped to rest, I also sharpened my axe." When you pause to enjoy your time investments, you too are sharpening your axe.

Here's to a lifetime of SOARing and axe sharpening!

Activity 9.7

Describe how you'll monitor and enjoy your time investments.

Answers to Focus Questions

1. Ralph Waldo Emerson (1904) said, "Every artist was first an amateur." This means that all great artists, athletes, scientists, philosophers, and students started out just like you—knowing nothing, having no skills—complete amateurs. Don't be intimidated by those farther along the talent path than you. You can catch up, but you must believe it's possible and take the leap.

2. *Follow your bliss* means to follow your dreams, not the crowd's, not someone else's. Don't play it safe. Come down from the bleachers and get out on the field.

3. Some people try to do too much. And their efforts are spread thin in several disparate directions. Focused integration means focusing your efforts on related and complementary things. For example, as a student, you likely have an academic major and want to join some college clubs and get some real-world experiences. Focused integration can allow all those things to happen without your being spread too thin. If your major is political science (pre-law), you might join the college's mock trial team and secure an internship with a local court judge.

4. A center of excellence is a place where like-minded experts assemble, places like the Juilliard School for music or Silicon Valley for technology. The productive scholars I studied gravitated to centers of excellence—top colleges and universities—for their training. At a center of excellence, you can learn from the best mentors and pass through the doors of opportunity that they open. You need not necessarily relocate to a center of excellence. You can link to those places and people in other ways, such as through visits, professional conferences, and electronic correspondence.

5. Deliberate practice is focused on subtle skill improvement. It is hard work and requires full concentration. It is often done alone and is usually not much fun. But it is the key to improvement and mastery. Most people do not practice this way. They practice casually. They play a round of golf or hit a few balls on the range without much thought as to why things go wrong or how to fix them. Casual practice or everyday experience does not bring improvement and can actually lead to worse performance over time.

6. Most productive or creative people have daily routines or rhythms that boost productivity. Most seem to work about 50 hours weekly but do so in efficient ways. For example, they accomplish their most creative work, like writing, in the morning when they feel most fresh. They save more rudimentary tasks, like meetings and correspondence, for the afternoon. They are adept at protecting their creative energy (e.g., turning off message signals while working), developing time-saving habits (e.g., cooking

food for multiple meals at one time), and shaping their space for success (e.g., removing distracting items and making sure all necessary materials are on hand).

7. Group study is effective because members share valuable study materials and ideas and offer feedback to one another. Study groups should be formed for each class and include 3–5 serious members. They should meet weekly. Members should create study materials and share them with the group. During group meetings, members should stay on task and be cooperative, but never hesitate to point out misguided ideas. Noncontributors should be dismissed, as they are pulling down the group.

8. Block schedules include (a) classes and commitments (such as your history class and work hours), (b) life tasks (such as chores and meals), (c) study times, and (d) leisure time.

9. When you are assigned a term paper that's due weeks or months in the future, it is best to invest early and invest daily. Invest early by getting started the week the paper is assigned, rather than procrastinating. There is much to do, so get busy. Invest daily by breaking the task into parts and setting personal due dates for each part. For instance, set a due date for outlining the paper, one for locating sources, and one for completing the literature review.

10. A semester planner shows each day of the semester, month by month. It records test and assignment dates for each subject. It also records self-imposed due dates for test preparation (e.g., read Chapter 6) and assignment completion (e.g., write first draft). A weekly planner is a matrix showing the days of the week across the top and your course names down the left margin. Information within matrix cells indicates when tests occur, when assignments are due, and which tasks are to be completed that week. Students should complete a semester schedule at the start of the semester and modify it as need be. They should complete a weekly schedule at the start of each week.

Figure Credit

CHAPTER 10

Epilogue

America's News, Avenue of the Americas, New York, NY
July 9, 2074

Reporter: Welcome, Dr. Kanter. Thank you so much for talking with me today. It's an honor to meet you and discuss your groundbreaking work in gene editing. Many scientists contend that this work could soon alter the course of disease treatments. Tell me briefly about your discovery, in terms we can all understand.

Dr. Kanter: Thank you for conducting this interview. And, please, call me Elisabeth. My team and I have been experimenting with a gene-editing technology that alters damaged, non-reproductive cells. It works in concert with the immune system's natural mechanisms by invading viruses and, like a pair of scissors, cutting out their infected DNA strands. After DNA strands are removed, new healthy DNA can be added in its place.

Reporter: And these gene modifications can potentially impact how doctors treat and perhaps cure life-threatening diseases like cancer, heart disease, and HIV?

Dr. Kanter: That's the hope. Our tests have shown successful treatment effects with a variety of animals harboring a variety of diseases.

Reporter: Fascinating, Elisabeth. I want to get into the intricacies of your research and its medical implications, but before we do, let's trace back to the beginning. What was life like growing up, and how did that early life perhaps influence your success?

Dr. Kanter: It influenced me a lot. My father was a mechanical engineer. So there was always talk of building new and better things. And, together, we did just that—building helpful devices for the house or for animals, such as outdoor warming beds and drink stations for the stray cats that came our way. We even jerry-rigged a prosthetic for a bird with a broken wing. So I'd say my "fix-it" mentality stemmed from Dad. My biggest influence, though, was my mom. She taught me so much in the early years and even homeschooled me through elementary school. She's a wonderful teacher. And she didn't just teach me subjects, like math and science; she taught me how to learn on my own. She taught me a lot of effective learning strategies dealing with note-taking, how to study, and how to regulate learning. Strategies I continue to use today in my work. She taught me how to manage time and, really, manage my life. And she taught me to have a growth mindset, telling me that my eventual success rests solely in my hands. She'd say: "Every talented artist and scientist began as an amateur, just like you." I think making me a strong learner was especially important to her because she was actually a really bad learner before turning things around later in college. Before that, she'd goof off in class and never make time to study.

Reporter: Hard to believe because your mother, Dr. Isabelle Kanter, is also famous in her own right as a historian, particularly for her books on the French Revolution. So glad she found her way and passed those things on to you.

Dr. Kanter: Me too. There is no gene therapy that teaches someone how to learn and succeed.

Related Readings by Chapter

Chapter 1

Bloom, B. (1985). *Developing talent in young people*. Ballantine Books.

Daher, T., & Kiewra, K. A. (2016). An investigation of SOAR study strategies for learning from multiple online resources. *Contemporary Educational Psychology, 46*, 10–21. https://doi.org/10.1016/j.cedpsych.2015.12.004

Dweck, C. S. (2008). *Mindset: The new psychology of success*. Ballantine Books.

Emerson, R. W. (1904). Progress of culture. In *The complete works of Ralph Waldo Emerson: Letters and social aims* (Vol. 8). Houghton Mifflin.

Flanigan, A., Kiewra, K. A., & Luo, L. (2018). Conversations with four highly productive German educational psychologists: Frank Fischer, Hans Gruber, Heinz Mandl, and Alexander Renkl. *Educational Psychology Review, 30*, 303–330. https://doi.org/10.1007/s10648-016-9392-0

Kiewra, K. A. (2019). *Nurturing children's talents: A guide for parents*. Praeger.

Kiewra, K. A., & Creswell, J. W. (2000). Conversations with three highly productive educational psychologists: Richard Anderson, Richard Mayer, and Michael Pressley. *Educational Psychology Review, 12*, 135–161. https://doi.org/10.1023/A:1009041202079

Kiewra, K. A., & Rom, B. (2019). A glimpse inside the lives of the academically talented: What Merit Scholars and their parents reveal. *High Ability Studies*. https://doi.org/10.1080/13598139.2019.1661224

L'Amour, L. (2003). *Ride the Dark Trail*. Random House.

Patterson-Hazley, M., & Kiewra, K. A. (2013). Conversations with four highly productive educational psychologists: Patricia Alexander, Richard Mayer, Dale Schunk, and Barry Zimmerman. *Educational Psychology Review, 25*, 19–45. https://doi.org/10.1007/s10648-012-9214-y

Reilly, R. (2005, June 20). *Strongest dad in the world*. Sports Illustrated. https://vault.si.com/vault/2005/06/20/strongest-dad-in-the-world

Sartore, J. (n.d.). *How did you get interested in nature and the environment? Joel Sartore*. https://www.joelsartore.com/about-joel/common-questions/how-did-you-get-interested-in-nature-and-the-environment/

Waitzkin, J. (2007). *The art of learning: A journey in the pursuit of excellence*. Free Press.

Chapter 2

Crenshaw, D. (2008). *The myth of multitasking: How "doing it all" gets nothing done*. Jossey-Bass.

Fiorella, L., & Mayer, R. E. (2015). *Learning as a generative activity*. Cambridge University Press.

Jairam, D., & Kiewra, K. A. (2009). An investigation of the SOAR study method. *Journal of Advanced Academics, 20*, 602–609. https://doi.org/10.1177/1932202X0902000403

Jairam, D., & Kiewra, K. A. (2010). Helping students soar to success on computers: An investigation of the SOAR study method. *Journal of Educational Psychology, 102,* 601–614. https://doi.org/10.1037/a0019137

Jairam, D., Kiewra, K. A., & Ganson, K. (2012). The SOAR study system: Theory, research, and implications. In M. Edwards and S. O. Adams (Eds.), *Learning strategies, expectations, and challenges* (pp. 71–92). NOVA Science Publishers.

Jairam, D., Kiewra, K. A., Rogers-Kasson, S., Patterson-Hazley, M., & Marxhausen, K. (2013). SOAR versus SQ3R: A test of two study systems. *Instructional Science, 41,* 409–420. https://doi.org/10.1007/s11251-013-9295-0

Kiewra, K. A. (2019, September 3). *7 tips on how to take better notes.* The Conversation. https://theconversation.com/7-tips-on-how-to-take-better-notes-120144

Kiewra, K. A., Colliot, T., & Lu, J. (2018). *Note this: How to improve student note taking.* The IDEA Center, IDEA Paper #73. https://files.eric.ed.gov/fulltext/ED588353.pdf

Kiewra, K. A., Luo, L., Lu, J., & Colliot, T. (In Press). Learning strategies that help students SOAR to success. In Zhang, L. (Ed.), *Oxford encyclopedia of educational psychology.* Oxford University Press.

Luo, L., & Kiewra, K. A. (2019). Soaring to successful synthesis writing. *Journal of Writing Research, 11,* 163–209. https://www.researchgate.net/publication/333132178_Soaring_to_Successful_Synthesis_Writing_An_Investigation_of_SOAR_Strategies_for_College_Students_Writing_from_Multiple_Sources

McDaniel, M.A., Anderson, J. L., Derbish, M. H., & Morrisette, N. (2007). Testing the testing effect in the classroom. *European Journal of Cognitive Psychology, 19,* 494–513. https://doi.org/10.1080/09541440701326154

Chapter 3

Dietz, S., & Henrich, C. (2014). Texting as a distraction to learning in college students. *Computers in Human Behavior, 36,* 163–167. https://doi.org/10.1016/j.chb.2014.03.045

Dunlosky, J., Rawson, K. A., Marsh, E. J., Nathan, M. J., & Willingham, D. T. (2013). Improving students' learning with effective learning techniques: Promising directions from cognitive and educational psychology. *Psychological Science in the Public Interest, 14*(1), 4–58. https://doi.org/10.1177/1529100612453266

Emanuel, R. C. (2013). The American college student cell phone survey. *College Student Journal, 47,* 75–81. https://psycnet.apa.org/record/2013-10664-008

Flanigan, A., & Kiewra, K. A. (2018). What college instructors can do about cyber-slacking. *Educational Psychology Review, 30,* 585–597. https://doi.org/10.1007/s10648-017-9418-2

Frey, B. A., & Birnbaum, D. J. (2002). *Learners' perceptions on the value of PowerPoint in lectures.* ERIC (ERIC Document Reproduction Service No. ED467192). https://eric.ed.gov/?id=ED467192

Fried, C. B. (2008). In-class laptop use and its effects on student learning. *Computers & Education, 50,* 906–914. http://doi.org/10.1016/j.compedu.2006.09.006

Froese, A. D., Carpenter, C. N., Inman, D. A., Schooley, J. R., Barnes, R. B., Brecht, P. W., & Chacon, J. D. (2012). Effects of classroom cell phone use on expected and actual learning. *College Student Journal, 46,* 323–332. https://psycnet.apa.org/record/2012-19556-009

Igo, L. B., & Kiewra, K. A. (2007). How do high-achieving students approach web-based copy and paste note taking? Selective pasting and related learning outcomes. *Journal of Advanced Academics, 18,* 512–529. https://doi.org/10.4219/jaa-2007-558

Katayama, A. D., & Crooks, S. M. (2003). Online notes: Differential effects of studying complete or partial graphically organized notes. *Journal of Experimental Education, 71,* 293–312. https://doi.org/10.1080/00220970309602067

Kiewra, K. A. (1985a). Investigating notetaking and review: A depth of processing alternative. *Educational Psychologist, 20,* 23–32. https://doi.org/10.1207/s15326985ep2001_4

Kiewra, K. A. (1985b). Learning from a lecture: An investigation of notetaking, review, and attendance at a lecture. *Human Learning, 4,* 73–77. https://psycnet.apa.org/record/1986-07638-001

Kiewra, K. A. (1985c). Providing the instructor's notes: An effective addition to student notetaking. *Educational Psychologist, 20,* 33–39. http://dx.doi.org/10.1207/s15326985ep2001_5

Kiewra, K. A. (1985d). Students' note-taking behaviors and the efficacy of providing the instructor's notes for review. *Contemporary Educational Psychology, 10,* 378–386. https://doi.org/10.1016/0361-476X(85)90034-7

Kiewra, K. A. (1988). Cognitive aspects of autonomous notetaking: Control processes, learning strategies, and prior knowledge. *Educational Psychologist, 23,* 39–56. https://doi.org/10.1207/s15326985ep2301_3

Kiewra, K. A. (2016). Note taking on trial: A legal application of note-taking research. *Educational Psychology Review, 28,* 377–384. https://doi.org/10.1007/s10648-015-9353-z

Kiewra, K. A., & Benton, S. L. (1987). Effects of notetaking, the instructor's notes, and higher-order practice questions on factual and higher-order learning. *Journal of Instructional Psychology, 14,* 186–194.

Kiewra, K. A., & Benton, S. L. (1988). *The relationship between information processing ability and notetaking. Contemporary Educational Psychology, 13,* 33–44. https://doi.org/10.1016/0361-476X(88)90004-5

Kiewra, K. A., Benton, S. L., Kim, S., Risch, N., & Christensen, M. (1995). Effects of notetaking format and study technique on recall and relational performance. *Contemporary Educational Psychology, 20,* 172–187. https://doi.org/10.1006/ceps.1995.1011

Kiewra, K. A., Benton, S. L., & Lewis, L. B. (1987). Qualitative aspects of notetaking and their relationship with information processing ability. *Journal of Instructional Psychology, 14,* 110–117. https://psycnet.apa.org/record/1988-34161-001

Kiewra, K. A., DuBois, N. F., Christian, D., McShane, A., Meyerhoffer, M., & Roskelley, D. (1991). Notetaking functions and techniques. *Journal of Educational Psychology, 83,* 240–245. https://doi.org/10.1037/0022-0663.83.2.240

Kiewra, K. A., & Fletcher, H. J. (1984). The relationship between levels of notetaking and achievement. *Human Learning, 3,* 273–280. https://psycnet.apa.org/record/1985-32060-001

Kiewra, K. A., Mayer, R. E., Christensen, M., Kim, S., & Risch, N. (1991). Effects of repetition on recall and notetaking: Strategies for learning from lectures. *Journal of Educational Psychology, 83,* 120–123. https://doi.org/10.1037/0022-0663.83.1.120

Kiewra, K. A., Mayer, R. E., DuBois, N. F., Christensen, M., Kim, S., & Risch, N. (1997). Effects of advance organizers and repeated presentations on students' learning. *Journal of Experimental Education, 65,* 147–162. https://www.jstor.org/stable/20152515

Knight, L. J., & McKelvie, S. J. (1986). Effects of attendance, note-taking, and review on memory for a lecture: Encoding vs. external storage functions of notes. *Canadian Journal of Behavioural Science/Revue Canadienne Des Sciences Du Comportement, 18,* 52–61. http://doi.org/10.1037/h0079957

Kobayashi, K. (2005). What limits the encoding effect of note-taking? A meta-ana-lytic examination. *Contemporary Educational Psychology, 30*, 242–262. http://doi.org/10.1016/j.cedpsych.2004.10.001

Kornhauser, Z. G. C., Paul, A. L., & Siedlecki, K. L. (2016). An examination of students' use of technology for non-academic purposes in the college classroom. *Journal of Teaching and Learning with Technology, 5*, 1–15. https://doi.org/10.14434/jotlt.v5n1.13781

Kuznekoff, J. H., & Titsworth, S. (2013). The impact of mobile phone usage on student learning. *Communication Education, 62*, 233–252. https://doi.org/10.1080/03634523.2013.767917

Lauricella, S., & Kay, R. (2010). Assessing laptop use in higher education classrooms: The laptop effectiveness scale (LES). *Australasian Journal of Educational Technology, 26*, 151–163. https://doi.org/10.14742/ajet.1087

Luo, L., Kiewra, K. A., Flanigan, A., & Peteranetz, M. (2018). Laptop versus longhand note taking: Effects on lecture notes and achievement. *Instructional Science, 46*, 947–971. https://doi.org/10.1007/s11251-018-9458-0

Luo, L., Kiewra, K. A., & Samuelson, L. (2016). Revising lecture notes: How revision, pauses, and partners affect note taking and achievement. *Instructional Science, 44*, 45–67. http://doi.org/10.1007/S11251-016-9370-4

Maddox, H., & Hoole, E. (1975). Performance decrement in the lecture. *Educational Review, 28*, 17–30. https://doi.org/10.1080/0013191750280102

McCoy, B. R. (2013). Digital distractions in the classroom: Student classroom use of digital devices for non-class related purposes. *Journal of Media Education, 4*, 5–14. https://digitalcommons.unl.edu/cgi/viewcontent.cgi?article=1070&context=journalismfacpub

McCoy, B. R. (2016). Digital distractions in the classroom phase II: Student classroom use of digital devices for non-class related purposes. *Journal of Media Education, 7*, 5–32. https://digitalcommons.unl.edu/journalismfacpub/90/

Mueller, P. A., & Oppenheimer, D. M. (2014). The pen is mightier than the keyboard: Advantages of longhand over laptop note taking. *Psychological Science, 25*, 1159–1168. http://doi.org/10.1177/0956797614524581

Nouri, H., & Shahis, A. (2008). The effect of PowerPoint lectures on student performance and attitudes. *The Accounting Educators' Journal, 15*, 103–117. https://www.aejournal.com/ojs/index.php/aej/article/view/99

Pettijohn, T. F., Frazier, E., Rieser, E., Vaughn, N., & Hupp-Wildsde, B. (2015). Classroom texting in college students. *College Student Journal, 49*, 513–516. https://eric.ed.gov/?id=EJ1095425

Peverly, S. T., Garner, J. K., & Vekaria, P. C. (2014). Both handwriting speed and selective attention are important to lecture note-taking. *Reading and Writing, 27*, 1–30. http://doi.org/10.1007/s11145-013-9431-x

Peverly, S. T., Vekaria, P. C., Reddington, L. A., Sumowski, J. F., Johnson, K. R., & Ramsay, C. M. (2013). The relationship of handwriting speed, working memory, language comprehension and outlines to lecture note-taking and test-taking among college students. *Applied Cognitive Psychology, 27*, 115–126. http://doi.org/10.1002/acp.2881

Piolat, A., Olive, T., & Kellogg, R. T. (2005). Cognitive effort during note taking. *Applied Cognitive Psychology, 19*, 291–312. http://doi.org/10.1002/acp.1086

Ragan, E. D., Jennings, S. R., Massey, J. D., & Doolittle, P. E. (2014). Unregulated use of laptops over time in large lecture halls. *Computers & Education, 62*, 24–31. https://doi.org/10.1016/j.compedu.2014.05.002

Rickards, J. P., & Friedman, F. (1978). The encoding versus the external storage hypothesis in note taking. *Contemporary Educational Psychology, 3*, 136–143. http://doi.org/10.1016/0361-476X(78)90020-6

Rickards, J. P., & McCormick, C. B. (1988). Effect of interspersed conceptual prequestions on note-taking in listening comprehension. *Journal of Educational Psychology, 80*(4), 592–594. https://doi.org/10.1037/0022-0663.80.4.592

Risch, N., & Kiewra, K. A. (1990). Content and form variations in notetaking: Effects among junior high students. *Journal of Educational Research, 83*, 355–357. https://doi.org/10.1080/00220671.1990.10885981

Tedx Talks. (2013, January 7). *Six keys to leading positive change: Rosabeth Moss Kanter at TEDxBeaconStreet. YouTube.* https://youtu.be/owU5aTNPJbs

Titsworth, S., & Kiewra, K. A. (2004). Spoken organizational lecture cues and student note-taking. *Contemporary Educational Psychology, 29*, 447–461. http://doi.org/10.1016/j.cedpsych.2003.12.001

Chapter 4

Atkinson, R. K., Levin, J. R., Kiewra, K. A., Meyers, T., Kim, S., Atkinson, L., Renandya, W. A., & Hwang, Y. (1999). Matrix and mnemonic text-processing adjuncts: Comparing and combining their components. *Journal of Educational Psychology, 91*, 342–357. https://doi.org/10.1023/A:1013176309260

Kauffman, D. F., & Kiewra, K. A. (2010). What makes a matrix so effective: An empirical test of the relative benefits of signaling, extraction, and localization. *Journal of Instructional Science, 38*, 679–705. https://doi.org/10.1007/s11251-009-9095-8

Katayama, A. D., Robinson, D. H., Kiewra, K. A., DuBois, N. F., & Jonassen, D. (2001). Facilitating text learning with adjunct displays. *The Journal of Research in Education, 11*, 54–61.

Kiewra, K. A. (1989). Matrix notes. *Educational Technology, 29*, 55–56.

Kiewra, K. A. (1994). The matrix representation system: Orientation, research, theory and application. In J. Smart (Ed.), *Higher education: Handbook of theory and research.* Agathon. Reprinted in R. Perry & J. Smart (Eds.), *Effective teaching in higher education: Research and practice.* Agathon.

Kiewra, K. A. (2012). *Using graphic organizers to improve teaching and learning. The IDEA Center,* IDEA Paper #51. https://www.ideaedu.org/Portals/0/Uploads/Documents/IDEA Papers/IDEA Papers/PaperIDEA_51.pdf

Kiewra, K. A., & DuBois, N. F. (1992). Using a spatial system for teaching operant concepts. *Teaching of Psychology, 19*, 43–44. https://doi.org/10.1207/s15328023top1901_10

Kiewra, K. A., DuBois, N. F., Christian, D., & McShane, A. (1988). Providing study notes: A comparison of three types of notes for review. *Journal of Educational Psychology, 80*, 595–597. https://doi.org/10.1037/0022-0663.80.4.595

Kiewra, K. A., Kauffman, D. F., Robinson, D., DuBois, N., & Staley, R. K. (1999). Supplementing floundering text with adjunct displays. *Journal of Instructional Science, 27*, 373–401.

McCrudden, M.T., Schraw, G. & Lehman, S. (2009). The use of adjunct displays to facilitate comprehension of causal relationships in expository text. *Instructional Science, 37*, 65–86. https://doi.org/10.1007/s11251-007-9036-3

Robinson, D., & Kiewra, K. A. (1995). Visual argument: Graphic organizers are superior to outlines in improving learning from text. *Journal of Educational Psychology, 87*, 455–467. http://doi.org/10.1037/0022-0663.87.3.455

Chapter 5

Casper H. (2007, September 10). *Mnemonic wizards: Incredible feats of memory. YouTube.* https://www.youtube.com/watch?v=6vsYCSmBcM0

Ericsson, A., & Pool, R. (2016). *Peak: Secrets from the new science of expertise.* Mariner.

Foer, J. (2011). *Moonwalking with Einstein: The art and science of remembering everything.* Penguin Books.

Chapter 6

Bauer, D., Kopp, V., & Fischer, M. R. (2007). Answer changing in multiple choice assessment change that answer when in doubt—and spread the word! *BMC Medical Education, 7,* 28. https://doi.org/10.1186/1472-6920-7-28

Bransford, J. (1979). *Human cognition: Learning, understanding, and remembering.* Wadsworth.

Karpicke, J. D. (2012). Retrieval-based learning: Active retrieval promotes meaningful learning. *Current Directions in Psychological Science, 21,* 157–163. http://doi.org/10.1177/0963721412443552

Keeley, J., Zayac, R., & Correia, C. (2008). Curvilinear relationships between statistics anxiety and performance among undergraduate students: Evidence for optimal anxiety. *Statistics Education Research Journal, 7,* 4–15. https://psycnet.apa.org/record/2008-17676-001

Roediger, H. L., & Karpicke, J. D. (2006). Test-enhanced learning. *Psychological Science, 17,* 249–255. https://doi.org/10.1111/j.1467-9280.2006.01693.x

Chapter 7

Luo, L., & Kiewra, K. A. (2019a). *A SOAR-fired method for teaching synthesis writing.* The IDEA Center, Idea Paper # 74. https://files.eric.ed.gov/fulltext/ED594168.pdf

Luo, L., & Kiewra, K. A. (2019b). Soaring to successful synthesis writing. *Journal of Writing Research, 11,* 163–209. https://www.researchgate.net/publication/333132178_Soaring_to_Successful_Synthesis_Writing_An_Investigation_of_SOAR_Strategies_for_College_Students_Writing_from_Multiple_Sources

Martin, S. (1978, January 21). *Steve Martin's monologue* [television transcript]. Saturday Night Live, Season 3, Episode 9. NBC. https://snltranscripts.jt.org/77/77imono.phtml

Chapter 8

Alfonsi, S. (June 18, 2017). *Chess instills new dreams in kids from rural Mississippi county.* 60 Minutes. Retrieved February 10, 2020 from: https://www.cbsnews.com/news/kids-fight-stereotypes-using-chess-in-rural-mississippi/

Arab Proverbs. (n.d.). Great Thoughts Treasury. http://www.greatthoughtstreasury.com/index.php/author/arab-proverbs

Archer, J. (n.d.). *Jeffrey Archer > quotes.* Goodreads. https://www.goodreads.com/author/quotes/4820.Jeffrey_Archer?page=2

Blaschka, A. (2019, November 26). *This is why saying 'no' is the best way to grow your career—and how to do it.* Forbes. https://www.forbes.com/sites/amyblaschka/2019/11/26/this-is-why-saying-no-is-the-best-way-to-grow-your-career-and-how-to-do-it/?sh=6a12406e479d

Bloom, B. (1985). *Developing talent in young people.* Ballantine Books.

Brown, S. (n.d.). *Sarah Brown quotes*. Brainy Quote. https://www.brainyquote.com/quotes/sarah_brown_170807

Brown, L. (n.d.-a). *Les Brown quotes*. AZ Quotes. https://www.azquotes.com/quote/1316041

Brown, L. (n.d.-b). *Les Brown > quotes > quotable quote*. Goodreads. https://www.goodreads.com/quotes/42181-no-one-rises-to-low-expectations

Bryant, J. (2015, May 29). *Dreams don't work unless you do — John C. Maxwell*. Selfmadesuccess. https://selfmadesuccess.com/dreams-dont-work-unless-you-do-john-c-maxwell/

Crosby, Stills, & Nash. (1964). Wasted on the way [Song]. On *Daylight Again* [Album]. Atlantic.

Cushing, R. C. (n.d.). *Always plan ahead*. Lead Masters Blog. https://leadmastersblog.com/2017/12/29/always-plan-ahead-wasnt-raining-noah-built-ark-richard-cushing/

de Saint-Exupéry, A. (n.d.). *Antoine de Saint-Exupéry > quotes > quotable quote*. Goodreads. https://www.goodreads.com/quotes/87476-a-goal-without-a-plan-is-just-a-wish

Day O'Connor, S. (n.d.). *Slaying the dragon of delay is no sport for the short winded*. Publicquotes. https://publicquotes.com/quote/36951/slaying-the-dragon-of-delay-is-no-sport-for-the-short-winded.html

Dweck, C. S. (2008). *Mindset: The new psychology of success*. Ballantine Books.

Dyer, F. L., & Martin, T. C. (2013). *Edison, his life and inventions*. Gutenberg. https://www.gutenberg.org/files/820/820-h/820-h.htm#link2H_4_0035

Emerson, R. W. (1904). Progress of culture. In *The complete works of Ralph Waldo Emerson: Letters and social aims* (Vol. 8). Houghton, Mifflin.

Ericsson, A., & Pool, R. (2016). *Peak: Secrets from the new science of expertise*. Mariner.

Fox, M. (2017, March 6). *Here's how Pete Kostelnick ran across the country in record time*. Runner's World. https://www.runnersworld.com/runners-stories/g20849234/heres-how-pete-kostelnick-ran-across-the-country-in-record-time/

Gardner, H. (1997). *Extraordinary minds*. Basic Books.

Half, R. (n.d.). *Forbes quotes: Thoughts on the business of life*. Forbes. https://www.forbes.com/quotes/8076/

Holmes, E. (n.d.). *Believe as though you are, and you will be…* . Quotefancy. https://quotefancy.com/quote/1241977/Ernest-Holmes-Believe-as-though-you-are-and-you-will-be

Jabr, F. (2011, December 8). *Cache cab: Taxi drivers' brains grow to navigate London's streets*. Scientific American. https://www.scientificamerican.com/article/london-taxi-memory/

Keller, H. (1903). *Optimism: An essay*. T. Y. Crowell & Co.

Kiewra, K. A., & Witte, A. (2018). Prodigies of the prairie: The talent development stories of four elite Nebraska youth performers. *Roeper Review, 40*, 176–190. https://doi.org/10.1080/02783193.2018.1466841

Lyman, D. (1856). *The moral sayings of Publius Syrus, a Roman slave*. L. E. Bernard & Co.

Mahalingam, T. V. (2015, March 13). *These five business icons got fired before they became legends*. The Economic Times. https://economictimes.indiatimes.com/these-five-business-icons-got-fired-before-they-became-legends/articleshow/46549923.cms

Markham, B. (1942). *West with the night*. Farrar, Straus & Giroux.

Maxwell, E. (n.d.). *Elaine Maxwell > quotes > quotable quote*. Goodreads. https://www.goodreads.com/quotes/717566-my-will-shall-shape-the-future-whether-i-fail-or

McGuire, E. A., Gadian, D. G., Johnsrude, I. S., Good, C. D., Ashburner, J., Frackowiak, R. S. J., & Frith, C. D. (2000). Navigation-related structural change in the hippocampi of taxi drivers. *Proceedings of the National Academy of Sciences of the USA, 97*, 4398–4403. https://doi.org/10.1073/pnas.070039597

Mirchevski, B. (2020, March 2). *One day or day one? It's your decision*. Medium. https://medium.com/the-logician/one-day-or-day-one-its-your-decision-87b3748061e9

Moore, C. (1921). *Daniel H. Burnham, architect, planner of cities* (Vol. 2). Houghton Mifflin.

More, M. (2014, January 24). *Midday motivation | Excuses are the nails used to build a house of failure (Don Wilder)*. Hot 107.9. https://hotspotatl.com/3369523/midday-motivation-excuses-are-the-nails-used-to-build-a-house-of-failure-2/

Nitze, P. H. (1991). *Paul H. Nitze on the future*. University Press of America.

Pinola, M. (2011). *Procrastination is like a credit card*. Lifehacker. https://lifehacker.com/procrastination-is-like-a-credit-card-5816391

Powell, C. (n.d.). *Colin Powell quotes*. Brainy Quote. https://www.brainyquote.com/quotes/colin_powell_121363

Ramsden, S., Richardson, F. M., Josse, G., Thomas, M. S. C., Ellis, C., Shakeshaft, C., Seghier, M. L., & Price, C. J. (2011). Verbal and nonverbal intelligence changes in the teenage brain. *Nature, 479*, 113–116. https://doi.org/10.1038/nature10514

Reed, S. (n.d.). *Scott Reed quotes*. Quotes.net. https://www.quotes.net/quote/2612

Reelblack. (2019, November 24). *Les Brown – It's possible (1991) | Make this your decade*. YouTube. https://www.youtube.com/watch?v=6P7f7wwbXNE

Richards, M. C. (n.d.). Pinterest. https://www.pinterest.ca/pin/122160208616732292/

Rolling Stones. (1964). Time is on my side [Song]. On *12 x 5* [Album]. Decca.

Robinson, K. (2009). *The element: How finding your passion changes everything*. Penguin Books.

Silverstein, S. (2003). Sick. *Shel Silverstein: Poems and drawings*. HarperCollins.

Taylor, C. (1897). *Sayings of the Jewish fathers*. Cambridge University Press.

Twain, M. (n.d.). *Mark Twain > quotes > quotable quote*. Goodreads. https://www.goodreads.com/quotes/219455-the-secret-of-getting-ahead-is-getting-started-the-secret

Vedantam, S. (2019). *Creatures of habit: How habits shape who we are — and who we become*. Hidden Brain (NPR). https://www.npr.org/transcripts/787160734?t=1588769290406

Waitzkin, F. (1988). *Searching for Bobby Fischer: The father of a prodigy observes the world of chess*. Random House.

Waitzkin, J. (2007). *The art of learning: A journey in the pursuit of excellence*. Free Press.

Wellcome Trust. (2011, October 22). *Brain scans support findings that IQ can rise or fall significantly during adolescence*. Science Daily. www.sciencedaily.com/releases/2011/10/111020024329.htm

Weisberg, R. W. (1993). *Creativity: Beyond the myth of genius*. W. H. Freeman.

Williams, P. (2002). *By the way – a snapshot diagnosis of the inner-city dilemma*. Xulun Press.

Winokur, J. (1999). *Advice to writers: A compendium of quotes, anecdotes, and writerly wisdom*. Vintage Books.

Wood, W. (2019). *Good habits, bad habits: The science of making positive changes that stick*. Farrar, Straus and Giroux.

Chapter 9

Allen, W. (1999). Down south. *Standup comic: 1964–1968*. Rhino Records.

Bloom, B. (1985). *Developing talent in young people*. Ballantine Books.

Csikszentmihalyi, M. (1996). *Creativity: The psychology of discovery and invention*. HarperCollins.

Ericsson, A., & Pool, R. (2016). *Peak: Secrets from the new science of expertise*. Mariner.

Flanigan, A., Kiewra, K. A., & Luo, L. (2018). Conversations with four highly productive German educational psychologists: Frank Fischer, Hans Gruber, Heinz Mandl, and Alexander Renkl. *Educational Psychology Review, 30*, 303–330. https://doi.org/10.1007/s10648-016-9392-0

Jobs, S. (2005, June 14). *'You've got to find what you love,' Jobs says* [Stanford commencement address]. Stanford News. https://news.stanford.edu/2005/06/14/jobs-061505/

Kiewra, K. A. (2019). *Nurturing children's talents: A guide for parents*. Praeger.

Kiewra, K. A., & Creswell, J. W. (2000). Conversations with three highly productive educational psychologists: Richard Anderson, Richard Mayer, and Michael Pressley. *Educational Psychology Review, 12*, 135–161. https://doi.org/10.1023/A:1009041202079

Kiewra, K. A., & Witte, A. (2018). Prodigies of the prairie: The talent development stories of four elite Nebraska youth performers. *Roeper Review, 40,* 176–190. https://doi.org/10.1080/02783193.2018.1466841

Levy, M. (2005). *If only it were true*. Atria Press.

Oppezzo, M., & Schwartz, D. L. (2014). Give your ideas some legs: The positive effect of walking on creative thinking. *Journal of Experimental Psychology: Learning, Memory, and Cognition, 40*, 1142–1152. https://doi.org/10.1037/a0036577

Patterson-Hazley, M., & Kiewra, K. A. (2013). Conversations with four highly productive educational psychologists: Patricia Alexander, Richard Mayer, Dale Schunk, and Barry Zimmerman. *Educational Psychology Review, 25*, 19–45. https://doi.org/10.1007/s10648-012-9214-y

Reelblack. (2019, November 24). *Les Brown – It's possible (1991) | Make this your decade*. YouTube. https://www.youtube.com/watch?v=6P7f7wwbXNE